The Next Gen Church

WILL THE CHURCH STAND?

Larry A. McMillan

authorHOUSE®

AuthorHouse™
1663 Liberty Drive
Bloomington, IN 47403
www.authorhouse.com
Phone: 1 (800) 839-8640

Published by AuthorHouse 12/07/2018

ISBN: 978-1-5462-3423-4 (sc)
ISBN: 978-1-5462-3421-0 (hc)
ISBN: 978-1-5462-3422-7 (e)

Library of Congress Control Number: 2018938442

ACKNOWLEDGMENTS

W E CAN NOT live alone, especially in the struggles to write a book. We are surrounded by saints of God, encouragers, leaders, and critics who call for the best in us. Even members can be a resource and some can be a distraction. We thank God for all people He places in our pathway to get the job done. And I set aside this space to give thanksgiving to some of them.

To James G. McMillan and Mrs. Marguerite McMillan both of whom are deceased and who's sanctified Afro-American marriage a successful church model has left an imprint on this author to share this book with the world. Since birth they instilled the vision for me to become a writer to the glory of God. They were able to read some of the notes of this book, and this book speaks to the heart of their teachings.

Marilyn McMillan, my wife, dear friend, and general editor of this book is either foolhardy or daring enough in love with me to take on this responsibility and contribute to this work, is to be commended. This June 7, 2018, we will celebrate fifty years of marriage. Many of our celebrations were refueled at the Hampton Ministries Conference since it took place on our anniversary date, June 7. Truly she is loved and I realize that it is love that we have made this journey through life together.

This writing of this took place in the midst of joys, burdens, sickness, and excitement. It took place in the midst of urban flirting within churches, in places like Jamaica, Germany, Las Vegas, Lake Meade, Switzerland, France, our cabin in the Poconos, PA., Churchville, MD, at our parents' home in Lake Waccamaw, NC, and Hallsboro, NC, Hampton Ministers Conference in Hampton, Va., and along the seashores of Myrtle Beach, S.C. But, now it is yours, and prayerfully to the glory of God ready to give a blessing to the reader. I am thankful for Mrs. McMillan's patience, and gentle encouragement, all of which I needed, for I am a man who spread on lots of words on a table and need someone to sort them out and present them as I intended.

I am indebted to Jhai Allen Thomas McMillan, my six year old grandson who knew I was writing a book, and when he came into the office he always asked this question; "Granddaddy, do you need any help! In my long suffering, he always gave me the kind of nudges needed to stay on task. Also, he would come to the office and speak the Hebrew words I taught him. This too gave me much encouragement. Yes, Jhai I need help to make this book a best seller.

To my three children, who are married and have their own families, I say thank you. Robert McMillan would say, "I really think you ought to do this." He was a staunchest human source of support and strength. Michael McMillan showed up with a coffee pot warmer and a popcorn machine, and said "you will be able to stay up longer if you did not have to travel to the kitchen to warm up your coffee." Larry McMillan, Jr. would challenge me with vibrant phone calls asking: "when will the work be finished."

Finally, I acknowledge all the unsung heroes and the people whom God poured His spirit upon to crystallize this work so His will and purpose will be done in my life. Thank you in advance for your financial support, encouragement, and prayers.

SPECIAL ACKNOWLEDGEMENTS

THIS BOOK IS a collective endeavor and a mandate from God based on the three churches God called me to be their pastor. Also, during those years I remained as a foundational member of the New Shiloh Baptist Church located in Baltimore, Md. Within a twenty five year span, God truly revealed many golden nuggets how the church can be equipped to make a difference in the lives of families, the world, and nations. Also, I owe a profound thanks to the various denominations of churches who allowed me to be recognized as a part of their organized church and openly taught me many of the trade secrets of their ministries that others were not afforded.

It is imperative that I give thanks to the late Dr. Olin P. Moyd, my homiletic professor at St. Mary's Seminary and University, Baltimore, Md. In 1991 he encouraged me in this work along with Dr. James Cone. Also I give thanks to Dr. Eugene Peterson of the same University who provided many rich moments of dialogue and mental simulations as he taught me about the churches as I studied the book of Revelation at the University. The late Rev. Dr. Harold A. Carter, Sr., my former pastor of the New Shiloh Baptist Church created an environment wherein this material lived as a potential model and many aspects were tested daily. The Rev. Dr. Harold Carter, Jr., the current pastor of the New Shiloh Baptist Church, is now providing immediate instructions on how the 21st century church should work according to God's word.

Today's Family, Inc. with location in Abingdon, Maryland was instrumental in giving this author much information and support with this project. Evangelist Marilyn McMillan, my wife and an Administrative officer gave strategic service as a research agent and technical adviser. In finality, I am grateful to God for all who assisted in bringing this work to fruition.

HONORARY STATEMENTS

I LOVE DR. McMillan's authoritative preaching voice. He is a prolific writer, teacher, and man of God. His book will add value to all churches to the glory of God.
Bishop Robert Johnson

The world in which we live offers few if any truthful model of a church as described in the Holy Word of God. If the church is to be successful in the eyes of God then many will have to reverse their model to be effective in the 21ˢᵗ century and beyond should God tarry. There is a get falling away and the percentage of those that are satisfied with the present model is absolutely too high. However, I submit that those who read and consider the facts researched in this book prayerfully will allow God's model to prevail.
Robert McMillan

This is your road map so that the church can stand up and demonstrate to the world how to be the head and not the tail. It is my prayer that those who read this book will find the answers to their questions and will stand up and make a better nation where love will prevail in the hearts of all believers.
Minister Michael McMillan

"The church son is in you, remember this always and look toward the hill from whence cometh your help. I'll pray you will be used by God to help the kingdom of earth become like it is in heaven."
The Late Deacon James G. McMillan

EDITOR'S PREFACE

THE CHURCH IS most important in this 21ˢᵗ century than ever in the history of humankind. God has called all of His people to be communicators and to shout a warning to the general populace. Everyone who has accepted the call of Jesus, the Christ is called to ministry. We are commissioned with the challenge to communicate our faith to the world without compromise.

This book brings all of the truths about the church into focus. The author is a scholar preacher, teacher, and pastor with outstanding abilities and talents to make the scripture come alive for individuals, groups, and leaders of the institution of the church.

The importance of the name of the church is crucible. The world's churches have many different names. They are derived in various ways. They may take on the names by particular doctrines they teach, the name of the organizer, the human-devised type of church they want to represent, the location of the church, the scope and size of ministry and the list goes on. The author believes that the church ought to represent the Holy Triune on earth in every way under God's directions.

On the night of Jesus' betrayal, He prayed for His church. The bible records the prayer as saying: "Holy Father, keep through your own name those whom you have given me, that they may be one, as we are. While I was with them in the world, I kept them in Your Name ... I have given them Your Word; and the world has hated them, because they are not of the world, even as I am not of the world. I pray not that You should take them out of the world, but that You should keep them from the evil. They are not of the world, even as I am not of the world. Sanctify them through Your truth: Your word is truth." (John 17:11-12, 14-17)

The author speaks of twelve separate places where the New Testament records that the true church has been kept in the name of God, the father, the Son, and the Holy Spirit. The first five refers to the entire church, or Body of Christ, as a whole. The next four speak of a specific local congregation, while using the term "Church of God." The final three reference the collection of all the individual local congregations. All of these references the term "Churches of God." They are listed in the book as scriptural commands of God.

The author is not being judgmental because God has already indicated that He is the judge and the final judge. He has made a gracious attempt to leave a road map for the upcoming leaders of the church and suggest that we as leaders take a self evaluation of our work in the Kingdom of God.

A growing renaissance in the 21st century church is being led by clergy and laity who is Biblical rooted, Christ centered, and Holy Spirit-empowered. However, the cultural wars within the world and insurgence of the unbelievers have caused the organized church to listen to the collected opinions of the marketing specialists of the media. The church seems to be silenced in the communities, the country, and the world at large. These days are most exciting for God is moving the church to the next dimension. This book is offering a primary resource for the new life that is on the horizon for the 21st century church.

This author has taken on the initiative to effectively communicate how we can find truly authentic leadership to emulate. We want to follow and emulate the ministries God has set before us and not the satanic ministries of the false prophets. This author has faced the same challenges and problems that every ministry has faced. God has given him wisdom and understanding and the experiences need to identify faithful and obedient disciples in personal evangelism, church renewal, and social responsibility.

I commend this book to you with gratitude to the author, my husband, my pastor, and friend through the many years we have ministered over thirty seven years and forty nine years of marriage. This book will allow you to experience a fine blend of scholarship in exposition and communication skills in the use of metaphors, contemporary parables, and short stories of people. You will truly appreciate the new insights into biblical text, the spiritual marketing skills God has given him, the financial insight, and theological scholarship. Revered and admired by clergy, church leaders, and the saints of God, he has been the clandestine pivotal person who has been guiding hundreds of churches forward toward following the precepts of God. Many call him "Bishop" of their church, but his humble spirit allows him not to be caught up in the grandeur of accolades. The Lord's indwelling power in his life is evident in all that he does and in the way he communicates to his friends in the ministry. He is an unsung hero in the courts of God. As you listen to him preach and teach, you will know that he spends quality time with God in his own personal devotions and in prolonged study of the scriptures. But, you will also sense something else. You will sense that he is able to laugh and cry, hope and hurt, tell the truth and not compromise the gospel, and listen attentively to others.

Evangelist Marilyn P. McMillan

INTRODUCTION

D R. LARRY MCMILLAN is not only a great preacher and pastor, he is an author that requires his readers to think. The grand topic "the churches of the 21st century" probed by this masterful expository touches things in which he could not be timelier. Today's world is in a puzzling chaotic condition. This world is leaving its mark on the foundation Christian doctrine in which God is not pleased. This message reflects and encases the questions ask most frequently upon people of faith. Are the contemporary programs presented by many churches actually incarnated by the scriptural persuasions of the first century church? This book explores the answer to this question and offers solutions to enhance the Godly growth of churches. The bible says that God will start judgment at the house of the Lord. The true Christian believes in the wrath of God. We all pay an opportunity cost for decisions made. The country pays a cost for engaging in military conflicts. There are consequences when a nation goes against God's commands. He believes that volcanic eruptions, untimely floods, earthquakes, famines, and so on can be at times a sign of God's displeasure with the actions of the world. The church is to be the light of the world.

This book explores the searing objections of the critics who claim that God is not concerned about the conduct of the church and the world simply because He is a loving God. God will answer them throughout these writings. Our own confusion, fear, and non-wisdom conclusions will either be dispelled or confirmed. To those who wait and trust God, this book will give eternal fellowship and the joy of the Lord will be their strength. Their joy will be complete and the world will not be able to take it away. The joy they will receive will be on a scale so large that the world will not be able to comprehend their attainment.

Many are convinced that the church must redefine itself as a modern, popularity, and world conscience and inclusive movement. They believe that the church is being molded in such a way for spiritual refinement. Since there are great numbers of ethnic populations emerging in America, some say that the church should be able to accommodate all religions. The book explores those ideas and points to conclusions that will guide the 21st century into the expectations of God for His church.

Throughout America a debate is raging over the political, social, and the liberating content of the faith that ought to be ascribed to Christian faith. There is a stand off amongst the Christian group. One group contends that the church is to maintain their religious city and spirituality. In John 18:36 Jesus says, "My kingdom does not belong to this world." Jesus focuses on the spiritual relationships between the human being and God. These relationships are translated in terms of sin or grace, conversion or hardening of the heart, saved or unsaved, and so on. Of course, there is disagreement, in which some say the church has the same scope as the salvation of which it is the vehicle. They believe that the church is concerned with the spirit, the body, and the world. This would include politics within religion. This author enters into this debate with eagerness and anxiety. He wonders which side of the scales the needle will incline.

Some are looking for the church to be more committed to the people and their desires. It is impossible to understand God's church in a vacuum. God laid the foundation and He is the founder. He established it by His own hands. But, there are those who want to correlate the world forces and the internal contradictions of the capitalist system in a formula that please them. Many would love to take out the conflict between the rich and poor, which is swiftly increasing. The role of the church is still an unglazed trail that is to be continued lead by the spirit of God by His purpose and will for the 21st century. The question is: "What should the 21st century church resemble?" The church commitment ought to spring from an imperative of faith in God to bring it to be a light in the middle of darkness. To compromise the church doctrines to be politically correct is written in the articles of faith presented to the church by God. The church can not afford to act as if God as change His mind concerning His charge to His church.

The church is the body of the risen Christ. The church is an organism animated by the Holy Spirit. This body of Christ is only alive in people when they live for the cause of Christ. This body of believes realize that their lives are only held in tact by the strength and power of the Holy Spirit. Everything done in the church must be done through the vitality of the Spirit.

In a history with the future unveiling, the church is to be on watch for the parousia or Second Coming of Christ. This can be no longer regarded as to happen in the distant future. The signs of the times tell the believer that the end is temporarily imminent. Until this happens, the church is called to "Make Disciples." Today, the church is ever more transparent. The gospel is intrinsically tied to this proclamation. The church is called to be the so-called defense attorney for human dignity, human rights, spirituality among fellow members, and to have a voice that rings loud and clear concerning, the cries of the less fortunate, and the making of Disciples of Christ. The church is called to stand up and lift up their voices united and to confront the power of wickedness in high places. The church that embraces a diakonia on behalf of the highest of human values will receive blessings from heaven. In this book there will emerge models for the 21st century church. However, the church will abide by following the commands of God. For these values are universally embedded in the souls and minds of God's true disciples. The church that genuinely succeeds in living out these commands will emerge as a successful church in the eyes of God. They will eventually become the universal spirit filled church of the 21st century that God is seeking.

This book advocates a sympathetic but critical relationship between attendee church and discipleship church. Dr. McMillan claims that this 21st century methodologies have almost been abandon and been replaced by posterity, interfaith, and greed from false teachers and false prophets. He also discusses the political dimensions of faith, the churches role in the 21st century, and makes bold reflections on various issues facing the Christian church. His book is considered vital reading for anyone concerned with the church of the 21st century and beyond, fostering equality to all humankind.

Yes, the church has been commanded by God to be the salt of the Earth. The churches are to make the world a better place because they follow God's Word. They have been called the salt of the earth which is equivalent to giving flavor to make a meal taste better. When the church is not attracting the lost, it becomes worthless. The salt has lost its savor. Now, it has become a great problem because the church is now repelling the saved. Some of the churches are running away the potential disciples from the church.

Perhaps not all will believe the center core of my superposition, but the middle road of this observation is enough to put the church on alert. The church has been so compromised that they have refused to demonstrate love to certain people. They have excused sin, misconduct, and other things so that the church will continue to multiply in numbers. Some churches have compromised and are so loose that they are excepting homosexuality and adultery in the church. Instead of making disciples they have changed the Word of God and are allowing a hammer made by man to break up the Word of God in many small pieces. They have traded their fishing poles for a sledgehammer so they can break up the Word of God into smaller pieces wherein it will have no substance for spiritual living.

Now in this 21st century, some churches have become a socially based, smooth, sensual, sophisticated, and Hollywood production. This kind of church is called a success in the eyes of those using a business formula to define success. But it is closer to be defined as a "pimping the ministry." Only the functional ignorant unlearned of the ways of Christ would termed this kind of church as being successful. My late father, Deacon James McMillan told me years ago, if it walks like a duck, and quacks like a duck, and looks like a duck, then it is most likely a duck. If the church takes on the Hollywood ideology and a world's concept, then it is not a church. I am asking a rhetorical question, what ever happened to the Gospel of power? If our churches are supposed to emulate Jesus, why are so many people being turned off by the actions of the church? If the fire that is burning in our churches is from the altar of God, then the church is Holy Ghost filled. But if the church is burning from the Wizard of Oz production, then she is not harvesting laborers for the Kingdom of God. Those that are hungry for God will not be drawn by the Spirituality of the church. Only God will be able intercede in this situation. Something is wrong!

We still have some old-fashioned preachers who preach under the anointing of the power of God. They do not rely on their stacks of disheveled notes. They do not rely on sermon they have purchased from traditional preachers. These preachers totally rely on the power of God to deliver the message.

It is a fact that numerous pastors in this 21st century follow social and marketing formulas to deliver a sermon to their congregations. They do not rely on the power of God to speak to the hearts of mankind. Some of these preachers have learned how to preach from colleges and universities that they learned in their homiletic classes. They learned to present a Gospel in a multi-media fashion with seven bullet points, a poem, and three jokes. Something is wrong!

Years ago, we relied on using the moaners bench. Now, it is the altar call. In many of our churches it has become seeking out a committee to entertain the question of salvation. What happened to the calls for repentance?

The spirit of God brought thousands to the altar to repent. They asked Jesus, the Christ to save their souls. This is a litmus test for Christianity. This is the essence of the Cross. This is the Great Commission that Jesus commanded us to have as the top priority in the church. If the church is not winning souls, then they are alike a barren woman. This is a shame before God and man how the altar call for repentance has been abandon by many churches. They have replaced God's church with a guided marketing religious principle manual and an economic assess religious thrift model. Something is wrong!

What happen to all the miracles that the church once had? When is the last time you've heard a genuine testimony? What we are hearing in a lot of churches is: "if it is God's will, you will be healed." What we have been hearing "your blessing is on the way." What we have been hearing is "name it and claim it." We have not seen the heavenly rim in faith. Many have placed all their hope on a "gradual healing" with doctors getting God's glory. They go to doctors weekly and fail to rely on the instant manifestation of the power of God. In Matthew 10:8 Jesus said to *heal the sick, raise the dead, and cast out demons, freely you have received, freely give.* Jesus commanded preachers *to preach the Gospel in season and out of season.* Preachers are to preach the unadulterated gospel. We as preachers are not given the privilege to take away or add any and everything to God's gospel. Jesus was not kidding or telling a joke. Jesus meant everything He said. Having preached the gospel of Jesus, the church ought to be flowing with miracle healing. Because this is not happening, then I'm sorry to say something is wrong!

When is the last time you have experienced the outpouring of the Holy Ghost? I heard some say that they did not even know that there was a Holy Ghost. Have you been taught about the power of the Holy Ghost? The book of Acts paints a beautiful picture of what happens when the Holy Ghost is poured out on His children. The room was filled with holiness and thousands of people began to speak in tongues. Or do we believe that the church is to have a world party like atmosphere? The marketing church gets someone to play a rewritten secular song, a charismatic preacher works the crowd with a prosperity message, a couple of woman dress in revealing silk dresses dancing to a secular song, and the audience get excited. The newcomers think they have attended a moving and inspiring church. This is not the case. The church has not witness the outpouring of the spirit for a long time. They do not know what the outpouring of the spirit really is. Something is wrong!

Many of the 21st century churches are out of order. The foundation is being ripped apart. Many of the churches have become sophisticated, politically correct, enamored with a social gospel, competitiveness, and pride. It seems that they are glad that the adversary has changed their mission priority. I am reminded of Gideon. Gideon was threshing his wheat in secret by the wine press of God. The fields had been taken over by a wicked king. But, because of his faithfulness and obedience, God gave him the victory. Again, I wonder out loud in this book "What happened to the miracles that our fathers experienced? Is there a vehicle to get the saints to here about these kinds of miracles in this 21st century? Something is wrong!

The 21st century church is loosing or has lost its fear of God. Many churches are constantly turning their backs on God. Has the church taken a backslider position on the Word of God? Have they abhorred after idol gods, especially money, power, and materialism?

The book of Isaiah 29 states that the Word of God became "*sealed unto us so that we no longer even grasp how far we have fallen.*" We read the Word of God, but we can't see past the surface of the page. How can we get back where we once were? The book attempts to answer all the questions lifted in this premiere narrative. What we need is a Holy Ghost filled revival.

I believe in the old fashion revivals that took place during my youthful days. We prayed that God would send a revival. We prayed that God would heal the land. The Word of God says in *2nd Chronicles 7:14, "If my people which are called by my name would pray, seek my face, turn from thy wickedness ways, then you will hear from heaven, and He will heal the land."* These churches must understand that they have strayed from God. The hymnologist said "It is me oh Lord standing in the need of prayer."

I was taught the four steps to revival by the late Rev. Dr. Harold Carter, Sr. He taught this by his actions from the pulpit. What did the spirit of God teach the church as we participated in revival services? This is what I saw in the Holy Spirit at New Shiloh Baptist Church on Fremont Avenue, Baltimore, Maryland. God revealed to me seven steps that must take place which will usher in a revival in the church. The seven steps to revival are Research, Recognition, Repentance, Re-dedication, Righteousness, Rejoice, and Revival.

The first step to research is why is there a need for a revival. God calls the church to spend time with God and find out what went desperately wrong with our church. Get two or three disciples to prayerfully partition God to inform them what was lost as they made their primary pursuit of success to obtain a super-sophisticated modern church. The church lost the vision and must ask God to show them the way back. This book will outline the research and the finding on this subject. The need for the seven steps to will be revealed in a special way as the book evolves.

God has a special place for the church in this 21st century. However, we must do the research, acknowledge our sins, trust God, and make the journey back to God's way. God has reserved a place for the church in this 21st century. We are living in the last days. We are living in perilous times.

This is not the first time that God's people have turned their backs on God and went astray. Listen to what God said in Revelations 3:14-19. *"And unto the angel of the church of the Laodiceans write; These things saith the Amen, the faithful and true witness, the beginning of the creation of God; I know thy works, that thou art neither cold nor hot: I would thou were cold or hot. So then because thou art lukewarm, and neither cold nor hot, I will spew thee out of my mouth. Because thou sayest, I am rich, and increased with goods, and have need of nothing; and knowest not that thou art wretched, and miserable, and poor, and blind, and naked: I counsel thee to buy of me gold tried in the fire, that thou mayest be rich; and white raiment, that thou mayest be clothed, and that the shame of thy nakedness do not appear; and anoint thine eyes with eye salve, that thou mayest see. As many as I love, I rebuke and chasten: be zealous therefore, and repent."*

TABLE OF CONTENTS

ACKNOWLEDGMENTS..v

SPECIAL ACKNOWLEDGEMENTS................................... vii

HONORARY STATEMENTS... ix

EDITOR'S PREFACE xi

INTRODUCTION..xv

CHAPTER 1 WHAT IS THE CHURCH? 1

CHAPTER 2 THE FOOT PRINT OF THE CHURCH................... 17

CHAPTER 3 THE TRANSPARENT CHURCH 24

CHAPTER 4 THE AGE OF CHALLENGE 35

CHAPTER 5 THE FLABBY CHRISTIANS 40

CHAPTER 6 WHICH IS OLDER GOD OR THE EARTH?.............55

CHAPTER 7 A COMFORTABLE CHURCH 67

CHAPTER 8 THE FEAR OF GOD 75

CHAPTER 9 GOD DOES THE WORK.................................89

CHAPTER 10 ONLY ONE BODY 102

CHAPTER 11 A VIRTUAL LOOK AT THE CHURCH.................. 114

CHAPTER 12 AN ATTENDEE VS DISCIPLESHIP 140

CHAPTER 13 THE FINAL PRODUCT 178

CHAPTER 14 THE POWER TO GET WEALTH 214

CHAPTER 15 FOR A STRONGER NATION.............................222

CHAPTER 16 JESUS IS COMING BACK FOR HIS CHURCH.....229

APPENDIX 257

SEMONIC OUTLINE 257

MAJOR POINTS OF INTEREST 259

REFERENCES 267

CHAPTER ONE

WHAT IS THE CHURCH?

I AM UNDER the impression that the institutional church is standing on its last legs. Statistically, the church is facing a constant decline in membership. Politics has leaked into the church and caused many leaders to try to be politically correct as they abandon the doctrines of Christianity. The public perception of the institutional church is lower than ever. I am being completely honest regarding the merits of church as we face more problems than have ever been recorded in history. *The Next Gen Church* book asks, "Will the church stand?"

Instead of asking, "What is the church?" perhaps the question should be *"Who* is the church?' The word *church* comes from the Greek word *ekklesia,* which is defined as "an assembly" or "called-out ones." The root meaning of *church* is not that of a building but of people. The universal church consists of all those who have a personal relationship with Jesus Christ. The universal church of God is all those who have received salvation through faith in Jesus Christ. The local church is where the members of the universal church can fully apply the "body" principles of 1 Corinthians 12: encouraging, teaching, and building one another up in the knowledge and grace of the Lord Jesus Christ. Who is the church? The church is God's regenerated people who were full of sin but saved of their free will by His power for His purposes and will for their lives in the world.

Many of the churches in America want to be labeled "Christian churches." But many of these churches have ignored the laws of God and have failed to adhere to the guidelines of the scripture regarding what a church ought to resemble. Many churches use professional marketing techniques to grow their congregations without any regard for the overall biblical teachings of Jesus, the Christ. The congregation and the world are suffering because of the lack of strong biblical teachings in these churches.

It is imperative that the church reflect the teachings of Jesus, the Christ. We are living in the last days, and perilous times are upon us. America is destined to witness a shift in the Christian world. Phyllis Tickle, in her book titled *The Great Emergence,* suggests that there is a historical pattern of a shift in Christianity every five hundred years. If she is correct, America is on the brink of a massive shift. Chronologically, America is about to experience a new dimension in Christianity.

Tickle suggests that the first shift began almost five hundred years after Jesus, the Christ, was crucified on the old, rugged cross. History records that the Roman Empire fell at this time. It is known as the "Constantine Christianity." The second shift occurred five hundred years later: the Great Schism of 1054. The division of Roman Catholicism and the Orthodox Church took place. The third shift took place in 1517. This was called the Reformation, and it gave rise to the Protestant Christian era. It is now the year 2018, and we are ready to witness another shift in the church. It is my belief that, based on this historical analytical posture, we are getting ready to witness another shift. I believe that this is scriptural as well as historically predicted to take place. Mere calculations indicate that it will begin around January 2017.

The people of God will continue to be blessed as God has given them promises. God has made a covenant with His people to be their God, and His people are to obey His commands. The church is to stand on the foundation that was laid by God. The foundation of their faith must be grounded in the personhood of Jesus, the Christ. The church is to keep its priorities in line with the Word of God. God has called on the church to follow the first-century commands as guidelines for His church. The scriptures state in Matthew 24:35 (KJV), "Heaven and earth shall pass away, but my words shall not pass away." His salvation is secure. "The heavens will vanish like smoke, the earth will wear out like a garment and its inhabitants die like flies. But my salvation will last forever, my righteousness will never fail" (Isaiah 51:6). Jesus tells us to have the proper priorities. "Do not store up for yourselves treasures on earth ... But store up for yourselves treasures in heaven" (Matthew 6:19–20). In these last days, it is imperative that the church be what God has called it to be.

What is the church? Is the church a building? Is it the place where believers gather to worship? Is the church the people who believe and follow Christ? How we understand and perceive the church is important in determining how we live out our faith.

Matthew 16:18–20 records Jesus saying,

> And I say also unto thee, That thou art Peter, and upon this rock I will build my church; and the gates of hell shall not prevail against it. And I will give unto thee the keys of the kingdom of heaven: and whatsoever thou shalt bind on earth shall be bound in heaven: and whatsoever thou shalt loose on earth shall be loosed in heaven. Then charged he his disciples that they should tell no man that he was Jesus the Christ.

Researchers contend that the Catholic Church interprets this verse to mean that Peter is the rock upon which the church was founded, and for this reason, Peter is considered the first pope. Protestants as well as Christians of other denominations interpret this verse differently. They believe in Romans 10:9 "that if thou confess with thy mouth Lord Jesus, and shalt believe in thine heart that God hath raised him from the dead, thou shalt be saved." They teach that everyone who confesses Jesus Christ as Lord is a part of the church. They also say, "We are the church." I believe that the New Testament church is a body of believers who have been called out from the world by God to live as His people under the authority of Jesus Christ (Ephesians 1:22–23). This body of believers—or "the body of Christ"—began in Acts 2 on the Day of Pentecost through the work of the Holy Spirit and will continue to be formed until the day of the rapture of the church. They were given the great commission and will work according to the command by Jesus to "make disciples."

Therefore, the local church is defined as a local assembly of believers or a congregation that meets together physically for worship, fellowship, teaching, prayer, and encouragement in the faith (Hebrews 10:25). This is a way of life for believers. With this being the matter, they are able to live in relationship with other believers. They break bread together (communion), pray for each other, disciple, and strengthen one another. Throughout the world, all believers are members of the universal church. This universal church is made up of every single person who has exercised faith in Jesus Christ for salvation, including members of every local church body throughout the earth (1 Corinthians 12:13; Ephesians 1:22–23).

THE PURPOSE OF THE CHURCH

The purpose of the church is threefold. It is to preach, teach, and evangelize. The church assembles to bring each member to spiritual maturity (Ephesians 4:13). The church reaches out to spread the love of Christ. The church is to evangelize, meaning to spread the gospel message to unbelievers in the world (Matthew 28:18–20). This is the great commission. So the primary purpose is to make disciples and to minister to believers and nonbelievers. Really, the church is universal, for it is responsible for reaching the world with the gospel. In a local sense, it is one of the main engines in which God carries out His purposes on earth. The church is God's heart, His mouth, His hands, and His feet for reaching out to an unsaved world. We are to be His mouth, His hands, and His feet reaching out to an unsaved world. Preachers are to preach the unadulterated Word of God. First Corinthians 12:27 (NIV) reminds the church, "Now you are the body of Christ, and each one of you is a part of it."

A CULTURE WAR

I feel the urgency to examine the efforts of churches to maintain their standards of biblical integrity with regard to marriage. And I examine the current conflict between American secular culture and the Christian faith as well as why Christians are losing the culture war. The term *culture war* is used to claim that there is a conflict between those values considered traditional or conservative and those considered progressive or liberal. It originated in the 1920s, when urban and rural American values came into clear conflict. "Culture war" is a translation from the German Kulturkampf, a term that was coined to describe the clash between cultural and religious groups in the campaign from 1871 to 1878, under Chancellor Otto Von Bismarck of the German Empire, against the influence of the Roman Catholic Church. From a strictly biblical perspective, all culture wars are between two major protagonists: God and Satan. The church cannot simultaneously embody justice and injustice. Values of what are right and wrong and good and evil are central to the culture war. The culture war will shape the moral values of American society for decades to come. I wrote a song sermon titled "Fighting a Culture War." This song captures the biblical views of the believers fighting this war for the kingdom of God.

For more than 2000 years, Christianity has been engaged in a war to convert and spread its gospel to as many followers as possible, but unless the church gets better at protecting the already saved, it is going to lose the battle *and* the war! Atheists are erecting monuments in favor of their non-belief and in opposition to religion. Gays/sodomites/homosexuals are becoming more prevalent in our society. Same sex marriages have been given a blessing by the Supreme Court. They have put themselves in the position to speak for God and for the American citizenry. Churches are watering down the gospel with 'feel-good' messages about self improvement and positive thinking, while failing to teach the essentials of Christ and Him crucified, along with a proper biblical worldview. Street preaching is a ministry that has become more UN-common within the past few years, is a relief at least in the current climate of moral decline. The church has retreated into the closet while the homosexuals have come out. Christians have been avoiding the culture war for so long that we now have to play catch-up.

There are many questions that must be asked if the church is to be the church that God is calling for in this 21st century. Will millions of preachers quit? Will thousands of ministries end? Will Christian media be reduced, if not eliminated? Will Christian schools go into rapid decline? I'm convinced the grace and mission of God will reach to the ends of the earth. But the end of the so-called church as we know it will go out of business.

There are three kinds of evangelical churches today: consumer-driven mega churches, dying churches and new churches whose future is fragile. Denominations will shrink, even vanish, while fewer and fewer Christian churches will survive and thrive. Emphasis will shift from doctrine to relevance, motivation, and personal success – resulting in churches further compromised and weakened in their ability to pass on the faith. It is time for missionaries to come to America from Asia and Africa. Will they come? Will they be able to bring to our culture a more vital form of Christianity?

John Adams stated: "Our Constitution was made only for a moral and religious people. It is wholly inadequate to the government of any other." Many people of the past and of the future have made significant statements about the church. Over the centuries many have had a mixture of ideas of what the church ought to be. Listed are a few that give their belief of what a church ought to be.

Yes, I see the Church as the body of Christ. But oh, how we have blemished and scarred that body through social neglect and through fear of being nonconformists.

Martin Luther King, Jr.

Where God builds a church the devil builds a chapel.
Martin Luther

The True Church can never fail. For it is based upon a rock.–
T.S. Eliot

The perfect church service would be one we were almost unaware of. Our attention would have been on God.–
C.S. Lewis

For years I thought my assignment or the ChurchHYPERLINK "http://www.brainyquote.com/quotes/quotes/m/maxlucado543045. html"HYPERLINK "http://www.brainyquote.com/quotes/quotes/m/ maxlucado543045.html's assignment was to articulate the Gospel and nothing more. Now I believe that if we donHYPERLINK "http://www.brainyquote.com/quotes/quotes/m/maxlucado543045. html"HYPERLINK "http://www.brainyquote.com/quotes/quotes/m/ maxlucado543045.html"t support the verbal expression of the Gospel with physical demonstration of compassion, we are not imitating Jesus.
<u>**Max Lucado**</u>

Hold firmly that our faith is identical with that of the ancients. Deny this, and you dissolve the unity of the Church.
Thomas Aquinas

The way to preserve the peace of the church is to preserve its purity.
Matthew Henry

The blood of the martyrs is the seed of the church.
Tertullian

And another thing is that I think as a church whenever we become politically driven, we alienate at least 50 percent of the people that God called us to reach with our political orientations.
T. D. Jakes

The gospel message itself—this message of love, redemption, grace, and mercy—was and is the main reason the church was and is disliked. I believe that the gospel is at war with a fallen humanity within the United States. Every time the real church apply the gospel to their communities, they are engaging in "culture warring." This is the battle that the church is called "the battle of light against darkness." The term "culture wars" simply refers to issues like abortion, gay marriage, same sex marriages, religious liberty, human poverty, immigration reforming human trafficking, racial injustice, urban renewal, prison reform, persecution of religious minorities and economic injustice.

That the gospel stay within the four walls of the church was not the intention of Jesus. He declared that his disciples are to love their neighbors, to care about human flourishing, and to embody the ethics of the kingdom of God. God has given the church the kinetic power shape government and public policy, to choose our political leaders with Christian behavior, and to influence the kind of policies they put in place. The church may not win every battle, and ultimately we fight not against flesh and blood, but against the powers of darkness, and this battle has already been won by our victorious King. The church can not escape the culture war; even if they try to remain behind the four walls. One of the primary principles motivating this work is found in Christ's words in Mark 12:17: *"Render under Caesar what is Caesar's and unto God what is God's."* Christians are called to obey the laws of the land in which they happen to live, unless those laws require a Christian to do something that stands in conflict with his or her faith.

Bibles were briefly banned from Walter Reed Medical Center. The Internal Revenue Service targeted Christian ministries engaged in pro-life activities. The government demanded to know the content of one group's prayers. A Wyoming church was ordered by government officials to turn over their membership roles. The list of attacks on the Christian church goes on and on – from students ordered to stop praying in front of the Supreme Court to chaplains being told they could no longer pray in the name of Jesus. The battleground has been expanded to pit gay rights groups against Christian-owned businesses that cater to the wedding industry. Christian bakers, florists and photographers have been sued and brought up on state discrimination charges for declining to participate in same-sex weddings. And in every single instance, lower courts have ruled that gay rights trump religious rights. "Christians have slowly given away their impact on culture by becoming more and worldlier instead of confronting the culture to conform to the biblical commands of God.

In Matthew 28:18-20, the resurrected Jesus says to His followers:" *All authority in heaven and on earth has been given to me. Therefore go and make disciples of all nations, baptizing them in the name of the Father and of the Son and of the Holy Spirit, and teaching them to obey everything I have commanded you. And surely I am with you always, to the very end of the age."*

The heaviest fighting is yet to come. In the midst of this 21st century we must stand up for righteousness. Our first step is to make sure that "no man or woman enslaves us using philosophy and empty deceit according to human tradition, according to the basic principles of the world, and not according to the Messiah" (Colossians: 2:8, KJV). We must evangelize, disciple, and raise up those who can lead the remnant.

There was a call for a shift to return to traditionalism. Theologians' leadership did not construct a systematic theology in favor of all Christians that would meet the needs of their people. The second shift was the incorporation of sociological, anthropological, and ethnographic methods to the study of American religion. They view Christianity through lenses of pluralism. There was a further shift called the dissolution of denominationalism and the ascension of a particular group having the right answer such as the "Born Again Christianity."

It is the responsibility of the followers of Christ to be the salt and light in a fallen world and this includes politics. It is the apparent duty of Christians to not abdicate their responsibility to be salt and light on today's contemporary moral issues. There is a divide among American Christians. The church *is* supposed to counter the culture.

For 185 years, American culture was friendly toward Christianity. America was considered a "Christian nation." America has never been considered an Islamic, Buddhist, or Hindu nation. But for the last 50 years, forces of humanism, atheism, evolution, social liberalism, pluralism, and "political correctness have assaulted the Christian church. They have been carving away moral and spiritual principles that once characterized society. So it is the religious, moral, and spiritual foundations are literally disintegrating.

The genuine church is fighting a spiritual culture war. The central issue is—God. The genuine church *is* in the throes of a life-and-death struggle over whether the God of the Bible will continue to be acknowledged as the one true God, and Christianity as the one true religion. This author believes the social and political liberals—from Hollywood to the University to the nation's Capitol—are openly hostile toward God. We who profess Christianity are facing the most perilous times ever faced in America. Forces have been mounted to bring about a full scale assault on traditional moral values. This author believes the evil forces are endeavoring to sanitize this society and break down all building connections for Christian unity. We live in a time far removed from the God Americans served in its origin. We are no longer the moral majority. We are a prophetic minority.

Who is the church? We find this answer recorded in the scriptures. Acts 2:41 reads, *Then they that gladly received his word were baptized: and the same day there were added [unto them] about three thousand souls."* I Corinthians 1:21 we read, *"For after that in the wisdom of God the world by wisdom knew not God, it pleased God by the foolishness of preaching to save them that believe."* We see from this, that this is God's plan to save people. They received the sermon Peter preached and were saved and baptized. This was a very effective sermon because 3,000 souls were saved. The saved souls are the church. Acts 2:44 *"And all that believed were together, and had all things common."* The believers stayed together, because they needed the strength of the each other and the apostles. Acts 2:47 *"Praising God, and having favor with all the people. And the Lord added to the church daily such as should be saved."* The Lord added to the number of the believers (church) every day. The apostles preached planted the seed), and God got the harvest. Acts 20:28 *"Take heed therefore unto yourselves, and to all the flock, over the which the Holy Ghost hath made you overseers, to feed the church of God, which he hath purchased with his own blood."* This assembly of people, the church, are not only responsible for themselves, but for their membership, as well. The Word of God are to be spoken to feed the flock is to be the un-compromised Word of God. Paul also reminds them that the precious shed blood of Jesus Christ has bought our salvation for us. The church of God is purchased by the blood of Jesus. I Corinthians 12:27 *"Now ye are the body of Christ, and members in particular."* The church is a group of people who once was filled with sin but Jesus made them well by His grace. An unbeliever can not be a church. There is no such thing as the church of the unchurched. Acts 2:46 *"And they, continuing daily with one accord in the temple, and breaking bread from house to house, did eat their meat with gladness and singleness of heart."* These Christians thought that Jesus would be back very soon and set up His kingdom. They had made the mistake of rejecting Jesus once, they did not want to take any chance that Jesus would return and them not know it. They all stayed with the twelve apostles. They ate together and had all things common. They were of one accord as they were at Pentecost. The church was the people, a family, saved saints of God, filled with the Holy Spirit, worshiping and praising God in spirit and in truth. This church was not a group of merchandising people in a mask using marketing tier methodologies to elevate themselves on a platform for recognition and financial prowess over people. The church is a biblical church family who subscribes to God's Word and commands realizing that God is the supreme authority over all things.

THE CHURCHES OF THE 21ST CENTURY

This author traveled far and near and came to a troubling problem facing the church. After consulting many spirit-filled preachers in the

United States and international, we agreed that the churches of the 21st Century do not resemble the historical church as recorded in the New Testament. For instance, the list of the Protestant churches in the United States is a non-exhaustive list and their focus is not predicated on the model set forth in the book of Acts. In this 21st century we have many Protestant churches has more than 2,000 members. Most of these churches are called mega churches and some fall outside this definition.

The Hartford Institute's database lists more than 1,300 Protestant churches in the United States. According to that data, approximately 50 churches on their list have attendance ranging from 10,000 to 47,000. Has the church become an established institution in the eyes of the world? Does the size make it successful? Should we emulate the patterns set forth by these church leaders for the 21st century model?

TOP 10 LARGEST MEGA CHURCHES

Have you ever wondered what the largest church congregations in America are? How many congregations make up this mega church? What is the salary of the pastor of this kind of church? This author found this information in public view listed in the Forbes Magazine. This book relates the following information for your consideration. He wonders if it fit the high calling of God as to how His church as been described in His Word. The author visited many of these churches. He surveyed many of the congregants to input for this book. He found some things unique and others things similar. With several visits and the Forbes Magazine, we found the answers to many questions. However, each and every day a church may move into a mega status and many churches do close due to foreclosures and other varying reasons. Forbes Magazine listed these ten as the largest mega churches in the United States as well as other books.

1: **Lakewood Church**
   Houston, Texas
   Pastor: **Joel Osteen**
   Average weekly attendance: 43,500
   Annual budget: $70 million

The largest mega church in the country is Lakewood Church. Pastor and televangelist Joel Osteen reaches approximately 7 million television viewers in the U.S. His broadcast reaches more than 100 countries. The church is nondenominational. Joel Osteen took over the church after death of his father in 1999. Under his leadership the ministry has seven times that of his deceased father. His congregants reflect the demographics of its diverse home city. He preaches positive life sermons, and makes millions from his inspirational books. Many in the preaching arena called him a "motivational speaker." He is often heard postulating that a pastor "needs not to be poor." *He* says more riches means greater influence for ministry. It is said that he does not take a salary as such. He and his wife, Victoria, are the largest donors to Lakewood.

2: **Second Baptist Church of Houston**
Houston, Texas
Pastor: **Edwin Young**
Average weekly attendance: 24,000
Annual budget: $53 million

Pastor Edwin Young started the congregation 30 years ago with 300 people. He has five campuses. His ministry focuses on youth. He says; "Only churches reaching kids are really growing." "All the rest of it is really fluff," he says.

3: **North Point Community Church**
Alpharetta, Ga.
Pastor: **Andy Stanley**
Average weekly attendance: 23,000
Annual budget: $38.5 million

This is a nondenominational "church for the unchurched." There are three campuses in the Atlanta area. Pastor Andy Stanley preaches practical applications of the Bible.

4: **Willow Creek Community Church**
Chicago, Ill.
Pastor: **Bill Hybels**
Average weekly attendance: 22,500
Annual budget: $36.2 million

The church was organized in the Chicago area in 1975, and in 2002 it has added four additional campuses. "Don't let our size overwhelm you," the church says, Pastor Bill Hybels.

5: **LifeChurch.tv**
Edmond, Okla.
Pastor: **Craig Groeschel**
Average weekly attendance: 21,000
Annual budget: $32 million

The church is the epitome of a mega-church and a multimedia evangelistic church. There are 13 campuses spread across the country. It also has a video content feeds and has supplementary materials to feed to "thousands" of start-up churches. The church has a virtual campus with an "online pastor" for services. The mini services held at lifechurch.tv; reaches some 3,000 people from 140 countries throughout the week. Pastor organized the church in 1996.

6: **West Angeles Church of God in Christ**
Los Angeles, Calif.
Pastor: **Charles Blake Sr.**
Average weekly attendance: 20,000
Annual budget: $15 million

Charles Blake is the Bishop of the International Church of God in Christ. Pastor Blake took over this Pentecostal church in 1969 with 50 members; they have 80 ministries today. In 1992, he founded the West Angeles Community Development Corporation. In 2001, he founded Save Africa's Children. This is an organization that provides direct care for children orphaned by and vulnerable to the pandemic of HIV and AIDS in sub-Saharan Africa. Amongst its congregants are celebrities Denzel Washington, Stevie Wonder, Magic Johnson, and Angela Bassett and husband Courtney Vance.

7: **Fellowship Church**
Grapevine, Texas
Pastor: **Ed Young Jr.**
Average weekly attendance: 20,000
Annual budget: $51 million

The church has five campuses in the Dallas area and one in Miami that it merged with in 2006, growing from 11 people to about 700. Young describes his services as young and edgy. He says of mega-churches: "I am fearful that too many churches are just shuffling sheep, [bringing in] people from other churches." Ed Young was involved in a church disputes, financial problems, and charged with crimes.

8: **Saddleback Valley Community Church**
Lake Forest, Calif.
Pastor: **Rick Warren**
Average weekly attendance: 19,400
Annual budget: $36 million

Formed in 1980, Saddleback carries the motto "One family … many locations!" Pastor Warren gave the inaugural invocation for President Obama. He authored *The Purpose-Driven Life*, a book that has sold more than 30 million copies. Warren and his wife practice reverse tithing, giving 90% of their earnings to the church, and keeping the remaining 10%.

9: **Calvary Chapel**
Fort Lauderdale, Fla.
Pastor: **Robert Coy**

Average weekly attendance: 17,000 people

Annual contributions: $40.3 million in tithes and offerings (2008)

The South Florida Mega-Church (Mecca) brings in an additional $19.8 million a year in revenue from the likes of a bookstore, café, thrift store and publications sales, tuition fees from a school and grants.

10: **The Potter's House**

Dallas, Texas

Pastor: **T.D. Jakes**

Average weekly attendance: 17,000 people

Annual budget: declined to release figure

The Potter's House has had an explosion of growth. Pastor Jakes started with 50 families in 1996. The nondenominational church's Prison Satellite Network Broadcasting is fed to some 260 correction centers in the country, according to the church Web site.

TWELVE RICHEST PASTORS

The author researchers found that many of preachers in the mega church settings have been reaping God's favor materialistically. Of course it is important to understand that God says that a "servant is worthy of his hire." Forbes Magazine points out that Bishop Edir Macedo is at the top of the list of being the richest pastor in Brazil. He is the founder of the Universal Church of Kingdom of God.

The doctrine, known as 'Prosperity Theology,' is in the foundation of the most successful evangelical churches in Brazil. Bishop Edir Macedo is part of this kind of ministry. His net worth is by several Brazilian business magazines* at $1.1 billion (one government arm in Brazil estimates an even higher sum). However, he is continuously involved in scandals, mostly due to allegations that his organization had siphoned off billions of dollars of donations intended for charity. They have also been official charges of fraud and money laundering.

The ETI News Celebrity Network compiled a list of the wealthiest pastors. Larry McMillan disclosed this list and called it "Net worth of Church Leaders of the 21st Century."

1. Edir Macedo net worth 1.1. billion
2. Kenneth Copeland 760 million
3. Bishop David Oyedepo - net worth - $150 million
4. Bishop T.D. Jakes -Net Worth – 147 million
5. Pat Robinson net worth 100 million
6. Chris Oyakhilome net worth 50 million
7. Joel Osteen net worth 40 million
8. Benny Hinn - net worth 42 million
9. E.A. Adeboye net worth 39 million
10. Creflo Dollar – net worth $27 million
11. Billy Graham - net worth $25 million
12. Rick Warren- net worth 25 million

Many of the young preachers observed the kind of money that is being earned from the pulpit and strive to be a carbon copy of those they see making a boat load of money from the organized church. Many are not waiting for the call of God on their lives. It is their mannerism to imitate the ministry and the pastor. God's will and purpose for their lives does not drive them to build up the kingdom of God. The institute of church suffers and the pews are suffering. The world has discounted the value of the church and its intent. In fact the world has taken to posture to dictate to the church. The question is: Is there a voice crying in the wilderness to show the way of Christ to the world that is living in darkness. Many are thinking they have moved to a higher dimension, but in actuality they have prostituted the pews and gospel for their personal gain. The question that Gardner Taylor asked the author one day was: "where are the minds and souls of those who present the Kingdom of God?" The salient point of this discussion is "What is the church and Who is the church?"

CHAPTER TWO

THE FOOT PRINT OF THE CHURCH

T HERE ARE SOME guidelines on reducing the need to be a carbon copy of another church. Robert McMillan, "the financial guru of church financially stability" wrote a simply financial spiritual plan for an upstart ministry as well a plan for a striving mega church that will stand the test of God systematical Word. The idea is to prayerfully present your plan to God with personal modifications and be blessed.

This chapter is intended to provide some initial guidance for churches having the desire to implement a carbon copy of another existing ministry. This author suggests any ministry that wants to duplicate a ministry should take giant steps to seek God's plan instead of their plan. We recommend a renewable energy system that only God can provide. Duplicating someone else ministry will eventually zap out all their natural energy. We further recommend that the individual ought to take concrete measures to eliminate the desire to produce a carbon footprint of somebody else ministry that was command by God for them to build. The author's idea is to help each person to identify the right starting points for organizing a church. This step should only be initiated if God has called the individual to undertake this mission. God is calling for churches to make an impact on the world according to His dictates.

What difference can churches make? Churches can potentially make a huge contribution to tackling societal, ethnic, integrity changes in America and throughout the world. Churches are to be the forum for Godly leadership in our communities. Every church has been given the command to allow it to be led by Jesus, the Christ. We are to strive in our churches to allow God to be on earth as it is in heaven. Every church has been commanded to leave a lasting Holy Spirit footprint that will point the future generation to subscribe the plan of serving God with their whole heart, mind, body, and soul. The church must leave proof that they conducted God's business in spirit and in truth as He commanded. God left us His plan and all the church has to do is to follow it.

WHERE SHOULD THE CHURCH START?

ESTABLISH THE GOD GIVEN SITUATION – These questions should be answered by the leadership of the church. What does it take to be successful in God's sight? What are your limitations? Will you compromise for the sake of the world and its agenda? Then, they are to develop a way to track the progress and prioritize the various objectives.

OPTIMISE THE HOLY ENERGY GOD SENDS- These questions should be answered. Is the church using all their talents and gifts to make disciples? Is the church educating the populace before sending them out to be disciples? Then, the leadership is to make sure that the disciples are properly trained and they will only advance the kingdom of God.

EXPLORE DISCIPLES, TRAINERS AND OTHER OPTIONS – The extent to which you can use on-site individuals is paramount. The supply and demand theory does come into play when disciples are needed to give instructions to the congregation. If the church has good dependable disciples, then it will with God's help make a high-profile impact on the future generation that will last for several generations.

ENCOURAGE OTHERS TO FOLLOW THE PASTOR'S LEAD- There are statistics that indicate that many churches and congregations want to engage in discipleship training programs. But, relatively few have succeeded as yet. Many churches do not understand how to evangelize the world in this 21st century. They do not know how to compete with the many opportunities afforded to the people of the world. They are faced with the problem of having to compete with the world's activities in order to get people to be trained as Disciples of Christ. However, the author firmly suggests that the church must manage to implement a successful discipleship program within the church. Having done so, it is imperative that they share their experiences with others so that the church can prayerfully use their success formula to bring more people into church.

This can have its foundation stance in the home of Christians. Parents have the responsibility to help their children to learn and live the gospel each and everyday. The church leaders and teachers assist parents in this important responsibility. Every parent has the responsibility to regularly provide their children with Biblical truth and carry them to church services and bible study. When this happens, and they are confronted with the questions of becoming a disciple, the answer will automatically be yes. We are to train up a child in the way they are to go. When this is done then the footprint of the church will pass on to the next generation.

This author was raised in the church. My mother and father were foundation members of New Light Baptist Church, Hallsboro, NC. My mother, Deaconess Marguerite McMillan went on to be with the Lord at the age of 94. She was the last of the foundation members. My father, Deacon James McMillan went on to be with God at the age of 85. They served the church their entire life. Research indicates that they were called the "founding members" of the church. Of course, we know that God is the founder of the church. My mother was caring me in her womb as she played the piano and directed the choir. I joined the church at the age of 12 on a Friday night at 12:00 am while on the "mourner's bench." The Holy Ghost filled the church and all who were in attendance.

God made it my purpose in life to preach my parents funeral. God got the glory out of their lives and their life testimonies allowed each person who knew them had a Godly picture of how God can use a family to His glory. God made this author a disciple of Jesus, the Christ. God orally called this author into His ministry. God called this author to pastor three churches. He served at the behest of God. His ministry was coached, mentored, and under the covering of the New Shiloh Baptist Church, Baltimore, MD. God opened the door for this author to have preached to congregations in the United States as well as aboard. It has been his honor and privilege to have preached the unadulterated gospel in churches of most church denominations in the Christian faith. God is faithful and all His promises are yes and amen concerning His church. God leaves a footprint in the sand for church leaders to follow as God leads them.

Some of the churches where this author preached spoke in dulcet tones, some spoke in tongues, some spoke Korean, some spoke German, and many had various colors of skin. Some sat quietly in the pews and others rolled in the aisles and were covered with white sheets. Some raised their hands in praise and others kept their hands on their wallets and coats. This author experienced ministering in mega churches and in the small churches in Europe. For thirteen years, this author was the pastor of what many called a "remnant church." Having shared these experiences, this author is not a stranger to any denominational church. God has blessed this author and he truly owes his life to God. This author must challenge the minds of God's leaders to think on the things that God has placed in his mind. God is calling for a revival to take place in the churches. Truly without a doubt, the church needs a Godly revival. This book has been written to seek assistance from Holy Ghost filled saints to expose the pathway that some churches have taken and to offer prayerful solutions to bring them back in line with the Word of God. Also, we must pray for those who have been blinded by the adversary tactics to take the church off focus.

The 21st century churches are facing many problems collectively. One is what the author calls the "Christian Stay Away Syndrome." There is a tremendous number of Christians who have decided to stay home on Sunday's instead of attending worship services. This trend is affecting the 21st century church. These Christian "Stay Away" individuals were once excited church leaders and were a threat to the adversary. They were actually big cups of the revolution that would help usher in the revival God is calling for in the Christian marketplace. Many have been praying for centuries and dreamed of for centuries for such a revival. But, now they have elected to become a part of the club called "Christian Stay Away Syndrome."

This author researched and gathered information from hundred of sources, both physical and personal testimonies. There are many groups, organizations, and Christian research groups that have collected data on the church. However, many have not taken the time to place it in a book that will help the Christian church press toward the mark of their higher calling in Jesus, the Christ. This author has been given the charge to place this information in books and this ought to prompt church leaders to allow God to direct the path of the church.

A portion of this research was conducted by The Barna Group. This is a California-based Christian research organization. Their research found that about 13 million Americans whom the researchers identified as being born again were "unchurched. These Americans have not attended a Christian church service, other than for a holiday at any time in the past six months." Genuine Christians will not turn their backs on the commands of God. Making disciples is the command of God for His believers.

Andrew Strom, a Revival historian and teacher found painful evidence of "a worldwide phenomenon." He spoke on a radio show about his findings. He dubbed his finding as the "Out of Church Christians." Strom wrote about it in one of his e-newsletters. He was bombarded with responses from people around the world telling him, "Me too."

But, Storm is still actively working and doing God's bidding. I have heard the saying that "a ship of fools adrift in the sea of confusion will eventually sink." This is the way that some might paint it. But, the church is not a ship, and God's children are not fools. The Word of God says, Matthew 5:22 (KJV) "But I say unto you, that whosoever is angry with his brother without a cause shall be in danger of the judgment: and whosoever shall say to his brother, Raca, shall be in danger of the council: but whosoever shall say, Thou fool, shall be in danger of hell fire." Call no man a fool. We do have problems. The church may drift but the true church will not drown.

The author's intention is to sound the alarm and those who are struggling will follow God, pray, believe, and apply Psalms 121 to their lives. Psalm 121 (KJV)

1.   I will lift up mine eyes unto the hills, from whence cometh my help.
2.   My help cometh from the LORD, which made heaven and earth.
3.   He will not suffer thy foot to be moved: he that keepeth thee will not slumber.
4.   Behold, he that keepeth Israel shall neither slumber nor sleep.
5.   The LORD is thy keeper: the LORD is thy shade upon thy right hand.
6.   The sun shall not smite thee by day, nor the moon by night.
7.   The LORD shall preserve thee from all evil: he shall preserve thy soul.
8.   The LORD shall preserve thy going out and thy coming in from this time forth, and even for evermore.

True Christians do not have the option of not attending an assembly of the righteous. God commands that we attend the assembly of the righteous. The question is what does withdrawal solve?

The second reason why many are staying home is because of the proliferation of the false teaching that is running rampant in American churches. These teachings must be run out of the churches of Jesus, the Christ. Many are allowing secularism to take root in the church. False teachers have created a "whiteout" for millions of potential believers. We must detect and overcome these destructive so called Christian doctrines and expose them as false teachings. God must get the glory out of the worship services. God will not send His spirit in an unclean church. We are living in perilous times, and time is running out. Jesus is coming back.

Steve Hill, an evangelist said in his book *Spiritual Avalanche,* that he received a prophetic vision warning the church of an impending "spiritual avalanche" that could kill millions. His vision also speaks of the coming of Jesus, the Christ again. Jesus is coming back for His church. He will be looking for a church without spot or wrinkle.

Years ago my wife, and I were driving home one night on the interstate when we were overcomed by what we called a never ending rain storm mixed with white snow. I was driving around a mountain slope with over a one mile drop. "I can hardly see the road," I shouted. We were experiencing a complete whiteout. There was no where to stop or turn around. This storm came on us suddenly. I couldn't see the road or other cars.

A normal drive turned into a mystical blizzard of white snow and rain. Occasionally, I thought I saw the white lines on the road. I thought about a minister who use to drive for the military. He told me about how he had to look for the white lines in an adverse situation. He said that he had to keep driving until the adverse weather seceded. So, armed with this information, I slowed down and prayed for God to intercede in our behalf.

By the providence of God we looked to the hill mentioned in Psalm 121 and kept driving. Suddenly, the storm lifted and we gave God the praise. Later, we found out that miles in front us and miles behind were accidents —too many to number. Many cars and trucks had slide off the road and some turned over. Many cars that had stopped were crashed by others running into them. We had received a miracle by God. It was by the hand of the Lord that he singled us out for a blessing.

This was a weather condition in which visibility was totally wiped out. God has made some promises to us. God has made some promises to His church. All His promises are yes and Amen in the Lord. The church is to stand on the promises of God. The church is to obey God. The church may not see their way, but we are not to follow the adversary's plan. We are to stand on the Word of God. We are not to allow the storms of this world to make us panic and let false teachings into the church.

The church of the 21st century is facing the same difficulty. There are many oblivious dangers that the church is facing. God is telling us that the church will face these dangers and many more are waiting on the horizon. In this spiritual whiteout, He has already given us reference points.

God told us not to forget the ancient landmarks. We hold onto the posted landmarks that brought us thus far. The church is to be aware of erroneous teachings. The church is witnessing lies spoken as truths. We are witnessing lies told by false teachers that cause the innocent believers to become disoriented and blinded.

We must speak with the unction and urgency of God. Preachers are dying men preaching to dying men. This whiteout hovering over the church has the potential to destroy everyone. The storm had layers of snow covering the car which means that these layers could be the covering of the traditional truth of Christ. The rain had the potential of washing the snow away and to give hope in the midst of any situation. God has the power to keep the church safe. We are not to let the church be lost in the flurry of the snow.

We are to realize that no one who loves God would willingly preach and teach deception to His believers. If a person has a real relationship with Jesus, they will preach and teach the Gospel of Jesus, the Christ. But, there is a spiritual whiteout taking place throughout the churches in the world. This can only mean that there is an unhealthy, unbalanced, unbiblical teaching going on in the churches that is blinding the many people in the church. This whiteout is growing rampantly in the church and the world is being lost because of the infiltration of lies being spreaded by the adversary. The footprint of the church must be so pronounced that the future generation will not have any trouble following and implementing them to their children. The next generation must be trained to be able to take up the discipleship making model and train the next generation to walk by faith and not by sight.

CHAPTER THREE

THE TRANSPARENT CHURCH

I T IS IMPERATIVE that the word transparency should be mentioned and discussed in the church. There comes a time when we are to take inventory of our church life. We are to ask ourselves what kind of church God wants us to be as we enter into the new millennium. Paul says that we as the church are to resist the temptation to be a church of sophistication, a wealthy church, a powerful church, a knowledge church in order to be attractive to the world. He says that we are to have the same attitude as Jesus, the Christ. Jesus says that we are to be His disciples. We are called to have a lifestyle of loving sacrifice for one another. We are not to have our focal point on impressing the world. We can live transparently before one another only as we live in perfect openness to God.

Passions easily ignite when the word transparency arise in sermons, bible study, and or general discussion within the church settings. A church is not real until it becomes transparent. A transparent church is not pretentious. The members of a transparent church will tell of their setbacks as well as their victories. The true believer values transparency. But, it causes concern also. In a transparent church, members are given the opportunity to share their struggles with one another. These members are loving and caring. This author values transparency and for good sound reasons. The church will grow stronger and the congregation will become more matured in their way with Christ. What we need in this 21st century is more transparent churches.

The transparent church will not be silent about what is wrong within the church. They are open and honest about sin. God is not pleased when a church does not preach and teach against sin. The church must have its focus on adding value to the spiritual character of its members. They are to refuse to participate in things that will destroy the souls of congregants. They will not plant bad seeds for they know that bad seeds will spring up and destroy the harvest. The transparent church knows that they can not entertain good and evil. Bad influences will eventually destroy good character. God is not pleased when a church is not transparent. We do not want Him to remove His anointing. But, we must admit that transparency can not be found in many churches.

The church is to condemn sin and to preach to sinners. Paul makes this principle very clear in his letter to the Ephesians when he says, "Do not participate in the unfruitful deeds of darkness, but instead reprove them. The transparent church cannot relegate certain groups as if they are different than others" (Ephesian. 5:11). In our culture the church that preaches against sin is called a church that is "judging people." They might as well have a sign over the entrance "we are a church that judge people." But, if the church does not preach against sin is really a church that is a "cover-up church." The end result of not addressing real sin is cover-up. This kind of church does not have transparency.

The transparent church does not marginalize groups in the church. When new believers join the fellowship in a transparent church, there is not a special group wherein they must participate called the new believers group. The transparent church is truthful. The church is to be united.

The greatest charge leveled against Jesus during his earthly ministry was that He was a friend of publicans and sinners. Jesus is a "friend of sinners, but He hates sin." The transparent is to openly let the congregation know that they do not embrace sin, but they will fight to get the sin out of the sinner. They will show love to homosexuals, but letting them clearly understand that God said the sin is a stink in His nostril. The transparent church will preach that people must get rid of the sin and become a new creation in God. It is the same with abusers, thieves, and murderers. Sins are not acceptable in the body of a transparent church. They believe that God is able to cleanse the sinner of all sin.

God is calling for Disciples of Christ. They can not practice sin. They must be the kind of disciple of Christ that God is seeking. The Gospel is grand in its depth for discipleship. The Gospel is grand in its breadth for evangelism. The transparent church love sinners for they realize that they can be saved by God's grace. So it is that the transparent church preaches to them the unadulterated gospel of Jesus, the Christ.

The transparent church will always apply biblical truth. The truth is taught from the pulpit, in the pews, inside classrooms, and even in the hallways. The truth is to be taught everywhere. The transparent church holds God's truth as its absolute guide for all conversation and action. God's truth is the essential ingredient that forms the foundation for the entire church.

The transparent church must confront sin no matter where they find it. It saddens my heart to say that I have witnessed that many churches choose to turn away and compromise truth so that their pew members can continue to be ignorant on the matters of the church. Some church leaders close their eyes to what they know is wrong and only speak on what makes the congregants feel good or comfortable in their sins in order to keep their numbers high.

The story of Hezekiah in 2 Chronicles 29 gives a tremendous example of this principle. Hezekiah was willing to expose the sin of the past regime. The priest was willing to expose the sins of the congregants. God exposes the sins of the world. It is unchristian to join others in the hiding sin. It is called in Ephesians the "ugly truth." (Ephesians 5:11). Sin is sin no matter where it is found. The transparent church points out sin wherever it is found. Sin maybe found amongst the chairman of the deacons, the treasurer, some longtime member or the pastor. The transparent church teaches the truth which is found in the Word of God.

It is a fact that unhealthy and destructive teaching can enter the church in various ways. Biblical truths can be taught excluding other related biblical truths. This kind of teaching will produce a dangerous imbalance. Also a biblical truth can be taught in an exaggerated way. This means that it is taught by adding more or less than what the scriptures mean. This kind of teaching does more harm than good. Biblical warnings are often ignored, misinterpreted, reinterpreted when it suits the need of the non-transparent church teacher. The true meaning is radically distorted and the meaning misconstrued. Yes, in non-transparent church biblical warnings are ignored or reinterpreted so radically that they lose all impact or effect. This kind of teaching leaves people vulnerable, exposed, and functionally ignorant. However, the leadership ought to know that they are not operating according to God's word. You can believe that Satan and his imps sees the accomplishments that they have made in their attempt to destroy the church.

Paul warned that the "time will come when believers will not endure sound doctrine, but according to their own desires, because they have itching ears, they will heap up for themselves teachers; and they will turn their ears away from the truth, and be turned aside to fables" (2 Tim. 4:3-4). The 21st century church may be indicted as the church that Paul was talking about. Christianity, as a whole in America is close to turning the faith community to be a fable. Research indicates that millions have already succumbed to these false teachings. It is crucial that the church identify the adversary's falsehood before we lose more souls. The church must agree and point out what we believe. We must point out these lies that have caused this whiteout. This book will point out seven greatest lies that have infiltrated the church and have led to the upcoming and present whiteout.

OVEREMPHASIS OF PROSPERITY

Those false teachers who overemphasize prosperity are motivated by greed. Their messages are riddled with overemphasized scriptures causing people to look for their prosperity rather than living a life pleasing to God. To these false teachers and preachers it is a means of financial gain. Paul rebuked these types of people in a strong way. He labeled them "as corrupt minds and destitute of the truth, whose suppose that godliness is a means of gain" (1 Tim. 6:5). 1 Timothy 6:5 (KJV), "Perverse disputing of men of corrupt minds, and destitute of the truth, supposing that gain is godliness: from such withdraw thyself."

There was an advertisement circulating in the town that a noted preacher was coming to the District of Columbia. This preacher was known for praying a financial blessing on all who attended his conferences. So, an entourage of men dressed in their finery decided to attend this conference. When the organized and hopeful men arrived at their destination, they witnessed a line of people almost a half of mile long. One of the men said "we might as well go back." There is not any way we can get into this prosperity conference," he said. But, this author was determined to observe and check out the validity of this ministry wherein God gives out monies through this ministry. This author stated, "I'm going to the front of the line. At the front of the line I saw prideful men standing at the doorway. I boldly peeked in the foyer. There I saw an associate standing in the foyer.

He immediately, said "let this man of God in." He said that he had a special seat for me. I beckoned to my friends to come in and follow me. Some of my friends followed me and others did not. Then, my long time associate said, "Follow me."

The fellow clergymen were dressed in splendid gowns trimmed in purple and gold. Their robes were king like and the finest jewelry was hanging from the neck. He, one of my friends and myself was escorted to the front of the elaborate church. Then, he pointed to a seat in the pulpit made of gold that stretched almost to the ceiling. There were more than 10 people seated in the pulpit. There were almost 5,000 people on the main floor dressed in finery of their custom. I was wearing a regular suit of clothing. I declined the seat in the pews and my friend and I took seats on the front row on the main floor.

Finally, my other friends took seats behind me with the exception of one. My associate friend quickly returned to the foyer. He came back leading the great processional of clergy. Then over 200 clergy marched in dressed in robes as if they were a part of the dynasty of the royal clergy. The trumpeters blew and the people stood up cheering. I could not stop wondering about the whereabouts of my other clergy friend. Finally, I saw him in the upper balcony waving his pocket handkerchief at us.

The processional of men robed in finery marched stately down the aisles on red carpet. The main guest preacher for the ceremony entered the pulpit from the side door carrying a golden rod. The attendee's stood to give him a king's ovation. One could hear the cheers for about four blocks. The prosperity preacher was now in the building. This author watched and wondered what would happen next. He thought about how his associate happened to get he and his friend a front seat on the main floor and why was he offered a seat on the pulpit.

After the sermon, it was now time to become a multi-millionaire. Having paid one hundred dollars as seed money, I was ready to let the main preacher lay hands on me for my fortune. I was elated. The message was that before twelve o'clock the very next day, a check would be in the mail. The theme was "Don't Doubt God." Of course, being young in the ministry, I got caught up in the moment. The next day, I looked for the check. However, there was not a check. In fact I never got the check. What did I learn from this encounter?

The danger is that many sincere people embrace this message. This message is still being proclaimed. It is called name it and claim it. It is called prosperity gospel. Many churches use this approach and use scripture to support their claim. They use false interpretations as proof to make their case. They point to the covenant blessing promised to Israel for their obedience. But they use it out of context. Also they use the scripture referring to financial prosperity recorded in (Deuteronomy) 28:1-13). They usually highlight verses in Proverbs and Psalms that link financial prosperity to generosity, hard work, godly living and faith (e.g., PS. 112). They remind us of wonderful promises, recorded in Proverbs 3:9-10. Then they linked them with verses in the New Testament that Jesus spoke of such as "Give, and it will be given to you" (Luke 6:38). And they quote Paul, who wrote about the financial principles of sowing and reaping (1 Cor. 9; 2 Cor. 8-9; Phil. 4:11-19).

This author realize that it takes money to run the organization of the church. But, God does not require money to keep His church in action. God does not want money to have you. There's more to the story than the carnal prosperity false teachers teach. The false teachers fail to mention the scriptures in the New Testament.

1. Jesus warned against storing up treasures on earth (Matthew 6:19-24) and covetousness (Luke 12:15).
2. Jesus emphasized caring for the poor (Matthew 25:31-46).
3. Paul and John both taught that we should not live according to this present age (1 Corinthian 7:29-31; 1 John 2:15-17).
4. Jesus did not die to make us financially wealthy but to save us from our sins (Matthew 1:21).
5. God chose the poor to be rich in faith and kingdom heirs (James 2:5).

The carnal prosperity preachers and false teachers have ignored other biblical warnings, like Paul's powerful words to Timothy: "Those who desire to be rich fall into temptation and a snare, and into many foolish and harmful lusts which drown men in destruction and perdition. For the love of money is a root of all kinds of evil, for which some have strayed from the faith in their greediness, and pierced themselves through with many sorrows. But you, O man of God, flee these things and pursue righteousness, godliness, faith, love, patience, gentleness" (1 Timothy. 6:9-11).

Carnal prosperity preachers constantly encourage God's people to seek after riches. They never cease to encourage God's people to seek after God for the purpose of riches. They judge the spirituality of God's saints by the kind of car they drive. This does-not have anything to do with the gospel of Jesus. They are destroying the very foundation of the church as they are on the payroll of the adversary.

EXAGGERATED VIEW OF GRACE

This hyper-grace teaching has become an epidemic. Many think that God's grace is designed to allow the Christian to participate in sin that Grace may abound. This false teaching has slipped into the church like a weed on the golf course. Even today, in many churches it has been unnoticed and has taken root. This exaggerated view of grace is hard to get out but must be dealt with immediately. I have counseled many young Christians that were on fire for the Lord and fell under the myth given to them by false preachers and teachers. Instead of them seeking a closer walk with God, they are partying. Some of these young Christians have stopped attending church and their young family are following in their footsteps. This will probably spread to the future generation. This will leave millions of lukewarm Christians who have traded their carnal passion for poison.

Research indicates that some hyper-grace preachers live in sin. They ease their conscience by preaching that God is all love and never condemns. They preach that God doesn't judge us by our conduct. These false teachers took on the character listed in Jude. They "turn the grace of our God into lewdness" (Jude 4). The New International Version describes such lewdness as "a license for immorality."

But not all hyper-grace preachers use this way to justify sin. Some truly love Jesus. They preach the truth mixed with error. They take the undeniable, glorious truth about God and present it in an exaggerated form that they nullify all divine warnings. They claim the word of Jesus does not apply to New Covenant believers. They encourage us not to judge and God is the only deity that can judge. However, Christians ought to understand that we are to know them by their fruits. We ought to know that we have a relationship of God through Jesus, the Christ or we do not have one. There is no between the sheets. If this seems judgmental, then it's time for honestly to be found in everyone's teachings. God gives us wisdom and understanding. Certainly we ought to know a biblical based teacher from an optimist. God did not call His children to just go through the Word; He said let this Word go through you. Why are we so afraid in this godless generation to confront fallacies?

These hyper-grace teachers rightly emphasize that we are saved by grace and not by works (Eph. 2:8-9), that while we were yet sinners Christ died for us (Rom. 5:6-8), that we are no longer sinners but saints in God's sight (1 Cor. 1:2), that God's love for us is not based on our performance (Rom. 5:9-10), that having begun in the Spirit we can't become perfect by human effort (Gal. 3:3), that we are now sons and daughters of God, joint heirs with Jesus (Rom. 8:15-17), and more!

But they ignore other scriptural truths. They do not draw biblical theological conclusions. Yes, Jesus died for all our sins—past, present and future. But, will not conclude that believers have to deal with sin. They do not preach or teach holiness. The Word says be holy as He is Holy. The Word also says in Galatians 6:7-9(KJV) 7 Be not deceived; God is not mocked: for whatsoever a man soweth, that shall he also reap. 8 For he that soweth to his flesh shall of the flesh reap corruption; but he that soweth to the Spirit shall of the Spirit reap life everlasting. 9 And let us not be weary in well doing: for in due season we shall reap, if we faint not. False prophets will be judged by God. Matthew 7:20 (KJV) 20 Wherefore by their fruits ye shall know them.

ANTINOMIANISM

Antinomianism means literally "against law." It is a hop from an overemphasis on the grace message to complete antinomianism. Actually, to the church it means that "anything goes," since Jesus has set us free.

This is the wrong interpretation of the scripture. Jesus did not set us free *to* sin. Jesus, set us free from sin.

Jesus died for us. He paid the sin debt. He broke sin's power over our lives. And by His spirit we can live righteous as required in the law commanded in (Rom. 8:1-4). False teachers spread the poisonous teaching that Jesus did not call us to live beyond the requirements of the law in His teaching. These teachers say that adultery refers to adultery of the heart and not just the physical act (Matt. 5:27-28). This is a false presentation of Jesus' intention and command for His disciples.

The church would want to understand that God's laws are perfect, holy, and glorious. The laws of God are not what are destroying the notions of the church. It is the sin of the flesh that is causing many to reject the church as an unidentified collection of disciples. Sin is the problem. But, many churches are not preaching about the sinful flesh being the problem. Sin will take you to places that you never intended to go. Sin has a high cost factor. Sin will make people losers. Sin will make you stay longer than you intended to stay. Sin is the reason why people will spend eternity in Hell. Sin promises the sinner that they will be rich and famous, but in the end the person will be bare. Sin loves to destroy and curse your very being. Sin loves you for a season, and eventually curses you for eternity. For the churches that embrace antinomians, they will not tell the people where they will end up. Does your church tell you the consequences of sin?

The Word of God says cry aloud, spare not, lift up thy voice like a trumpet, and shew my people their transgression, and the house of Jacob their sins. –Isaiah 58:1 Some pastors frankly admit they must preach against sin. Preachers are to preach against sin for four reasons. First, God is against sin, born again Christians are against sin, the Holy Bible is against sin, and the moral consciences of the secularism is against sin. Second, preachers are to preach against sin because God commands them to preach the whole counsel of God. Thirdly, Jesus, the Christ preached against sin, and preachers are to be like Him. Fourth, to preach against sin is the only way to bring revival in the land and salvation to the sinners.

DEIFICATION OF MAN

Research pointed out that the false teachings in the 21st century starts with man. It never was started by God. Paul was inspired by God to write the gospel message in Romans. He started with God and then wrote about man. God is holy. We are called out to be Holy as God is Holy. He is righteous and we are called out to become righteous. It is God who is the supreme judge of all mankind. We need His mercy and grace. We ought to know to cry out for God's mercy and grace.

In this 21st century gospel especially in America, has been changed to suit the various churches. They do not preach about sovereignty of God. In fact in many of the churches they preach the "ME GOSPEL." It is all about "me." I call it the "Me Gospel Syndrome." The American way is to make things bigger and better. The churches have concentrated on devising a way to make their congregants think that Jesus came to make you, the church bigger and better. Years, ago it was prognosticated that there would become a time when everyone would believe that they could become a god. They called it living in the Age of Aquarius. I ask some questions: "If everything is about them, then what about others?" Who will look out for the have not's? Martin Luther King spoke about our obligations to help the least of these.

Jesus said to His disciples, "If anyone desires to come after Me, let him deny himself, and take up his cross, and follow Me. For whoever desires to save his life will lose it, but whoever loses his life for My sake will find it" (Matt. 16:24-25).

America is in grave danger. The world is on the brink of collapse. Millions upon millions gaze upon man rather than God. A closer look at the Congress of the United States, political system, and the entire government will point to the fact that Godly principles have abandoned the minds of the politicians. The truth is constantly called lies and lies are being called truth. It is impossible to hear words like Messiah, Lord, Savior, and Anointed One used in their discussions. The fruits of the spirit are not evident in their output for the country. God is responding to this absence of love for His children. God will unleash His wrath as recorded in His word. What is being produced is the setup for the Antichrist. The church must stop the custom of worshiping man and return to worship

Him and Him only. The Antichrist is being maneuvered in as the church is sleep. The question is: Does your church worship man or God? We can not worship two; we either love one or hate the other. The church must be transparent for the eyes of God and prayerfully get it right, for God is coming back again. The church must have transparency in this 21st century as we seek to save the next generation.

CHAPTER FOUR

THE AGE OF CHALLENGE

GOD'S WORD IS under attack. The church and the secular world are challenging His Word. This challenge really started in the Garden of Eden. It started with the challenge given to Eve by the serpent in the Garden of Eden. The scripture states: "Has God indeed said, 'You shall not eat of every tree of the garden'?" (Gen. 3:1). There is the satanic challenge that is taking place in the 21st century all over again. The church is entertaining a twofold challenge. Two questions are asked for the church to respond. Satan asks then, and is asking now: Did God really say that? And, God really did not mean what He said, did He? "You really will not die if you eat from the tree of good and evil. (Verses 1-5).

This twofold challenge is on the plate of the church today. Be not deceived, God is not mocked; you shall reap what you sow. The non-believing church is under attack again by the adversary. This is an ongoing assault on the church. Today there is an attempt to challenge the authority of God to even be God. Since the wealth of the righteous is stored up in the hands of the wicked, they are printing more books indicating that God does not have the authority to be God. So it is that the "Best-selling" report to the media is that the biblical text isn't reliable. They further state that the biblical manuscripts are hopelessly contradictory, and that there is not anyway we can know about the historical Jesus. Other authors of the same persuasion says that the Bible is only a collection of religious traditions. These same critics say that God is nothing but a religious myth. They say that the bible is nothing more than a collection of religious traditions.

For the most part, they say that the Bible must live up to their standards.

They judge the bible based on their morality. When the scriptures go against what they believe and feel, then, they will judge it based on their morality. They do not have any problem in questioning God and His Word. They question God's Word and His authenticity. Yes, they challenge the authority of God's Word.

REJECTING HELL

There are churches and so-called Christians that reject the notion of Hell. Therefore, many will say that God is a God of love and He will not allow anyone to spend eternity in Hell. This became prominent in the 21st century because many preachers preached an unbalanced gospel. They emphasize God's love. This kind of church will not speak of God's wrath. They make it a habit of emphasizing His mercy. Never do they speak of His justice. Hell is not welcome as a part of their theology. Even in there contradiction, hell has no place in their church, but heaven is a place where all will go.

This kind of church has neither room for hell nor the future punishment of God upon those who refuse Him as their personal Savior and proclaim that there is no God.

Jesus used strong language when He taught about the fire of hell and about people weeping and wailing and gnashing their teeth (see Matt. 8:12)? Jesus taught that there is a place prepared for those who reject His salvation plan. He said: "it is more profitable for you that one of your members perishes, than for your whole body to be cast into hell" (Matt. 5:29) Other New Testament writers warn us repeatedly about the wrath of God. (Ephesians 5:1-6)

Many churches debate about the existence of hell. But, there are churches that downplay it and even eliminate it from the Word of God. God's Word will not be reversed because certain churches have that desire. Again, there is a coming judgment, a dreadful and eternal consequence for rejecting God's salvation plan.

Revelation 20:11-15 clearly warns about unbelievers facing the Great White Throne Judgment. Yet, in the 21st century false teachers have instituted the falsehood that there is no heaven or hell. We are living in the age of when the authority of a sovereignty God is questioned. This is the age of challenging the Word of God and His existence.

UNIVERSAL RECONCILIATION

There is the wrong theological conclusion of universal reconciliation. This means that in the end everyone will go to heaven. It simply means that one can continue to sin and not pay for their sins. This is like getting out of jail without paying for the crime.

Universalism concludes that all paths lead to God. There is future suffering, but it will be purged. Rather than be punished, ultimately everyone will be saved. This type of church teaches that God reconciled "all things to Himself, by Him, whether things on earth or things in heaven, having made peace through the blood of His cross" (Col. 1:20). And they point out that just as in Adam all die, in Jesus all will live (Rom. 5:12-21).

Using this definition, would you think that Adolf Hitler was in heaven? Would you think that confessed mass murders are in heaven? Of course, the believers of universal reconciliation would preach this as absolute. I call this an "avalanche snow syndrome theory." This foundation of this kind of church will deteriorate and the foundation will cord and melt down and crumble to the ground.

During this 21st century, we ought to be celebrating the life, death and resurrection of Jesus. We ought to glorify Him, give Him the Honor, and respect. It is His command that we follow Him. However, a gentle breeze of false teaching has turned into a strong wind of blasphemous error, heretical, and a bold face doctrinal deviation, and a massive deadly whiteout of the facts.

This author recommends and strongly urges that the church stay committed to sound biblical teachings of Jesus. Do not permit false teachers to weave into the church and plant seeds of deceptions. Do not permit the "avalanche snow syndrome theory" destroy your faith in the God's promise. This is one of the purposes for writing this book. I am warning the church through the Spirit of Jesus, the Christ. The church must stand against the idea of universal reconciliation. Yes, Jesus said in the last days even the elect could be deceived.

America remains deeply religious relative to Europe, Russia, and other countries. There is an anti-God campaign launched years ago by satanic organizations to strike God out of the functioning body of the United States. Its primary mission is and was to overthrow the foundation belief that God is in charge of the world. It wants to destroy the belief that God is sovereign, Holy, and the origin of all things present both past and present and future.

There is not a single self-professed atheist among the 535 members of the US Congress. It is must be mentioned that US presidential candidates are expected to believe in God. God echoes from their speakers, even though the candidates' actions may not be as the Word of God commands. Just as the church is to be transparent so is the governing body.

According to the Pew research group, one third of Americans aged 18 to 29 say they have "no religious affiliation", compared with less than 10 per cent of their grandparents' generation. Many faiths have flourished in the United States; including imports spanning the country's multicultural heritage as well as those founded within the country, and have led the United States to become the most religiously diverse country in the world. The majority of Americans identify themselves as Christians (76%), while non-Christian religions (including Buddhism, Hinduism, Judaism, and others) collectively make up about 4% of the adult population. Another 15% of the adult population identified as having no religious affiliation. According to the American Religious Identification Survey, religious belief varies considerably across the country: 59% of Americans living in Western states report a belief in God, yet in the South (the "Bible Belt") the figure is as high as 86%. The United States has more Christians than any other country in the world. Catholics represent the largest Christian denomination in America with over 68 million members.

A new petition urges lawmakers to fight a "perverse" wave of anti-religion moves that effectively are outlawing "the faith that formed the moral foundation of our nation."

While the fight is being funded and encouraged by clandestine donors, the church can not afford to sit idly by and watch the tide submerge the people of God. The author wants to remind and warn the church to be vigilant in all that they do.

Yes there are many challenges facing the church of the 21st century. All of them are of equal importance and the church must deal with them according to the Word of God. For instance, there is the challenge of broken marriages, cynicism, proclaiming the truth, technological revolution, moral confusion, apatheism, and sexual saturation of culture, just to mention a few. Jesus taught, "When these things begin to take place, stand up and lift up your heads, because your redemption is drawing near." (Luke 21:28) Let us pray with purpose, and act in Faith. To God be the Glory!

CHAPTER FIVE

THE FLABBY CHRISTIANS

W HAT IS A spiritual matured Christian? This is what the church's mission ought to be. We are to make disciples. They are to be spiritually matured. Spiritual maturity is achieved through becoming more like Jesus Christ. After salvation, every Christian begins the process of spiritual growth. The believer is to eventually become spiritually matured. According to the apostle Paul, it's an ongoing process. The process will not end in this lifetime. In Philippians 3:12–14, he tells us that he himself has not *"already obtained perfection, but he press toward the mark of the higher calling which is in Jesus, the Christ. Brothers, I do not consider myself yet to have taken hold of it. But one thing I do: Forgetting what is behind and straining toward what is ahead, I press on toward the goal to win the prize for which God has called me heavenward in Christ Jesus."* Like Paul, we have to press continually toward deeper knowledge of God in Christ.

Paul says, knowledge puffs up. Love, by contrast, builds up. Discipleship means that soon they will become matured in the gospel and will no longer drink milk made for babes in Christ. The goal is to be matured disciples of Christ. They will know and *do* something with what they know. The definition of maturity in Christ needs to be clarified.

Christian maturity requires a reordering of one's priorities. Christian maturity requires a changing over from pleasing self to pleasing God and learning to obey God. The key to maturity is being consistent. Another key is to persevere in doing those things we know will bring us closer to God. We do these things by Bible reading/study, prayer, fellowship, service, and stewardship. All of these things are manifested by the Holy Spirit within us. Galatians 5:16 tells us that we're to "walk by the Spirit." The Greek word used here for "walk" actually means "to walk with a purpose in view." Paul tells us again that we're to "walk by the Spirit." Here, the word translated "walk" has the idea of taking things "step by step, one step at a time." Being filled with the Spirit means we walk under the Spirit's control. As we submit more and more to the Spirit's control, we will also see an increase in the fruit of the Spirit in our lives (Galatians 5:22–23). This is characteristic of spiritual maturity. We are to become disciples of Jesus, the Christ.

JESUS COMMANDS TO THE CHURCH

An authentic disciple should reclaim:

1. Jesus commanded us to **make** disciples, not **be** disciples.

For instance, we are to make a cake, not be a cake. If we continue to be a cake and not make cakes, then the multiplication formula will not work. It is apparent that Jesus wants more and more disciples. By making disciples, we become more and more what God wants us to be. Then, we will be transformed into new creations.

2. Discipleship is simply linked to evangelism.

One can not be an evangelist without being a disciple. Dr. Harold Carter, Sr. said: "The disciple must evangelize or die." But many disciples would rather be disciples without being evangelists.

3. A mark of an authentic disciple includes getting it wrong.

The Word of God says that Peter did not get it right all the time. Peter was in the company of Jesus. Peter needed to be corrected. Many leaders in the early church had to be corrected. Paul corrected Peter about his unwillingness to eat with Gentiles. However, Jesus, the Christ chose to allow them to be pillars in the building of the early church.

4.   A morally mess up may be inevitable.

One stinging criticism of churches is that the church does not resemble the Jesus of the bible. Yes, it may look like the secular world. The church in Corinth struggled with *every* problem thinkable. This denotes that the church is making progress. The church can make the change and be a church that Jesus will help to become the church He loves.

5.   Maturity takes time and is not linear.

One can not expect a 3 year old to have the maturity of a 13 year old. When you place expectations on people wherein they are not able to bear them, then you crush them and/ or confuse them. They may grow at different rates. They may grow in different measures. For instance, a person trying to loose weight, may loose in inches before you will be see the total weight loss. One may not see the maturity in a month and not even a few years. The church may not be on track until years, but the primary application ought to be in place.

6.   Christian maturity was never about making a certain person a matured specimen.

Christian maturity is not really about the church or the individual peruse. It is about how Jesus is working in lives of people.

7.   **Love compels us**

The primary motivation for discipleship and evangelism is love. If we advance discipleship as being primary, then the church and our culture would be transformed.

THE CHURCH VIRTUALLY UNCHANGED

Research by the McMillan Consultants found that David T. Olson discovered that "of the 200,000 U.S. Churches, it added 52 million people in 16 years. They noted that the church is virtually unchanged. This suggest that the American church is in a crisis. It is time to sound the alarm. The reality is that the American church is losing ground as the population continues to surge. What is happening in the churches in America? What is happening in America that is influencing the church? What is being transposed into the churches? We must make a response to God's command to make disciples.

There are some starring statistical information concerning church growth. In 2012, one hundred and eighteen (118) million Americans attended a Christian church on any given weekend. Two years later, the attendance dropped. The United States population in 2012 had 312.8 million people (or exactly 312,780,968) people according to US News and World Report, December 30, 2011. The U.S. Population is growing, but church growth is in decline. Few people will argue that church attendance in many churches in America is declining. Our own research indicates that the majority of churches in our country are not growing. Many have suggested that our nation is shifting away from its Christian roots, and thus the churches are declining as a smaller proportion of our country are believers in Christ. This is not good news for the Christian church. What does this author suggest?

These five suggestions have proven to be the most helpful in hundreds of churches:

1. Raise the expectations of membership
2. Require an entry class for membership
3. Encourage ministry involvement
4. Offer more options for worship times
5. Monitor attendance of each member
6. Show much love for all members and communicate with them regularly
7. Organize prayer cells among members especially Disciples of Christ

The growth process will get better if churches follow the committed membership covenant of what the Apostle Paul mandates in 1 Corinthians 12. It is important to set Discipleship training as the primary priority in the church. Discipleship training must be the first priority. All churches should have a manual for discipleship training.

Out of all the people who attend church, how many are disciples or being trained to be a disciple? How many will go to heaven and how many spend their time in hell? Statistically looking at the United States and over the sea of humanity, what do I see? A scene from Revelation comes to mind: "I looked, and behold, a great multitude which no one could number, of all nations, tribes, peoples, and tongues, standing before the throne and before the Lamb" (7:9). The question is how many Americans will someday be in heaven? Truly, I do not know.

THE UNITED STATES CHURCHES RESPOND WITH SIZE

Most Christians believe that large churches are growing. They believe that smaller ones are declining. This is not statistically true. Large churches (those with more than 1,000 in attendance) are still growing. So called small churches (less than 75 in attendance) are growing. Unfortunately, midsize churches are struggling. On average, churches with 100 to 299 people decline in attendance by more than 1 percent per year—a trend that has accelerated over the last seven years. Research indicates that many of these congregants are making a mass exodus to the larger churches and mega churches.

One reason why small churches are growing is that everyone can know each other by name. Another reason for growth in the small church is that they open the door for intimate bonds. Although most large churches are not usually intimate, but they usually offer a wide range of high-quality ministries. Small churches are great because bonding takes place among its members and with families.

Research indicates that midsize churches are too large to be intimate, and too small to offer the range of services that large churches provide. Midsize churches are being squeezed by both sides of the continuum. What are midsize churches to do? Discipleship can be very effective tool to make the church commendable in the sight of the community.

Midsize churches comprise 50 percent of Protestant church attendance.

These churches (100 to 299) must learn how to embrace both intimacy and ministry excellence if they hope to grow. Prayer and discipleship is imperative in the growth of the midsize church. Of course, the Word of God must be preached with clarity and they must stand up for the truth of the gospel. The church must be a leadership style church.

THE AGE OF VARIOUS CHURCHES

Most people in their 40s begin to show signs of advancing age. They show signs such as graying hair and presbyopia. This is the case with churches that were established before 1965. They show and demonstrate signs of growing older. A recent study divided 75,000 Protestant churches into the decade in which each church was started. The researchers found that churches were most likely to grow during their first four decades of life (years one to forty). Those beginning at age 40, a period of persistent decline were likely to occur.

Churches do not have to follow this human pattern. People older than 40 may practice five healthy habits; these are proper diet, regular exercise, good relational connections, mental stimulation and spiritual vitality. Many of the negative effects of old age may be delayed. These habits promote health while showing little decline.

These five factors can be correlated to the habits of healthy churches. A church's proper diet is God's unadulterated Word being preached and studied. The spiritual food that its members receive is through teaching, preaching and Bible study. Regular exercise strengthening is obtained by the body's active ministry involvement. The healthy personal connections are enhanced by the inside and outside of the church God's relationships. The mental stimulation takes place by the study of the gospel to show them rightly dividing the Word of God and transforming the world and culture. Spiritual vitality occurs by knowing Jesus as Lord of their lives and being filled with the Holy Spirit. When using the five habits, the natural effect of deterioration diminishes.

SURVIVAL OF THE SPECIES

What is the future of the American church? Dodo birds, great auks, passenger pigeons, dinosaurs, are species forever lost. They could not adapt to the environmental changes humans brought. Is your church headed for extinction? The church is a living creation by God. Jesus said "upon the rock I will build my church and the gates of hell shall not prevail against it." God will and has determined the life of a church. Since the church is a living creation, there are three indicators that forecast a species' future: its mortality rate, the health, and reproductive rate of its adult members, and its birthrate. What is the future of the American church, based on those indicators?

RESEARCH INDICATES THAT THE (MORTALITY RATE)

Approximately 3,700 churches close each year. A little more than 1 percent of all churches disband annually. This is similar to the human mortality rate. The Adult Health and Reproductive Rate of churches indicate that Evangelical churches of more than 40 years old are declining in attendance at slightly more than 1 percent per year. Mainline churches are declining at more than 2 percent per year. By 2020, these churches will decrease in size by 20 percent. In addition, most established churches do not leave a legacy for the future by reproducing themselves through church planting. Without using a formula for church planting, many churches may be without knowing putting into motion a way for demise. Planting churches is biblical.

Approximately 4,000 churches are started annually. They survive at least one year. Many are very small, and have "low birth weight" and have a high infant mortality rate. To keep up with population growth caused by new Americans, our country needs an additional 2,900 churches started each year. The church planting can be used.

The critical factor is the birthrate. The mortality rate and decline rate of established churches will remain the same. The only solution to counteract that decline is to start new churches that flourish for generations. How will the 21ˢᵗ century church take advantage of this research? Historically, the American church has grown through three types of births:

- Physical births: church families having children, causing biological growth
- Spiritual births: people who repent, believe the good news and follow Jesus through the ministry of the church, causing conversion growth
- Congregational births: healthy established churches that parent new churches, causing multiplication growth

Does your church attract and connect with young adults and families resulting in a significant natural birthrate? Does your church seek out new followers of Jesus? Is your church birthing a sizable numbers of healthy new churches because of your covering? Are the churches praying that God will help them in securing the best mortality rate that will be great in His sight. To make it plain, we are discussing the franchising of churches in America under the brand of the senior church.

A MESSAGE TO THE CHURCH

The church's most critical challenge in the next 10 years is to restore Jesus' words and actions to their proper place of centrality. My research of more than 200,000 churches over the last few years, indicate that their sermons, statements, visionary statements, and music, have failed to clearly communicate to their congregants the total unadulterated gospel of Jesus, the Christ.

Much of the church's public discourse has been altered and Jesus' words have been changed to suit man's endeavors. They have allowed Jesus Words to become trite, whereas His actual words and actions to have the power to cut deep into a person's heart.

Jesus' Word has become a shallow and narrow understanding of the message and mission of Jesus. Instead of painting a glorious vision of Jesus, the focal point of many sermons coming from the pulpit is used to fulfill life of the listener and allow the preacher to be advanced financially, and give power to the leadership. These types of messages failed to possess the power to transform lives through the spirit and to call for the necessity to worship God in spirit and in truth.

How will our world see Jesus and make Him their personal Savior? How will they experience His living power? The 21st century church needs to embrace the dream and vision that the world will meet Jesus, and know Him as their personal Savior. The whole united church needs to embrace the vision that the whole world will hear the gospel message, and will be taught the same gospel message. The united church must unite in the vision that the hearers and be saved and become matured disciples of Christ, and make disciples for the Kingdom of God.

The 21st century church is deceiving itself in some very crucial areas. They have adopted some practices that are not sanctioned by the Word of God. We are not fighting these practices, but are these practices working to foster the advancement of the Kingdom of God? For instance, are the practices listed below really fostering the advancement of the Kingdom of God?

1. "Asking Jesus into our heart" is not in the Bible. "Give your heart to the Lord", or repeating a "sinner's prayer" are not in the bible. These doctrines are a fabrication. These are man made to make salvation "quick and convenient".

2. Church buildings were invented around 200-300 AD. The church was in serious decline. Church buildings are anti-New Testament. The church fell into the hands of Rome and the concept of the "cathedral" came into being.

3. The concept of "one pastor running everything in the church is not biblical. In the book of Acts the word "pastor" is not used. The early church had strong leaders and elders. But, the church was not a one man band and it was not so controlled by man.

4. "Tithing" is not a New Testament practice. In the New Testament we are told to give cheerfully. There is not any evidence that the apostles taught or preached giving a 10 percent tithe. It was regarded as an Old Testament practice.

5. Jesus did not use the words "prosper" or 'prosperity' as He taught in the market place. It was used a couple of times in the New Testament. Yet, some preachers have built the whole kingdom on "prosperity gospel."

6. There were no bible colleges, seminaries or degrees in the New Testament. But, the Scribes and Pharisees had schools! The apostles were simple fishermen and tax collectors. Their "qualification" for being in the ministry was that they spent time with Jesus, and He had called them. I believe that many of the "professional clergy" today with their degrees has driven the church over the cliff. The real called out of God is facing much difficulty in getting a chance to ministry because of reptroprochey of the lettered. They are void of the paper that is needed to qualify them for active work in the church.

7. The early church did not have special seating on Sundays. In fact they gathered together 'from house to house' virtually every day! Love and fellowship and 'koinonia' were as natural to them as breathing. The apostles in Jerusalem preached every day at huge open-air gatherings. They were not "hidden away" inside four walls.

8. They did not try to replace the Holy Spirit with man made programs. The early church had much more of God and much less of 'man'.

9. Many churches preach a 'humanistic' Jesus sermon. They preach about a Jesus who exists mainly for their "happiness". They preach a Santa Claus type of Jesus who exists to give out blessings. A lot of preachers are well aware of this. God is about to bring "Great Reformation". There is a reversal on the way. God is not going to allow these 'hirelings' to destroy His church. God will replace the old leadership and the old lies. It is like David replacing Saul. In fact it is happening now.

There is a new leadership arising. The hour is now here. Now, I know why God has been using this author to spread the word about His intentions. The church has sunk so low that they have forced God to start His judgment on the church. Some have sunk so low that God had to send His disciples and leadership team to rescue His people out of some of these churches. It is true, because He has used this author to rescue families from being totally destroyed because of the types of doctrines being taught. They are mired in deception – an entire system of deception.

In Luke 11:33, the bible says *"No man, when he hath lighted a candle, putteth it in a secret place, neither under a bushel, but on a candlestick, that they which come in may see the light."* This scripture shines light in the very face of those who are asleep. The church has been asleep in the interpretation of this scripture. Jesus asked His disciples to pray, but they went to sleep instead. Most believers have gone to sleep spiritually worldwide, especially in America. This author is saying consider waking up to righteousness. 1 Corinthians 15:34 says, *"Awake to righteousness, and sin not; for some have not the knowledge of God: I speak this to your shame." I want to help you in the spirit of meekness* (Galatians 6:1)

Many churches have hid their light within the church walls. The church has become a secret place. Some meet secretly every week and do not reveal to the congregants their real plans. The church congregants do not have any idea of what their leadership is planning. The communities are functionally ignorant of the plans for the church and the communities. The communities do not have any idea of what the church believes.

A church called this author to pastor their church. For a number of years, the membership worked diligently to grow the church as God would have it. The church grew in leaps and bounds and discipleship classes bursting to the seam. However, the former pastor had left a considered amount of clandestine members in the church as spies. Earlier, the pastor had purchased in the church name without many knowing waterfront property. The old pastor had plans to use this property as a retirement tool for his personal advancement. The clandestine members did not want to jeopardize or lose their share of the potential wealth flow. Being that they were relatives and had helped in concealing the records they arranged to have this pastor removed.

We are supposed to honor and worship God at all times. The church is not to be used for pastor's own self-aggrandizement. We are to live righteous lives before God and congregants. There is not any room for pimps and crooks in the Kingdom of God. We ought to know of whom we believe and what we believe. The church is not to have the secular courts decide the truth of God's word.

Many American churches have swallowed the lies that the devil has placed before their mouths. The devil has said that the church should not force our beliefs upon people. This is not the case. God has commanded that we stand up against the evil doers. *Who will rise up for me against the evildoers or who will stand up for me against the workers of iniquity?* (Psalms

94:16) Every church in America should clearly state what they believe and what they stand for within the community and the world. We are to stand up for we are soldiers in the army of the Lord.

THE EARLY CHURCH WAS PERSECUTED FOR THEIR FAITHFULNESS TO CHRIST

The early church stood up for what they believed and shared it with the communities. The book of Acts gives us an example. People were getting saved because preachers were preaching the gospel. (Acts 2:41) The Word says that 3,000 souls were saved. They were preaching what they believe and told the community absolutely what the facts were. Satan was very concerned. In Acts 4:4, the Bible tells us that 5,000 men were saved (not including women and children). The Devil was going ballistic and made up the lie that they are not to force their beliefs on others. King Herod killed James with the sword. (Acts 12:2) In Acts 12:3 the bible says that the Jews were pleased with James' execution, which prompted Herod to also put Peter on death row.

This is happening in the 21st century church. The wicked would love to see Christians get their heads chopped off. Many leaders do not want to get into confrontation with political authorities so they accept the lie Satan put out. Many of the Churches today are mainly concerned about making money. So they go through the religious motions, but their candle is well hidden. When God says in 2nd Timothy 3:12, *"Yea, and all that will live godly in Christ Jesus shall suffer persecution."* If you are not experiencing persecution in this apostate world, then you are not living Godly in Christ Jesus.

CHRIST-HONORING CHURCH STIRS THINGS UP WITH THE TRUTH

The early church in the Book of Acts was rocking the boat. They were sinking ships with the gospel. They were making people angry by preaching the truth. Some Christians were martyred and willing to die for the cause of Christ. In acts 19:19 many who had been involved with the occult brought their "curious arts" and burned them in a bonfire. The worth of the books and items were 50,000 pieces of silver (about $48,000 in today's value, and millions in Bible times). A piece of silver was a day's wage in the New Testament.

The local idol makers were so enraged at Paul, that the other believers had to keep him from the angry mob waiting to tear him to pieces (Acts 19:30). In this 21st century, if the churches were making disciples, then beer and alcohol companies would be going out of business, pornographic perverts would be going out of business, taverns and prostitution houses would be closed down, the drug dealers would be out of business, and the corrupt politicians would be voted out of office. The country would not entertain the idea of putting a sinner, racist, adulteress, gambler, and so on as the president of the United States. Think about it, abortion would be at an all times low. There would not be any need for rosary makers. There would not be any need for palm readers, the tarot card readers, and the psychics. There would not be any need for satanic video games, and machines. Hollywood and their imps like Walt Disney movie houses would have to find a decent way to earn billions of dollars. It would put the gambling casinos out of business along with its CEO. The Gospel of Jesus, the Christ will put the strip joints and nightclubs out of business. The bible tells us that when Jesus returns at the Second Coming, He will put all these evil people out of business! He will put the heroine and drug growers out of business. The church needs to take a stand. We are living in the last days. This is the Word of God for the people of God. Until Christ returns, we are responsible to stand against the evils of our day. (Psalm 94:16) 2nd Thessalonians 2:10 tells us that we are to speak the truth and the truth will set us free. The church ought to love the truth. The church is to know the truth.

THE CHURCH HAS THE CONSTITUTIONAL RIGHT TO PROCLAIM THE TRUTH

A man of God will proclaim the truth and tries to reach people for Christ. In America, when he or she does this they are simply exercising his Constitutional *Bill of Rights*, as well as his God-given call. The police department under the guise of the State or Federal does not have the authority to bring out billions of dollars of military equipment to stop the believer from exercising their constitutional rights. If the church does not want to be the church, then God says that they are liars. EVERY believer is commanded to speak against wickedness's of our day! Every disciple of Christ is to witness to the lost and speak out against wrong doings. It is not only the preacher's command. The devil uses his imps. God is giving His church a wake up call. Wake up! The church is not "forcing our beliefs" on others; we are simply calling Satan a liar. We are preaching against wickedness's. We are attacking the backbone of sin, but never the sinner. God HATES sin, but not the sinner. No one hates sin any more than God, yet no one loves sinners as much as God. Disciples of Christ will know the difference because they were taught by Godly people. The church's priority ought to be making disciples.

THE DEVILS PARADES WICKEDNESS FOR THE WORLD TO SEE

The devil writes and plays by his rules. The homosexuals write their own rules and proudly march up and down our streets promoting their wickedness's. Their rules and position can not be justified through the word of God. This being written, then the church has been given their command in the word of God and must stand up for what they believe. If the devil can have a parade, then the church ought to have a parade when the Holy Spirit leads. The question is: "Will the Church Stand Up." Ephesians 2:2 explains that Satan's spirit works in the hearts of the unsaved ("*… the spirit that now worketh in the children of disobedience*"). The righteous and the wicked will NEVER co-exist in harmony ("*An unjust man is an abomination to the just: and he that is upright in the way is abomination to the wicked,* Proverb 29:27"). We can't stand each other.

Larry A. McMillan

AMERICA'S CHURCHES NEED TO
SPEAK THE TRUTH PUBLICLY

As Christians, it is our responsibility to get the truth out. Every church in America should have the reputation of speaking the truth of God's message to the world. Sin is sin. There is not any big sin and little sin. The "Flabby Christians" are under the microscope and the world is getting a good look at them.

Paul compares the Christian life to running a race and the goal is to make it to the finishing line. To be Christian runner requires that the person be discipline. The are some days that the runner does not want to exercise. They make excuses. It may start out as legitimate excuses, but time after time more excuses are offered. The runner get flabby. This is what I call a "Flabby Christian." There are likely days they just don't want to exercise. We must not become a "Flabby Christian." Paul says in **1 Corinthians 9:24-27** *Do you not know that those who run in a race all run, but one receives the prize? Run in such a way that you may obtain it. And everyone who competes for the prize is temperate in all things. Now they do it to obtain a perishable crown, but we for an imperishable crown. Therefore I run thus: not with uncertainty. Thus I fight: not as one who beats the air. But I discipline my body and bring it into subjection, lest, when I have preached to others, I myself should become disqualified.*(NKJV) We must have daily quiet times with God, we must share the gospel with our neighborhoods, we must make disciples, and obey God commands to be active in the kingdom of God. We must speak the truth to the world and exercise our faith in public. If we fail to do so, then perhaps we will become a "Flabby Christian."

CHAPTER SIX

WHICH IS OLDER GOD OR THE EARTH?

THE REAL QUEST is to realize who is really in charge of the world in which we live. If the earth is older than God, then we are to give the earth all the praise. If God is the creator and is older than the earth, then we owe God all the praise. Without any hesitation or reservation, I firmly believe that God is older than the earth. Therefore, God is in control and certainly not man. Wisdomatically, God comes first, then the earth, and after which man comes into play.

We cannot make a comprehensive, conclusive statement as to how old the earth is. Is it six to seven thousand years old? Could it be millions or billions of years old? We do not know. I believe the earth is probably a lot older than we think. Christians can not agree on the age of the earth. But no one loses their salvation if they think the earth is only six thousand years old or 2.9 billion years old. In the eyes of God time is not an issue. He was here before time ever existed. The essentials of the faith are really all that matter. What is essential is Jesus died for our sins and He established the church. Christ and His dying for sinners is paramount. If you are born again or not, if you will live in heaven or in hell is so important. The destinations are drastically different (Rev 21; 22; Rev 20:11-15). To live with God for all eternity, is as simply as believing on the Lord Jesus Christ (Rom 10:9-13). To die without Christ, you will live in a Christ-less eternity (John 3:18). The choice of attending a church within God's Holy Spirit is a choice to make. God is the creator of all things. Man can not create anything nor will he ever create anything. It is God who made us and not we ourselves.

GOD COMMANDS DOES NOT CHANGE

Hebrews 10:25 (KJV) *not forsaking the assembling of ourselves together, as is the manner of some, but exhorting one another, and so much the more as ye see the Day approaching.* We as the body of Christ are to attend the fellowship with others to get strengthened. When Christians do not attend the assembly of believers, they are apt to loose some strength waiting for them from their fellow believer. Satan is happy when attendance is falling. He has planted the seed of discourse, discouragement, disagreement, and distrust among fellowship believers. Yet, we witness decease in the number of church attendance. We are to obey God for His commands does not change.

Why is their a decease in the number of church attendance? Joani Schultz and Thom Schultz wrote a book to answer this question entitled "Why nobody wants to go to Church Anymore?" The question is still being asked. In a recent issue of a Christian magazine Ed Stetzer wrote an article entitled," The State of the Church in America: Hint: It's Not Dying." He states: "The church is not dying … yes … in a transition … but transitioning is not the same as dying." I believe that there is a great reversal taking place in America. Stetzer, according to the Hartford Institute of Religion Research, says more than 40 percent of Americans "say" they go to church weekly. However, less than 20 percent are actually in church. More than 80 percent of Americans are finding more fulfilling things to do on weekends.

Statistically, approximately 4,000 and 7,000 churches close their doors every year. Southern Baptist researcher, Thom Rainer, in a recent article entitled "13 Issues for Churches in 2013" puts the estimate higher. He says between 8,000 and 10,000 churches will likely close this year. Research indicates that between the years 2010 and 2012, more than half of all churches in America did not add a single new member. Nearly 3 million more previous churchgoers enter the ranks of the "religiously unaffiliated." We must admit that something is wrong within our churches. Our research can point out seven changes or trends that are impacting church-going in America. These are trends that contribute to the decline.

DEMOGRAPHIC REMAPPING AMERICA

Immigration is clearly a challenge to the church attendance. Whites were the top in attendance at a 64 percentage. The coloring of America is changing this drastically. In 30 to 40 years, White Americans will be in the minority. Hispanics will be one out of every three people in the United States. In other words reaching Hispanics today, will add to the churches attendance. Making disciples out of Hispanics will add to the church discipleship numbers. This author predicts that by 2046, if the Lord tarries, then the population of the United States will not have a so called superior white race. Of course the evil forces will attempt to make this statement false by exporting minorities to other countries. In fact there will be a brownish race of people as the major skin color. Certainly, we will not be able to point to "a white race of people as being totally white in color or genealogies. This will be impossible to stop because God has already placed this trend in action. God is in control and not man.

The fact that America is aging is another factor. The attendees of church today are a disproportionate number of gray-headed folks in comparison to all the others. According to Pew_Research, "every day for the next 16 years, 10,000 new baby boomers will enter retirement." The demographic remapping of America is causing a decline in the numbers of those who attend church.

TECHNOLOGY

Technology is changing the operational style of the church. There are churches that are operating in the age of the Industrial Revolution void of technology. People who attend worship service and see that the church is void of computers, I phone, smart phones, and so on, are not connecting and/or communicating with other churches and the world. Making discipleship initiatives ought to include technological advancements. The Millennial have little or no interest in what they have to say because they appear to be out of touch. The absence of the use of current technology is contributing to the decline.

LEADERSHIP CRISIS

Clergy abuse, the cover-ups, pimp preachers, false prophets, and satanic congregations have been driving people away from the Church. The church is in need of Godly called out leaders. This is what drive people away faster than any other trends. The real church has to agree to point out those who are not adhering to doctrines and practices of Jesus, the Christ. The real church must put a stop on the practice of driving people away from the church. Christians must not refuse to follow the law of God. The absence of not practicing the truth in churches is driving people from the church. The church need Godly trained, dedicated, and Holy Ghost filled leadership in God's church.

COMPETITION

The world has given people more choices on weekends than going to church. Further some churches are openly competing against other churches for their members. There is not any "Blue Law" being adhered to anymore. Competition comes from those who say they are cultural Christians. These are those who "believe" they are Christians simply because their culture says they are. Competition comes from those who say they are congregational Christians. These are the misguided group who think they are better off than those in biblical days. They lost connection with other churches. Competition comes from which call themselves the conventional Christians. They believe that they are the only group that is actually living their faith. They left the church to preserve their faith. (Matt. 7:1). Competition is coming from within and without the church.

Competition comes from the infiltration of religious pluralism. Again, people are given more choices in the 21st century church. People are meeting others of different faith, traditions, cultures, persuasions, and are finding that many who confess to being Christians are not any better than those attending their church. Competition ought not be a problem.

Diana Eyck's, the Harvard scholar and researcher, concludes in her book entitled A New Religious America, that the "Christian Country" has become the world's most religiously diverse nation. The debate is whether it is true. Some would question if this country has ever been religious. We are to put aside competition and concentrate on making disciples for the kingdom of God.

However, competition is seen in the choice of the Contemporary Worship Experience or the traditional service. Churches are lending to the trend for the last couple of decades to pretend to be something they're not. They have experimented with praise singers, praise bands, the installation of screens, praise music, leisure dress, and compromising sermons to grow the congregations. They have been competing for members. It has largely proven to be a fatal mistake. Of course, there are exceptions in those churches with the UN-traditional look, staging, an amphitheater-style seating, and have hired the finest musicians to perform for worship. Many churches are attempting to follow this model only to discover that they are missing the mark.

Competition in using phony advertising is causing a decline in the churches. There are many churches that advertise that all are welcome. But, when people arrive, there are few mixed races and/or no mixed couples. We have all Black churches, all white churches, and so on. This is false advertisement because what they really mean you are welcome as long as you are like the rest of the congregation. They are not really interested in making disciples out of those that God sends to their church. The primary focus of the church ought to be mentioned. The church ought to honestly and prayerfully try to be an influence on the culture and the society.

There are those who will ask what do you base your writing on. We based it on the author and the finisher of our faith. Research leads us to also ask a question about the earth. In fact the question was, "How old is the earth? What the bible has to say about church has its basis also on how old is the earth. Bodie Hodge on May 30, 2007 featured an article as to the age of the earth. They have been debates on Internet debate boards, TV, radio, classrooms, in many churches, Christian colleges, and seminaries as to the age of the earth. The highest agreed con-sense agreed that the earth is about 6,000 years. The old -earth proponents of the secular age agree that the earth is about 4.5 billion years. They say that the universe is about 14 billion years old. It is apparent that we really do not know.

The difference is immense! God's word says the world is about 6,000 years old. If we rely on man's fallible (and often demonstrably false) dating methods, we can get a confusing range of ages from a few thousand to billions of years. Cultures around the world give an age of the earth that confirms what the Bible teaches.

If the churches can not agree as to the age of the earth according to the bible, then it seems that it is not able to agree what God has said about the church. We must use our faith to trust and obey God. In Revelation 22; 13 God says, *I am Alpha and Omega, the beginning and the end, the first and the last.* In the book of Acts 5:29 KJV, *Then Peter and the other apostles answered and said, we ought to obey God rather than men.*

Church today has become predictable, says bestselling author and influential preacher Francis Chan. "You go to a building, someone gives you a bulletin, you sit in a chair, you sing a few songs, a guy delivers maybe a polished message, maybe not, someone sings a solo, you go home," Chan says in his latest "BASIC" video. This should not happen if God is the center focus of the praise and worship service.

"When you read the New Testament, you see the Holy Spirit was to change everything so that this gathering of people who call themselves Christians had this supernatural element about them," Chan explains in the video series, produced by Flannel. His talk on the Holy Spirit premiered recently on "Relevant." Competition in the church will give certain returns that is not of God.

In the book Acts the Holy Spirit, which came down after Jesus ascended to heaven, empowered Christians thousands of years ago. Through the power of the Holy Spirit, people began speaking in different languages, people were being healed, and believers had a supernatural love for one another. The fire that came down from heaven, that rush of wind, however, seems to have disappeared, Chan points out. "Do you really see this supernatural power at work when the believers gather together for what we call church?" he asks. "Isn't it the same Holy Spirit that's supposed to be available to us today? Why is it so different?"

Chan's frustrations with the church today are what inspired this author to write about his church experiences over the forty plus years. I discovered that Chan was successfully leading a mega-church in Simi Valley, Calif., when he began to question and rethink, "how we do church." He began feeling uncomfortable with people driving long distances just to hear him speak every weekend and with church having become a once-a-week routine. After 16 years at Cornerstone Church, he let go of the reins in 2010 and traveled to Asia where he and his family spent time with persecuted Christians and orphans.

Chan has yet to announce his next ministry move but an update on his blog revealed that he is currently residing in San Francisco. "I am working on some projects that I believe can help the overall health of the church in America," he wrote earlier this year.

Chan filmed a seven-part short film series with Flannel that is aimed at challenging Christians to be the church that is illustrated in Scripture. The videos are being slowly released and the Holy Spirit installment is the third and latest one in the series being made available. In it, Chan observes what church looks like today and what it's suppose to look like, according to the Bible. "I heard one person say the church nowadays is neither super nor natural," he says. "Everything is predictable and everything is expected."

"There's a truth to that," he admits. "I feel bad about it. Being around a church culture, even leading a gathering of believers, I've gotten pretty good at predicting what's going to happen in a church service. Was that the way it was supposed to happen?" "When Jesus said this power (of the Holy Spirit) would come upon you, it really did come upon them and they were powerful beings (Jesus' disciples)," Chan points out. "Why is it that in the church so many people are weak or defeated, or we get so insecure because we look at ourselves rather than God? It doesn't make sense."

Though Christians believe in an almighty and all powerful God who places His spirit in believers, the response among His people today is: "Hi, welcome to church. Here's your bulletin. We'll get you out in an hour. Come back next week." "I mean, really? Is that all God intended for us?" Chan challenges. While pondering whether Christians really believe the Holy Spirit exists today and can work powerfully, he asks one poignant question: "What would the church look like today if we really stopped taking control of it and let the Holy Spirit lead?" So, I asked God to give me the answer to this dilemma.

WHERE IS GOD'S TRUE CHURCH TODAY?

Roderick C. Meredith wrote his book asking an important question. Where is God's true church today? He speaks about where all races can enjoy and be in the company of God. He prose's a lot of questions, but this author is not really looking to name a particular church. He wants to establish the qualifications, backgrounds, and characteristic of the kind of Jesus will be looking for when He returns.

Thousands of different denominations claim to be following Jesus Christ. Yet they teach thousands of different "gospels" and disagree on countless points of doctrine. Is Jesus Christ the Head of all these denominations? Is Christ divided? Or is there a true Church of God that stands apart from this religious Babylon? How can you recognize God's true Church? This book will help us understand the merits of a true church!

Have you ever wondered why you were born? What will it be like to live in the after life? What you will actually be doing for eternity? Will you sit around all day, playing a harp, or staring passively into the face of God? Or does God have something far more awesome and wonderful planned for you? Is it possible to experience the true church on earth?

Have you ever wished you could find a church that truly understands the end-time prophecies of the Bible—how they apply to today's headlines and how the near future events affecting your life? Have you searched for a church that could help you understand the genuine meaning of life itself—and could explain where you and your nation will be headed in the next few years? Have you ever wished that you could find a church where the ministers actually preach right out of the Bible and help you "make sense" of its words—including its many specific prophecies? Do you long for a church where virtually all the members bring their Bibles to services, and where everyone actually believes what the Bible says and is trying to live by the true "first-century Christianity" that Jesus Christ and His apostles lived and preached? Have you hoped to find a church where people of all races and backgrounds are accepted with warmth and love, and where Christ's command us to love one another is reflected in the "family atmosphere" when church members gather for worship and fellowship?

My friends, there is such a church that genuinely believes in the divine inspiration of the Holy Bible and is actually trying to do what the Bible says in every phase and facet of life. It is a church that has no other "holy books" or church "traditions" that take the place of the Bible on anything. This church is not a building or a corporation or an invention of human beings. It is a spiritual organism with a history going right back to Jesus Christ and the apostles. It is a very small church—the "little flock" described by Jesus Christ (Luke 12:32)—but it has always existed since the time of Christ and will exist at the end of the age when its faithful members are taken to a "place of safety" (see Revelation 12) before the Great Tribulation actually begins. Do you want to be part of such a church, whose members will soon become the kings and priests helping rule this earth under Jesus Christ? (Revelation 5:10).

WHERE ARE GOD'S PEOPLE?

The man sitting across from me was sharing his thoughts earnestly. "I used to think that God's people were just scattered all through the various denominations," he exclaimed. "However, the more I read the Bible, the more I feel there must be a true church somewhere on earth composed of people who really do what the Bible says. But how can I know? How can I be sure where God is working today?"

Now, the big question is: How can you know? How can you be sure? Today, many churches call themselves Christians. Some practice baptism by immersion in water. Others just "sprinkle" or pour water on the head of baptismal candidates. Many churches keep what they call the "Lord's Supper" every Sunday morning. Others observe this custom once a month or quarterly, or only once a year.

Most churches observe Sunday as their day of worship, while a few observe the Sabbath from Friday sunset to Saturday sunset. Others say that the day of worship does not matter at all. Churches are called by all kinds of names: Episcopal, Baptist, Holiness, Lutheran, and Presbyterian, Catholic, Methodist, Pentecostal and others. More importantly, the various churches of this world have different concepts of God. Some feel that God is a fierce autocrat who roasts sinners in an ever-burning hellfire. Others think of God as simply the "divine spark" that somehow started all life but that has very little to do with everyday events and does not care about mankind's "lifestyle." Yet these differing churches all call themselves "Christian"—they use the name of Christ.

Does it make any difference? Has God left it up to human beings to search out and call their churches by various names, and come up with various days upon which to worship, various modes of baptism and different doctrinal teachings? Where are God's people?

WHERE IS GOD?

Does God have anything to say about all of this?

Yes, He does!

Somewhere on this earth, God has true servants who faithfully and fully proclaim the end-time warnings to which we should all be paying attention. God inspired His prophet Amos to tell us: "Surely the Lord God does nothing, unless He reveals His secret to His servants the prophets. A lion has roared! Who will not fear? The Lord God has spoken! Who can but prophesy?" (Amos 3:7–8).

Today, staggering events are on the immediate horizon. They are prophesied in your Bible. One-fourth of the entire Bible is devoted to prophecy. And the Apostle Paul wrote: *"Preach the word! Be ready in season and out of season. Convince, rebuke, exhort, with all long-suffering and teaching. For the time will come when they will not endure sound doctrine, but according to their own desires, because they have itching ears, they will heap up for themselves teachers; and they will turn their ears away from the truth, and be turned aside to fables"* (2 Timothy 4:2–4). Does your minister preach the full message of the Bible? Does he regularly explain, and make clear to you and your loved ones, the powerful end-time prophecies of the Bible? The Bible lists many specific events for which true Christians should be watching. These events will soon clearly demonstrate that humanity is at the very end of this present age—the age of man's rule over the earth under the influence of Satan the Devil (Revelation 12:9).

Many religious leaders talk about the "end times." But, in all honesty, who is telling you the specific events for which you should watch? And who is helping you, today, to understand the real meaning behind the traumatic upheavals in the weather, the increasing earthquakes, terrorist attacks and the awful wars in Africa, the Middle East and elsewhere that are increasingly threatening this planet? Who is truly "making sense" out of all of this? Jesus said: *"If you abide in My word, you are My disciples indeed. And you shall know the truth, and the truth shall make you free"* (John 8:31–32). Again, if you are to abide in Christ's "word," who is really making that word "come alive?" Who is continually quoting—not from the secular writings of this world—but from the inspired word of God? Who is constantly challenging you: *"Prove all things; and hold fast that which is good"* (1 Thessalonians 5:21, KJV)?

Another vital issue to consider: where is the full truth being preached today? "Oh, all churches have the same basic beliefs!" many will say. Or: "No one has a monopoly on the Truth. We can't really know about these things anyway, so all religions are essentially valid as long as people are sincere!" I am sure many of you have heard this type of reasoning before. If there is not a real God, or if the Holy Bible is not truly inspired, then such reasoning might stand up. But such is not the case! Perhaps the most basic instructions of Jesus Christ are these words: *"Man shall not live by bread alone, but by every word of God"* (Luke 4:4). God's true Church must necessarily acknowledge this most fundamental of all Christian teaching! Church leadership, and individual Church members, may not yet be perfect, but they must at least acknowledge that God's word is the basis for knowing the ultimate truth their Creator intended. For without the Bible—without the inspired instruction from God Himself in His inspired word—all that remains are the billions of human opinions: "This is the way I feel!" or: "This is how it seems to me!"

Do you get the picture? So if God does have a true Church on this earth, it must acknowledge the inspired authority of the Bible, and must base its teaching solidly on that foundation! As the Apostle Paul was inspired to write: *"But if I am delayed, I write so that you may know how you ought to conduct yourself in the house of God, which is the church of the living God, the pillar and ground of the truth"* (1 Timothy 3:15).

Again, what is the Truth? Jesus said in your Bible: *"Sanctify them by Your truth. Your word is truth"* (John 17:17). Wherever the true Church is, it is the pillar and "bulwark" (as the word "ground" ought to be translated in 1 Timothy 3:15) of the Truth. It is the protector of the Truth. Paul also tells us that true Christians—those who compose the true Church—are *"fellow citizens with the saints and members of the household of God, having been built on the foundation of the apostles and prophets, Jesus Christ Himself being the chief cornerstone"* (Ephesians 2:19–20). If, as Paul wrote, the true Church is built on the foundation of the apostles and prophets, Jesus Christ Himself being the chief cornerstone, then the writings of the apostles and the prophets—not human opinions or "feelings"—must be the basis of doctrine and practice.

Paul's inspired statement about the true Church being the pillar and bulwark of the truth is enormously important! For through God's Church, people should come to understand the supreme purpose for mankind's existence. They should learn in detail about God's great plan for humanity and how He is working out that plan. They should come to understand the vital one-fourth of the Bible that is prophetic. They should then grasp the real meaning of current events as they relate to Biblical prophecy. This will make their newspaper reading and world news viewing on television truly "come alive."

Then, members of the true Church of God will know how to follow Jesus' command: *Watch-therefore, and pray always that you may be counted worthy to escape all these things that will come to pass, and to stand before the Son of Man"* (Luke 21:36). These truly converted people will then have the divine protection of God Himself during the horrifying Great Tribulation that Jesus Christ specifically prophesied would occur just before His return (Matthew 24:21–22). These true Christians—members of the true Church, learning the full Truth—will be spared from the horrifying "hour of trial" that will soon descend on this earth! For Jesus promises to people in this Church: *"Because you have kept My command to persevere, I also will keep you from the hour of trial which shall come upon the whole world, to test those who dwell on the earth"* (Revelation 3:10).

Do you, personally, want to be protected during the traumatic years just ahead? Or would you rather be "comfortable" attending whatever church you grew up in—or that you now attend—whether or not it understands the real truth? God is the truth and He is the beginning and the end.

CHAPTER SEVEN

A COMFORTABLE CHURCH

S HOULD YOU LOOK for a church where you can easily "fit in" and where you can be "comfortable?" A *Charlotte Observer* columnist recently wrote: "'Comfortable in church.' Really, I do not like the implications of this phrase. I was told that that attending church should cut a person and having heard the entire gospel then that same person would be healed. Why would one leave home to attend a church that makes them comfortable in their sins? 'Comfortable' is what I want when I put my feet up and listen to music of my choice. Comfort for the believers is to know God for themselves.

Churchgoers ought not be comfortable. They have a certain education level and what to be challenged in the comfort level. Church is not to be comfortable as if they are a specialty club. Church is not be comfortable for those of a certain race or nationality. To find these people linking up for miles to get for man made reasons is not what God intended. Going to church to find a political contact is not what God wanted for His worshipers. But there are those who like to worship with people who think like them, look like them, and drive the same kinds of cars they drive." This happens in a lot of churches around the country. They want to be most of all comfortable in their sins and actions. But is *this* the kind of church that Jesus Christ taught His true followers to model? Of course the answer to this question is absolutely "no."

Listen to Christ Himself: *"If anyone comes to Me and does not hate ["love less"] his father and mother, wife and children, brothers and sisters, yes, and his own life also, he cannot be My disciple. And whoever does not bear his cross and come after Me cannot be My disciple … So likewise, whoever of you does not forsake all that he has cannot be My disciple*" (Luke 14:26–27, 33). Going to church looking for comfortablity in the sanctuary is a recipe for impending disaster. Looking for comfortablity as reason for going to church is a stumbling block, robs us of our strength and dependence on God. Our life is not about our comfort. It is about loving God, loving others, and spreading the word of God.

Jesus Christ does not intend that we strive for a "comfortable" existence in following Him! This is the slanted gospel that many preachers expose for the pulpit. It is called "the peace and prosperity" gospel. Jesus Christ tells His believers to come out of the world. The saints of God need to prepare for persecution. We are to serve God and Him only and be prepared to live with Him eternally.

The true Church is composed of people who have genuinely *surrendered* their lives to God through Jesus Christ. They have walk by faith and not by sight and work out their own salvation with fear and trembling. They are to be inspired by the Word of God and command every Word that comes out of the mouth of God. They are to be Holy as God is Holy. Jesus Christ instructions are: "*Man shall not live by bread alone, but by* every word *of God*" (Luke 4:4). Jesus of Nazareth was *God in the flesh*: that He died to pay the penalty of sin for all humanity, *rose from the dead* after three days and three nights in the grave (Matthew 12:40) and now sits at the right hand of God the Father as our active High Priest, the mediator, living Head and soon-coming King.

The true believers will repent, be converted and surrender to Christ as "Lord"—the only One whom they will obey. Therefore, Jesus, the Christ is to live *within them* through the Holy Spirit (Galatians 2:20), they are commanded to live by the teachings of the Bible. As quite as it is kept, these are the people who make up the true Church of God! Jesus said wide is the road that leads to destruction, but narrow is the path that leads to righteousness, but few find it.

So if you want to keep it real, then we must interpret the Word of God rightly. God *does* have a true Church here on earth. That Church is genuinely preparing its members for eternal life. That Church is *genuinely* doing the work of God in this 21st century. This church has several signs that mark its identity as God's true church. What are the signs? We must be willing to listen, pray, and have an open mind to hear and see the signs of God's churches in this 21st century.

ATTENDING THE 21ST CENTURY CHURCH

In this 21st century many people are turned off from what is called "organized religion." Its doctrines, message, and mission has become confusion for the world and the churchgoers. This is a sad day in hearts of true believers. Many families have decided to stay at home and worship God in the confines of their own homes. The pastor is the father and the children are being trained to follow the precepts outside of "organized religion." Many mega churches have concluded that they are the Church that God's desires, but God has not sanctified many so called mega churches. Is there anything wrong with families worshiping at home instead of the organized church?

Many sincere people are trying to justify the practice of forming a "stay at home church." Forming a "stay at home church," maybe biblical. But, overall they are not what God taught in His Word. We are not to forsake the assembling in worship with other worshipers. We have to mediate, pray, and wait on God to lead our families to the place of worship He has set aside for you and your family. Yes, it can be at home, but we must take our instructions from God.

Jesus Christ is "light" whom God sent into the world. He is our example. His fully converted apostles, disciples, and followers were used as examples. The 21st century church must be the kind of church that God has declared in His Word, and if the have changed it for their purpose then it is not God's church.

The bible gives us this intelligence. Jesus, the Christ *"So He came to Nazareth, where He had been brought up. And as His custom was, He went into the synagogue on the Sabbath day, and stood up to read"* (Luke 4:16). Jesus' own practice was to attend worship services regularly with others in an "organized" synagogue or Church setting! For God had already called the Sabbath a "holy convocation. This is a "commanded assembly." So Jesus, the Christ obeyed His father's command. This sets up the example of the model church that He commands.

God's Word clearly states that after Jesus' resurrection, Peter and the early apostles met regularly in the temple on both the weekly and annual Sabbaths. The New Testament Church did not have its beginnings on Christmas Day or Easter Sunday. God actually gave a command for Holy Days, and the Day of Pentecost! (Acts 2:1) The early disciples met regularly with others in the temple at Jerusalem (Acts 2:46–47). We are to meet regularly together for the purpose lifted in the scriptures.

God had the time set for Paul to become active in ministry. The Word of God says, "Then Barnabas departed for Tarsus to seek Saul. And when he had found him, he brought him to Antioch. So it was that for a whole year *they* assembled *with the church* and taught a great many people. And the disciples were first called Christians in Antioch" (Acts 11:25–26). Paul and Barnabas "assembled" with the "Church." This organized church under the directive and command of God meet together regularly. The scripture further states: *"then Paul, as his custom was, went in to them, and for three Sabbaths reasoned with them from the Scriptures."* (Acts 17:2)

The inspired writer of Hebrews seals the command of God regarding church assembly: *"And let us consider one another in order to stir up love and good works, not forsaking the assembling of ourselves together, as is the manner of some, but exhorting one another, and so much the more as you see the Day approaching. For if we sin willfully after we have received the knowledge of the truth, there no longer remains a sacrifice for sins."* (Hebrews 10:24–26). This vital scripture in God's word tells us not to forsake assembling with others. It also tells us to "stir" one another to love and "good works."

Some have twisted these words to believe that if they met at home with family and friends, they could stir up each other to good works. This approach goes against the biblical examples of God. God called every father of a Godly household to be the first pastor of His home. They are to train his family in the fear and admonition of God. God did not say that every layman could appoint himself to be a called out preacher and to organize a church in their home. They can not call themselves to be an ordained *true* minister of Jesus Christ! The Bible is emphatic that *"no man takes this honor to himself, but he who is called by God"* (Hebrews 5:4).

In my more than 37 years in Christ's ministry, I have thought of withdrawing from "organized religion." It was very difficult to witness the many pastors, Bishops, and other self appointed leaders making up their own rules and regulations for their organized church. They willingly decided to establish their own clear pattern of leadership, servant hood, pastoral duties, and directions of the church. Having done this, they adopted the policy of "just Jesus, me, and my family" approach to the church. They forced the people in the pews to believe and approve their plans for dynasty church. They sought to use a clear pattern of leadership in their church and attempted to keep their plans as an under cover venture. Many of the so-called church leaders refused to hear sound counsel and to allow God's called out workers to be a vital part of their ministries. *They* assumed all the duties of the ministry and appointed loyal subjects for them as co-workers. Some even called themselves "God Father" as if they were running Mafia operation. These so- called ministries were **self**-*willed*, hardheaded and genuinely unwilling to be taught and led by spiritual leaders. They desired to be important and wanted to be in the spot light. As these church sprung up throughout the land, many had the idea to leave these churches and establish a "home church." But, as indicated this is not what God commanded for His church. God is still in business of building His church.

God will not bless people who reject His leadership. God calls out whom He wants to be a spiritual leader for His people. Every man does not have the right to act as if God has called them to be a spiritual minister. The bible tells us that some self-willed individuals challenged Moses and Aaron with these words: "You take too much upon yourselves, for all the congregation is holy, every one of them, and the Lord is among them" (Numbers 16:3). God showed *His* attitude toward this falsehood. This "every man is a minister" did not set well with God. He allowed the earth to open up and *swallow alive* these hardheaded rebels (verses. 28–34)!

In this 21ˢᵗ century we are called to identify God's true ministers. The question is: are they preaching the Gospel to "all the nations" (Matthew 28:19–20). If they are shirking their responsibility to be part of the true *active body* of Jesus Christ and have separated themselves from God's unadulterated Word, then God is not pleased. They are to be constantly working together with the believers as part of the body. They are to be learning the full Truth of God in a *balanced* way. They are to be humble and receive and act upon the needed *exhortation* and *corrections* that all Christians receive from the creator. The leadership has the responsibility for making God's church the place where the unadulterated word of God to be preached and practiced.

But, what is happening is that many are ending up on the fringe. Too many are not interacting and learning what it means to be a real part of God church engaging in Holy fellowship. Many churches are self-appointed religious leaders, and their followers, usually become sidetracked by odd ideas and doctrinal novelties. Many churches in this 21st century are showing their lack of **faith** in God's ability to lead His Church, and have the gauge to tell God *His* responsibility (Ephesians 1:22–23; Colossians 1:18)!

The Church Jesus Built

Jesus asked His disciples: "'Who do men say that I, the Son of Man, am?' So they said, 'Some say John the Baptist, some Elijah, and others Jeremiah or one of the prophets'" (Matthew 16:13–14). But Peter answered: "You are the Christ, the Son of the living God." Then Jesus continued: "You are Peter, and on this rock *I will build* **My church**, and the gates of Hades shall not prevail against it" (v. 18).

Jesus said very plainly that He *would* build the "church." This means which is inspired by Greek language a "group" or "crowd" of people. Jesus called it "**My**" church—not just *any* group or crowd or church.

Throughout the New Testament, God clearly indicates that *His* people, *His* Church—would be *small* in number during this age. The church would face persecution. Jesus said: "You did not choose Me, but I chose you … If you were of the world, the world would love its own. Yet because you are not of the world, but I chose you out of the world, *therefore the world hates you*" (John 15:16–19). It is obvious that God's true people will not "fit" into world. Jesus continued: *"If they persecuted Me, they will also persecute you"* (v. 20). And Jesus called His people the *"little flock"* (Luke 12:32). Jesus said: *"Enter by the narrow gate; for wide is the gate and broad is the way that leads to destruction, and there are many who go in by it. Because narrow is the gate and difficult is the way which leads to life, and there are few who find it"* (Matthew 7:13–14). Remember, then, only a few go in through the straight gate. Only a few *truly understand* and are part of God's true Church today!

Jesus says: *"Not everyone who says to Me, 'Lord, Lord,' shall enter the kingdom of heaven, but he who does the will of My Father in heaven"* (Matthew 7:21). Jesus plainly stated that His true people must be *obedient* to the Father's will. They must do what God the Father commands. This *applies* to the true Church. All through the New Testament, the term "woman" is used as a *symbol* of a church. In 2 Corinthians 11:1–2, the true Church is pictured as the affianced "bride" of Christ. In Revelation 17, the great false church is called a "harlot" (v. 1) and the "woman" (v. 3) sitting on a scarlet colored beast.

Scholars acknowledge that in Revelation 12, the *true Church* is pictured as the bride, and I agree with these scholars. She is being "persecuted" by the "dragon"—described in verse 9 as Satan the Devil. Although the zealous members are taken to a place of safety, in verse 17 God describes the devil as going to make war with the "remnant" of the true Church—*those left behind*. I suggest that this war is already being felt in the "remnant" church.

In Revelation 14:12, God describes His faithful people. He describes them as being His "patient saints." They keep the commandments of God, and the faith of Jesus. *"They* are the people of God. God will protect *them* from the soon-coming Great Tribulation and the horrifying **plagues** of God that immediately follow! This is the church that Jesus built.

Does it *make any difference* how you worship God? *Of course* God has given all of us free will; you can worship in the church of *"your* choice." Because of freewill, you can follow the ideas of your relatives, friends and associates. But they will not be able to protect you during the coming world upheaval. More importantly, they will not be there to "save" you in God's judgment. The Bible is the *inspired revelation*, from God, the Creator. Without the bible humankind would not have the basic spiritual knowledge. It would be inaccessible to humankind. This is what the Bible has to tell the world about where God's true Church is today.

IDENTIFYING "SIGNS"

Jesus said *He* would build *His* Church. The Bible describes that Church as a small and persecuted Church. The church is not a part of the world. God church is a Church that does the will of God the Father. It **keeps** the Ten Commandments given as a basic *way of life* by the Almighty God.

Many differing churches are small. Many are persecuted. Some are persecuted because they seem to deliberately *provoke others. They* bring unneeded persecution upon themselves. Why? They bring persecution because of thoughtlessly and arrogantly trying to "cram a made up religion" down the throats of other people.

Many small, unorthodox religious groups believe that they are not "part of this world." They wear distinctive attire, black hats, black bonnets, robes, and special made clothes to prove that they are head of religious groups. A biblical "key" to properly understanding and applying the above principles is revealed in the Apostle Paul's statement that God has given Christians the spirit of "a *sound mind*" (2 Timothy 1:7). But apart from the above general description of the true Church, are there any specific *identifying* signs that point unmistakably to where God's Church is today? Yes, there are identifying signs.

CHAPTER EIGHT

THE FEAR OF GOD

T HE AUTHOR OF Ecclesiastes, Solomon writes, *"Let us hear the conclusion of the whole matter: Fear God and keep His commandments. For this is man's all"* (Ecclesiastes 12:13). The Apostle John writes, "God is love," (1 John 4:8). But there is not a contradiction in the writings of these authors. What is this fear that God is speaking to us about?

God loves us. He hates sin. Those who choose to practice it in defiance of His law will die (Ezekiel 18:4). Now that is something to be afraid of. So it behooves us to obey God. Yes, many obey out of fear of the alternative—death. However, the more we keep God's law, the more we come to understand God's love for us. We will soon discover that He gave us His good laws because following them will give us the best life possible.

The Hebrew word for "fear" in Ecclesiastes 12:13 is *"Yare." It does not mean to be afraid.* It means to stand in awe of, to reverence, honor and respect. God does not want us to be in terror of Him. We are to have a healthy reverence and respect for the most power being in the universe and the laws He has set in place that we may be blessed. We fear and keep His commandments because God is love. We do not deserve His love so we stand in awe for the depth of love He has for us.

God created humankind, but before He did this, He created Lucifer—one of the three cherubs, or super archangels, who originally surrounded His throne. In Latin, "Lucifer" means "light bringer" or "shining star of the dawn." Lucifer was originally created as a powerful, beautiful super archangel with tremendous wisdom and capacity (Ezekiel 28:11–15). In Isaiah 14:12–15, *Lucifer is described: "How you are fallen from heaven, O*

Lucifer, son of the morning! How you are cut down to the ground, you who weakened the nations! For you have said in your heart: 'I will ascend into heaven, I will exalt my throne above the stars of God; I will also sit on the mount of the congregation on the farthest sides of the north; I will ascend above the heights of the clouds, I will be like the Most High. Yet you shall be brought down to Sheol, to the lowest depths of the Pit."

Many theologians agree that Lucifer's ability and beauty led to a great deal of pride. It is evident that his pride led him to *rebel* against his Creator. His name was changed from "light bringer" to *Satan*—which literally means "adversary" in Hebrew. Lucifer is God's greatest *enemy*. Throughout the entire Bible, God shows us that He is determined not to allow *anyone* to come into His Kingdom who is a potential *adversary*—a potential *Satan!* We all should recognize how vital this is to God. He wants *unity* and *peace* in His Kingdom and His Spirit-led family! He is the Author of *love, joy* and *peace*. Any being who would be a potential rebel might eventually destroy that peace.

God reveals that He will make *absolutely sure* that any potential son of His will come to have the correct "fear" of God! As God's word indicates, this fear is **not** "terror" or being "afraid" of something bad! Rather, it is a profound *reverence*, humility and willingness to **obey** the Creator. We are to never rebel against His laws and His righteous ways. His way always brings peace and joy. Hell was created for Satan and his imps.

One of the first "tests" that Abraham, the "father of the faithful," had to pass is described in Genesis 22. Here we find how God "tested" Abraham (v. 1) to see whether he would *be totally submissive* to his Creator. He tests him to see if he would be willing to sacrifice his only son. At the very last minute—when Abraham had proved his total submission to God—God sent an angel who said: *"Do not lay your hand on the lad, or do anything to him; for now I know that you fear God, since you have not withheld your son, your only son, from Me"* (v. 12). Then, God gave Abraham the magnificent blessing that tremendous *physical* wealth and power would come upon his descendants, as well as *spiritual* blessings through the "seed," Jesus Christ (verses. 15–18).

Abraham *proves* that he "feared" God and had enough faith to willingly and t*otally surrender* to God and do His will. Abraham believes in God. Proverbs 1:7 says: *"The fear of the Lord is the beginning of knowledge,* but fools despise wisdom and instruction." Proverbs 9:10 says: "The **fear** of the Lord is the beginning of wisdom, and the knowledge of the Holy One is understanding." The awe and deep *reverence* before our Creator is the starting point of true knowledge and true wisdom. We must have it to get into His eternal Kingdom!

This author believes that the church that has this kind of awe and profound reverence and willingness to obey is the kind of church God is looking for in this 21st century. They must be as faithful as Abraham demonstrated-willing to forsake all to obey the commands of God. Also, members of the true Church realize that the true meaning of Hebrews 11:6: *"But without faith it is impossible to please Him, for he who comes to God must **believe** that He is, and that He is a rewarder of those who diligently seek Him."*

The true church of God totally believes in the Word of God as it is described in the Bible. And we must believe that, as the Bible says, He is a "re warder" of those who *diligently seek Him. God word did not say we are to be half-heatedly,* do what is convenient, and to believe whatever religious fad is currently in vogue! He did not tell us to be interfaith believers. God is a jealous God and they that worship Him are to worship Him in spirit and in truth.

The authentic Christian will know the truth, for Jesus said: *"Man shall not live by bread alone, but by every word of God"* (Luke 4:4). The genuine Christian will *surrender themselves* to follow what Jesus said, and to **do** what God says in His inspired word. They know that God "reveals" Himself *through His word,* **not** through our human imagination. They will understand and respond to 2 Timothy_3:16–17: *"All Scripture is given by inspiration of God, and is profitable for doctrine, for reproof, for correction, for instruction in righteousness, that the man of God may be complete, thoroughly equipped for every good work."*

God makes it clear the scripture is given just for our encouragement but for reproof and for correction as well as "instruction in righteousness." The 21st century church must base its beliefs totally upon God's inspired word! She must accept the Jesus, the Christ as revealed in the Bible as both Savior and Lord. We are to obey Him and not man. This author believes that those who have failed to do so have instituted thousands of different competing denominations. All of them have their own doctrines, practices and concepts of what God is like. As quiet as it is kept to avoid from saying that they are being judgmental-many are counterfeits using the church as a front to exploit the weak and fevered.

THE FOUNDATION OF TRUTH

Dr. Harold Lindsell in his book entitled "The Battle for the Bible" lays out this fundamental proposition: "Of all the doctrines connected with the Christian faith, none is more important than the one that has to do with the basis of our religious knowledge. For anyone who professes the Christian faith the root question is: From where do I get my knowledge on which my faith is based? The answers to this question are varied, of course, but for the Christian at least it always comes full circle to the Bible. When all has been said and done, the **only** true and dependable source for Christianity lies in the book we call the *Bible*."

This author believes that truth is vital to the success of the church in this 21st century. With all the earthquakes, wars, upheavals in Ferguson, New York, Baltimore, Chicago, and so on- the answer to all our problems can be found in the Word of God. This is absolutely vital to true Christianity and we are to be in leadership. This is a vital "key" that *must* be taught and practiced by any church that calls itself the true Church of God! Again, the *true* people of God will only be those who surrender to actually do what God commands. They will obey God's word even *if* it brings them *"problems" or* severe persecution!

The point must be made that the early Christians put their lives on the line *when* they followed Jesus. The original apostles did likewise. They were continually persecuted. Many of them were martyred. They were often hounded out of their jobs, their cities or even their families. Jesus warned them as He told them: *"If anyone comes to Me and does not hate ["love less"] his father and mother, wife and children, brothers and sisters, yes, and his own life also, he cannot be My disciple. And whoever does not bear his cross and come after Me cannot be My disciple"* (Luke 14:26–27). He gives us the power to follow and obey His every command.

When we are challenged about our "power" think of what Peter said about the healing of a crippled man, he said: *"Let it be known to you all, and to all the people of Israel, that by the name of **Jesus Christ** of Nazareth,* *whom you crucified, whom God raised from the dead, by Him this man stands here before you whole. This is the 'stone which was rejected by you builders, which has become the chief cornerstone.' Nor is there salvation in any other, for there is no other name under heaven given among men by which we must be saved"* (Acts 4:10–12). There is power in His name and gives power to His called out disciples.

To be in God's *true Church*, one must sincerely follow Peter's inspired instruction on the day of Pentecost: *"Repent, **and** let every one of you be baptized in the name of Jesus Christ for the remission of sins; and you shall receive the gift of the Holy Spirit. For the promise is to you and to your children, and to all who are afar off, as many as the Lord our God will call"* (Acts 2:38–39). When one comes to the point of being willing to heartfelt repent of breaking God's holy law—for *"sin is the transgression of the law"* (1 John 3:4, *KJV*)—*one must be baptized in the name of Jesus Christ, and receive the Holy Spirit through the laying on of hands.* At that moment, the new Christian will be *totally forgiven* of past sins, and will become a member of God's Church.

For you cannot "join" God's true Church! You must be put into the Church—baptized into the Church—by God Himself, through His filling you with the Holy Spirit. Paul said *"Now if anyone does not have the Spirit of Christ, he is not His"* (Romans 8:9). Also: *"For by one Spirit we were all baptized into one body—whether Jews or Greeks, whether slaves or free—and have all been made to drink into one Spirit"* (1 Corinthians 12:13). Through the total surrender of your heart, mind and body to God *through* Jesus Christ as Savior, you will be plunged into—*put into*—the Church of God, which is Christ's body. Then—with Christ as your Lord—you will not belong to yourself anymore. "Or do you not know that your body is the temple of the Holy Spirit who is in you, whom you have from God, and you are not your own? For you were bought with a price; therefore glorify God in your body and in your spirit, which are God's" (1 Corinthians 6:19–20).

I can hear the late Reverend N.B. Benjamin saying early at 6:00 am baptismal service at the New Light Baptist Church, Hallsboro, N.C., "I baptize you in the name of the Father, Son, and the Holy Ghost. Noting last evening you had been on the mourners bench praying and prayed over until the Holy Ghost filled the room. Then, he would say, "when you come out of the water shout Jesus, for you have been submerged in God's name,

God's Son name, Jesus, the Christ, and the name of the Holy Spirit. And remember you have been also baptized in Jesus' name. He said, "Now, you belong to Him and Him only." "Now shout amen and say so mote it be." Then, after the baptism service he would teach and preach until the power of the Holy Spirit fell heavily on those who were baptized.

COMPLETE SURRENDER TO JESUS CHRIST

God's true Church is composed of people willing to surrender fully to Christ. They must also be willing to follow Jesus' instruction: *"If anyone desires to come after me, let him **deny** himself, and take up his **cross**, and follow Me. For whoever desires to save his life will lose it, but whoever loses his life for My sake will find it"* (Matthew 16:24–25). This author has observed that many professing Christians today seemed to be interested in "saving" their lives—having a "good time" and fitting into this present society. This makes it very difficult for them to obey the powerful teaching of the Son of God.

One of the preachers and my friend at St. Mary's Seminary & University in Baltimore, Maryland was granted the opportunity to conduct a series of small evangelistic meetings in London, England. This author wanted to go but I was not really offered the opportunity. My friend told me that among the attendees was a very compassionate Scottish couple who came every night for four weeks. This couple seemed very interested and enthusiastic. They shouted loudly "Praise the Lord!" and acted very pleased with what my friend had to say throughout the weeks. We had prepared the seminar outline and content before he had departed. In fact I carried him to the airport. The couple told him after each session that they wanted to do "whatever" the Lord had in mind. By the end of the sessions my friend said he taught the outline I had given him on God's Ten Commandments. He said that suddenly the couple's attitude changed. They became somber and defensive. They declared that my friend had gone too far.

He said that he and his wife who went with him tried to convince them of the merits of the Ten Commandments after the session. He shared with them that what he said came directly from the bible. But they said because of their employment, it would be "too difficult" to obey God. So they failed to show up for the last couple of meetings, and eventually faded away into the mass of Londoners. God's direct command seemed "too hard" for them. It demanded *obedience* in a way to which they were not prepared to respond. My friend was so disappointed that the couple refused to even consider God's commandments.

During the years of ministry, I have learned to accept that "God will not 'save' anyone who will not accept Him as their personal savior. We must have a willingness to surrender our lives to Him and a willingness to obey Him like Abraham did.

I do not mean to convey the idea that every person has to have this *almost perfect attitude* of submission to God **before** becoming a member of His true Church! But the basic *understanding* and willingness to *grow* in that perfect submission to our Creator ought to be present. We must be willing to let Him in when He knocks at our heart. When we accept Him, then we will become a new creation in Christ. Then, we can call Him Lord, Father, Abba Father, and He will be our Shepherd. Jesus, the Christ said: *"But **why** do you call Me 'Lord, Lord,' and **not do** the things which I say?"* (Luke 6:46).

Jesus, the Christ also said: *"Not everyone who says to Me, 'Lord, Lord,' shall enter the kingdom of heaven, but he who **does** the will of My Father in heaven. Many will say to Me in that day, 'Lord, Lord, have we not prophesied in Your name, cast out demons in Your name, and done many wonders in Your name?' And then I will declare to them, 'I never knew you; depart from Me, you who practice lawlessness!'"* *"Depart from me, you who practice lawlessness!* (Matthew 7:21–23).

I submit that those who pretend to teach the Ten Commandments and invent all manner of excuses to "water them down **for t**heir own purpose is in *deep trouble*! The Apostle James was inspired to write: *"For whoever shall keep the whole law, and yet stumble in one point, he is guilty of all. For He who said, 'Do not commit adultery,' also said, 'Do not murder.' Now if you do not commit adultery, but you do murder, you have become a transgressor of the law. So speak and so do as those who will be judged by the law of liberty"* (James 2:10–12).

James was referring to the Ten Commandments. *These* commandments teach against murder and adultery. James stated that all of us must obey all ten of God's commandments. We are not to compromise and initiate new commandments to suit our personal needs and desires. We are not to come up with clever reasons as to why it should be abandoned, modified, compromised, modified, and tampered with to suit the lifestyles of the modern and so called famous.

What is God's true church composed of in this 21st century? God's true Church is composed of those who have the *genuine* "fear of God," those who are tired of "playing games" with religion, those who are willing to *diligently seek* the God of the Bible, those who will obey His commandments and those who truly yield themselves to Christ to live *His obedient life* within them through the Holy Spirit. Paul cited the best one-verse definition of a true Christian. He states *"I am crucified with Christ: nevertheless I live; yet not I, but Christ **liveth** in me: and the life which I now live in the flesh I live by the faith of the Son of God, who loved me, and gave himself for me"* (Galatians 2:20, *KJV*). *This* is the very basis of *true Christianity. This* is the foundation of the **true** Church of God!

THE TRUE CHURCH HAS GOD'S NAME

God names things what they are! Before Satan rebelled, he was called "Lucifer," which means "light bringer." After he tried to dethrone the living God, however, his name was changed to "Satan." His name means "enemy" or "adversary." He has become exactly what he is, the fallen cherub. The name "Jacob" means "usurper" or one who "supplants" another. After he wrestled with God's Messenger and began to ask God for help, God *changed* his name to "Israel." This means "over comer" or "prevail" with God. Throughout the Bible God demonstrated the naming guidelines. Names are *very important* to God. *God names things what they are!*

Research tells us that many years ago, in 1517; a young Catholic priest in Germany became upset at the selling of "indulgences"—the Roman Catholic practice of promising forgiveness of sins upon payment of money. He nailed to the church door 95 theses expressing why the practice of selling indulgences was wrong, and explaining his other disagreements with the Roman Catholic Church. This person was Martin Luther. He unwittingly started what became the Protestant Reformation. Later, after a break with the Roman Church, his followers called themselves "Lutheran" after this reformer. They decided to *name* their church the *"Lutheran Church."*

Years later, John Wesley came of the scene. He set out preaching about a different approach to God and religion. Eventually, his followers decided to name their church after him. The term "Wesleyan" was widely used. Wesley and his followers became noted for their "methodical" and organized manner of conduct. This became their nickname. Eventually the church became the name of their whole denomination, "The Methodist Church."

Presbyterians are named after their form of church government by the elders, or "*presbyters*." Baptists are named after one doctrine: *baptism*. Seventh Day Adventists are named after *two* of their doctrines—belief in the seventh-day Sabbath and the "advent" or return of Jesus Christ. Many other churches take their names from their town, their form of government, or some point of doctrine.

What, then, should God's true Church be named? Should it be named after some man? Should it be named after some *country* or geographic location? Should it be named after some *doctrine* or practice of the Church? Does God give us any indication in the *Bible* what His Church should be called? Some may be surprised to learn that *He does!*

THE CORRECT "NAME" IS LISTED TWELVE TIMES

When the Apostle Paul was instructing the elders of the Church in Ephesus, he wrote: "*Therefore take heed to yourselves and to all the flock, among which the Holy Spirit has made you overseers, to shepherd the church of God which He purchased with His own blood*" (Acts 20:28). Heed what? "Heed the "*Church of God.*""

Does it seem too obvious that God's true Church would be called *just that*: "The Church of God"? 1 Corinthians 1:1–2. In his official address to the church, the Holy Spirit inspired Paul to write: "Unto the *church of God* which is at Corinth ..." Later in the letter, he tells them: "Give no offense, either to the Jews or to the Greeks or to the *church of God*" (1 Corinthians 10:32). We are to stress that the church belongs to God and not to any man.

In 1 Corinthians 11:16, Paul describes the many congregations *collectively* as "the *churches of God.*" In verse 22 of this chapter, Paul again refers to them as "the *church of God.*" And in 1 Corinthians 15:9, he wrote: "*For I am the least of the apostles, who am not worthy to be called an apostle,* because I persecuted the church of God." 2 Corinthians begins with the same official address: "*To the church of God which is at Corinth.*" And in 1 Thessalonians 2:14, Paul refers to the original Christians as "*the churches of God which are in Judea in Christ Jesus.*" The introduction to both of Paul's letters to the Thessalonians refers to "*the church of the Thessalonians in God the Father,*" for they were His churches and must be *in union with Him.* In 1 Timothy 3:5, Paul tells the young evangelist Timothy that if an elder does not know how to rule his house, "*how shall he take care of the church of God?*" Finally, in 1 Timothy 3:15, Paul tells Timothy that he is writing to tell him how to conduct himself in "*the house of God, which is the church of the living God, the pillar and ground of the truth.*" Again, the church belongs to God and Him only.

Throughout the New Testament—in *twelve distinct passages*—the true Church is called "the church of God," "the churches of God," "the church of the Thessalonians *in God*" and, at pagan Ephesus where stood the idol to the goddess Diana, "the church of the *living God.*"

Often, in business or industry, the founder or owner's name is given to an enterprise as the identifying "sign" of ownership or control: for example, "The Bank of Morgan" or "Lever Brothers." God's *name* is always attached to *His* true Church. Christ is God, so in one or two passages we also find the appellation "church of Christ."

One of the absolute prerequisite identifying signs of God's true Church is that it *must bear God's name*! The name *alone* is not absolute proof of its identity. But, taken together with the four other identifying signs we shall discuss, it is an absolutely *vital* designation. For *God names things what they are.* In fact, just before His crucifixion, Jesus prayed for His followers: "*Holy Father, keep through Your name those whom You have given Me, that they may be one as We are*" (John 17:11).

GROWTH IN GRACE AND KNOWLEDGE

The Apostle Paul wrote: "*Now if anyone does not have the Spirit of Christ, he is not His*" (Romans 8:9). And again: "*For as many as are led by the Spirit of God, these are sons of God*" (v. 14 To be truly "Christian" and a child of God, one must be filled with and *led by* the Holy Spirit. The Bible shows clearly that each child of God must *grow spiritually.* So must the true Church of God genuinely grow in spiritual *understanding* and *depth*? And they must be *led by* the Holy Spirit.

How does the Holy Spirit work? Jesus explained that the Holy Spirit is "the Spirit of truth." He said that when the Spirit of truth has come, it would guide Christians into all truth, and that it would even tell them of things to come (John 16:13). The Spirit "guides" us *into* all *truth*. It also helps us to understand *prophecy*— "things to come."

It is a process of *growing* and changing; a process of becoming more and more like God in our character, our thoughts and habits. Perhaps the Apostle Peter expressed it most clearly: *"But grow in the grace and knowledge of our Lord and Savior Jesus Christ"* (2 Peter 3:18). The true Church of God is made up of truly *converted* Christians—people who have been and who are certainly *being* changed by the power of God's Holy Spirit. As each individual must "grow" in grace *and in knowledge*, so the unified body of those individuals—the true Church—*must also grow.*

For instance, Daniel was given awesome visions and dreams involving events to take place on earth at the end of this age—probably just a few years from now. He asked: *"O my Lord, what shall be the end of these things?"* And God's angel answered: *"Go your way, Daniel, for the words are closed up and sealed till the time of the end"* (Daniel 12:8–9). Now, with humankind having the capacity to destroy all life from off this planet, we are certainly in the prophesied "time of the end."

WHO REALLY UNDERSTANDS?

In this 21st century, the church of God is truly growing into such knowledge and understanding of Bible prophecies. The question is: "Are churches really growing in knowledge and understanding? Do you know of any church that has been willing to change and grow, not to become more like the world, but rather to more deeply understand the Master Plan of God that is in action today? Is there a church that truly understands *where we are headed? The* United States and Great Britain are slowly but inexorably sliding from their pinnacle of national greatness. A powerful union of nations in Europe will soon become *the* force to reckon with. The

United States is searching for the answers of not collapsing in these last days. This author believes that they will have to get their directions from the church. God wants His church to be ready, willing, and able to shine its light for this dark world to see His plan of salvation.

There is a Church that grasps why we were actually born and place on this earth. There is a church that understands the incredible human potential. There is a church that understands the amazing truth that God is *literally reproducing* Himself. This Church knows *why* most people in this present age never join any type of "Christian" church or organization, and why God *is not rendering a supernatural miracle to* "save" the world during this 6,000-year period when, as the *Almighty* God, He clearly has the power to do so if He wants to.

God's true Church *understands* these matters, and can give *clear biblical answers* to these most basic questions. It is a Church that *keeps on learning and* growing in vital knowledge and understanding. Most "mainline" churches seldom *if ever* change or grow in true knowledge. When they do change, it is nearly always in the direction of secularism— "watering down" what little bits of biblical truth they may once have had. But the true Church of God *grows* continually into a deeper and fuller understanding of the Bible, of the great purpose being worked out here below and of the exciting fulfillment of biblical prophecy now starting to occur.

THE "SIGN" OF GOD'S PEOPLE

Speaking of true Christians having to flee the coming Great Tribulation, Jesus said: *"And pray that your flight may not be in winter or on the Sabbath"* (Matthew 24:20). *Why* would Jesus be concerned about His followers keeping the Sabbath day? It is because it is a "test. It is a test to determine if each of us will just *obey God because He says to do it.* And therefore it is an identifying "sign" of His people. Also, it points to the *true* God, the Creator of heaven and earth.

Jesus observed the Sabbath, "As His custom was" (Luke 4:16). The Apostle to the Gentiles always preached and had religious services on that day (Acts 17:2). In the Old Testament, a special Sabbath covenant was made with Israel: "Speak also to the children of Israel, saying: *'Surely My*

Sabbaths you shall keep, for it is a sign between Me and you throughout your generations, that you may know that I am the Lord who sanctifies you. You shall keep the Sabbath, therefore, for it is holy to you. Everyone who profanes it shall surely be put to death; for whoever does any work on it, that person shall be cut off from among his people. Work shall be done for six days, but the seventh is the Sabbath of rest, holy to the Lord. Whoever does any work on the Sabbath day, he shall surely be put to death. Therefore the children of Israel shall keep the Sabbath, to observe the Sabbath throughout their generations as a perpetual covenant. It is a sign between Me and the children of Israel forever; for in six days the Lord made the heavens and the earth, and on the seventh day He rested and was refreshed'" (Exodus 31:13–17).

In addition to the weekly Sabbath, God gave His people seven *annual* Sabbaths or Holy Days. These spiritual "feasts" of rejoicing picture God's great plan of salvation. Those who fail to observe them do not understand God's great plan and purpose. They do not know, for instance, *why* God is not "saving" everyone now. And they do not know the exact time when, in God's Master Plan, all human beings who have ever lived will be given *genuine understanding* of God's word and of true Christianity—and the *vast majority* will respond!

One of these spiritual feasts is the Passover. Most churches have *changed* its time and manner of observance and call it the "Lord's Supper," "Eucharist," or some other name. Jesus kept it as the "Passover" (Luke 22:15–20). The Apostle Paul kept the Passover and the accompanying "Days of Unleavened Bread" (1 Corinthians 5:7–8).

The Passover lamb of ancient Israel pointed to the *death* of Jesus Christ—the Lamb of God—for our sins. Right after the Passover, the "Days of Unleavened Bread" were observed. In putting out leaven, Christians are to picture *putting out sin* and growing in grace and knowledge—the next step after accepting Christ's sacrifice!

Paul taught the Gentile church at Corinth *how* to keep the Feast of Unleavened Bread: "Therefore let us **keep** *the feast*, not with old leaven, nor with the leaven of malice and wickedness, but with the unleavened *bread* of sincerity and truth" (1 Corinthians 5:8). This is a New Testament command—not *to* Jews—but to a primarily *Gentile* church to observe the Feast of Unleavened Bread. God's *true* Church should be observing this God-given festival just as Christ, the apostles and all the early Christians did! We need a "Put Out Sin Revival." The author is widely known for His put out sin workshops and revivals.

The point is that these *annual* Sabbaths and Holy Days are also part of God's "sign" by which *His people* would be identified. God said: *"It shall be as a sign to you on your hand and as a memorial between your eyes that the Lord's law may be in your mouth ..."* (Exodus 13:9).

Wherever God's true people are—wherever *His Church* is—His servants will have the identifying "sign" of God's true Sabbaths, weekly and annual. The weekly Sabbath points to the true God—the Creator— and the annual Sabbaths set forth His marvelous plan.

God's true church must be willing to obey the fourth commandment, which tells us to keep the seventh day of the week as "holy time. The church is not to set around arguing or "reasoning" away God's commands. His true Church flees *to safety just as Christ indicated* in Matthew 24:20! And you will become *very thirsty* as the millennial rule of Christ begins and He is forced to bring *total* drought on *all* nations and peoples who *refuse* to keep His commanded Holy Days—especially the Feast of Tabernacles (Zechariah 14:16–19)! For your *own* sake—and the sake of your loved ones—please do not underestimate this huge issue! The true church is willing to surrender and obey the Creator.

CHAPTER NINE

GOD DOES THE WORK

ONE OF THE "signs" Jesus gave of His coming, and of the end of this age, was this: *"And this gospel of the kingdom will be preached in the entire world as a witness to all the nations, and then the end will come"* (Matthew 24:14).

Just before Jesus' Second Coming, His true servants will be preaching with increasing power the message of the coming world-ruling Kingdom of God! They will preach the message of heartfelt repentance and total surrender to God and to His laws. This is what Jesus preached when He was on earth being both fully human and fully divine. They will explain how true Christianity involves not just accepting Jesus Christ as personal Savior, but *genuinely* accepting Him as our *Lord*, our *High Priest* and our soon-coming King. For Jesus' coming Kingdom is a *real* Kingdom. A kingdom is a *government*—and from one end of your Bible to the other, God's message is about His coming government, which will utterly crush all the governments of this world and will rule forever. (Daniel 2:44; Revelation 11:15)

Jesus Christ will soon return in mighty power to *govern this earth* and save man from destroying the world his by hand. (Matthew 24:22)! Jesus said: *"He who overcomes, and keeps My works until the end, to him I will give power over the nations—He shall rule them with a rod of iron"* (Revelation 2:26–27). *"And have made us kings and priests to our God; and we shall reign on the earth"* (Revelation 5:10). *Christ and His saints will rule "on the earth"—not up in "heaven"!*

God's true Church will proclaim the vibrant message of His soon-coming world ruling the government. This message will not convert everyone, but will be proclaimed so when it actually occurs, humanity will understand their plight. The true church has always known of Jesus' eminent return.

Also, through the true Church, God is training men and women so they will be "ready" to serve under the living Christ when He returns as King of kings. The Apostle Paul alerted true Christians to this *vital* truth and told them of the type of *preparation* and *training* members of the true Church should be receiving. Paul wrote: *"Do you not know that the saints will judge the world? Now, the world will be judged by the true Christians, and then are you worthy to judge the small matters of the church?"* (1 Corinthians 6:2–3). In order to rule others, one must first learn to rule oneself. God's *government* is based upon His spiritual law—the Ten Commandments. So *that* is why God says of the true saints: "Here is the patience of the saints; here *are* those who *keep the* commandments of God and the faith of Jesus" (Revelation 14:12). Another absolutely vital part of the work of the true Church is to understand and proclaim the *prophetic messages* of the Bible. Approximately *one-fourth* of the entire Bible is devoted to prophecy! God's says: "For the testimony of Jesus is *the spirit of* prophecy" (Revelation 19:10).

God's real church understands and proclaims the real *meaning* of current events. They have been given the wisdom and understanding to explain **why** the U.S. and other British-descended peoples are increasingly losing their power and prestige. They know the prophecy recorded in the Word of God. They know where these nations are heading. They can explain *why* the mainly Catholic nations of continental Europe are increasingly uniting. They know the destiny of Britain. They have been told that Britain will *get out* or be "pushed out" of the European Union. The United States and Great Britain in Prophecy is known by the true church.

Another vital part of the prophetic commission of God's true church concerning the end-times is called the "Ezekiel commission." This is the warning message that God indicated His true servants should give to the twelve tribes of Israel. According to prophesy, the Anglo-Celtic peoples of the U.S. and the British Commonwealth nations are the descendants of the so-called "Lost Ten Tribes" of Israel. Along with the Jewish people, *they* will bear the brunt of the soon-coming Great Tribulation. *They are to be* warned about this coming holocaust!

The true church is the end-time watchman: "When she sees the sword coming upon the land, if he blows the trumpet and warns the people, then whoever hears the sound of the trumpet and does not take warning, if the sword comes and takes him away, his blood shall be on his own head. He heard the sound of the trumpet, but did not take warning; his blood shall be upon himself. But he who takes warning will save his life. But if the watchman sees the sword coming and does not blow the trumpet, and the people are not warned, and the sword comes and takes any person from among them, he is taken away in his iniquity; but his blood I will require at the watchman's hand. So you, son of man: *I have made you a watchman for the house of Israel; therefore you shall hear a word from My mouth and warn them for Me*" (Ezekiel 33:3–7). This is a vital part of the responsibility of God's true servants in these "last days." This author is sounding the trumpet in this book and preaching where God's leads him to declare His word for this untoward generation.

Only God's true church is equipped to understand and give the genuine understanding of these and other world-changing trends that will soon *dramatically affect the world.* God's *true* Church is be consistently teaching, training and genuinely *preparing* its members for their future as kings and priests in Christ's soon-coming world government (Daniel 7:27; Luke 19:15–19, Revelation 1:5–7;5:10;20:6). If you can find that Church - become part of it. Your life is important do not play church! Be that church, that God is looking for.

GOD'S TRUE CHURCH HAS IDENTIFYING "SIGNS"

God's true Church is one spiritual organism. It is normal and biblical for churches to exist in several different "fellowships" or "branches" at the same time. In chapters 2 and 3 of Revelation, Christ reveals the characteristics of the seven ages or "eras" of God's true Church. He finds some fault with most of the seven churches or "eras." He spoke highly of Philadelphia. These "eras" represent attitudes in God's Church. We can look and see the progression of "dominant" attitudes in the churches today. Today, many churches resemble the Laodicea era. Christ condemned this church for being "lukewarm" even though it has most of the Truth. Jesus

Christ said: "I know your works, that you are neither cold nor hot. I could wish you were cold or hot. So then, because you are lukewarm, and neither cold nor hot, I will vomit you out of My mouth" (Revelation 3:15–16).

The church in this book that author is producing is by the power of God expressing Himself in these pages. He strives to retain the Philadelphia emphasis even in our Laodicean age. He wants God's church to be *zealous* in doing God's work. It is his desire to do the will of God and get this book in the hands of whom God desireth. So I must focus on accomplishing the work of God the Father, Son, and Holy Spirit in these last days.

Apostle Paul said in 1 Corinthians 12 that God's church is the "body" of Christ, the *physical instrument* through which Christ is working today to accomplish His Work and to prepare the future kings and priests for His Kingdom. This body of Christ, "the true Church" has *always* existed. Jesus said: *"And I also say to you that you are Peter, and on this rock I will build My church, and the gates of Hades shall not prevail against it"* (Matthew 16:18).

Ever since Christ ascended to heaven and became the *living* Head of the Church, He has guided His "little flock" through trials, tests and persecutions down through the ages. By examining the "fruits" of the church, one can know how God is using the Living Church of God today to accomplish His purposes. Apostle Paul wrote: *"For as the body is one and has many members, but all the members of that one body, being many, are one body, so also is Christ. For by one Spirit we were all baptized into one body—whether Jews or Greeks, whether slaves or free—and have all been made to drink into one Spirit"* (1 Corinthians 12:12–13).

DIFFERENT "BRANCHES" OF GOD'S CHURCH

To be in the body of Christ, one *must fully surrender* to God and be led by His Spirit: *"Now if anyone does not have the Spirit of Christ, he is not His"* (Romans 8:9). Again, God gives the Holy Spirit "to those who **obey** Him" (Acts 5:32). Yet down through the ages, there have been many different

Church of God fellowships— "branches" of the true Church—that sometimes coexisted. For example, during the 12th and 13th centuries, God's true Church existed among the Bogomils in Hungary even while those believers were unaware that a similar group of Sabbath-keepers existed simultaneously in Great Britain.

In the U.S. there is church called "the Seventh Day Church of God." Over the years it underwent various "splits." Before World War II it ended up with one group headquartered in Stanberry, Missouri, and another headquartered in Caldwell, Idaho. Herbert W. Armstrong became the leader. They used the name "the Church of God." Mr. Armstrong acknowledged different fellowships as "branches" of the true Church.

During Mr. Armstrong's ministry, the people asked two vital questions:

(1) Was the truth of the Bible most clearly being preached?
(2) Was the "Work" most powerfully being done?

The "Work" consists of preaching the truth of the Bible, proclaiming to the world the soon-coming Kingdom of God (Matthew 3). 24:14), giving the "Israelite" nations a strong warning of the impending Great Tribulation, "feeding the flock" with the "whole counsel of God" (Acts 20:27) and genuinely teaching, training and preparing God's people to be "kings and priests" in Christ's Kingdom (Revelation 5:10). Was the work being done?

Jesus tells us, regarding *any* religious organization: "By their fruits you will know them" (Matthew 7:15–20). So it is up to the true Christian readers to carefully ask: *Where* is Christ primarily working today? *Who* is preaching the truth of God's Word? *Who* is most effectively doing the Work of proclaiming the Gospel to the public all over the world?

Wherever God's true people are, they will be those who have *surrendered their lives* to live by "every word of God." Within the greater body of Christ, God's true people must genuinely **love** one another as Jesus loved us all (John 13:34). Where those people are gathered into different corporate fellowships, there will be differing strengths and varying emphases. But out flowing love, brotherly kindness and the spirit of service should be present in converted members of God's Church, no matter where they live and to which particular fellowship they belong. The *genuine* love of God is based on the Ten Commandments. Apostle John said: *"For this is the love* *of God, that we keep His commandments. And His commandments are not burdensome"* (1 John 5:3).

The true people of God will follow this path. They will not argue and make excuses to be disobedient to His Word. God's true church does the **work** of proclaiming "the message of salvation *through* **Jesus Christ** and the *good news* of the soon-coming kingdom *of God* based on His law.

As world events move inexorably toward the **end** of this present age, one must know where they are headed. *Only* the *true* Church of God has been given the *understanding*, the *courage* and the boldness to proclaim the full Truth. (Revelation 1:6) I

THE NEED TO ACT

The living Jesus Christ tells *all* of us to *bear fruit*: *"By this My Father is glorified, that you bear **much fruit**; so you will be My disciples"* (John 15:8). This author prays that His readers and fellow unsaved people will be inspired to be an *active part* of the work that Christ is now accomplishing through *His* body, the true Church of God on earth today. We are living in the last days; we must be ready when Jesus comes. We can not afford to be confused and misguided. It is now time to make a decision to spend eternity in Heaven with God. God is able to make every person who calls upon Him partakers of the Heavenly treasure.

"THERE IS NOTHING WRONG WITH AMERICA THAT CANNOT BE CURED BY GOD.

The true church is to be the light. The "Light" is the truth of God's Word. It is to get the truth out. What is the truth? It is certainly not what many churches are saying. The truth is not:
1. Material Messiah
2. Mystical Messiah (Jump off this mountain and angels will bare you up)
3. Political & Militaristic Messiah (compromise)

Jesus is the Suffering Servant. He did not come to bring people wealth just for asking and tithing. He is not a God that you can tempt and conceive to be in partnership with Him. He does not compromise His Word for the sake of individuals and to be politically correct.

Some Believers Are Preaching Lies

Many Christians have their own concepts of what the Bible teaches. Obviously, some are correct and others are very wrong. Truth is intolerant! There is no compromise. There is no diversity. The modern-day neo-evangelical church preaches a watered-down gospel, and little else. I heard a pastor preach a sermon that was most disturbing. Truly, I would not call him a pastor, so I use this term very loosely. This author was ashamed to be in the same pulpit with him. He was a disgrace to his profession and to the faith.

The only way one would know that he was preaching is that he was introduced as such. He never touched upon any basic doctrine. He did not call out the name of Jesus; mention the blood, the crucifixion, the deity of Jesus, the Christ, the virgin birth, and so on. The pastor simply said, it will get better. He'd say things like, "Give your life to the master and you'll never have any problem again." Becoming a Christian doesn't guarantee a smoother life. On the contrary, becoming a Christian, the Word of God guarantees you persecuted. *"Yea and all that will live godly in Christ Jesus shall suffer persecution."* -2nd Timothy 3:12 This person continued talking and said "I never missed a good Hollywood movie. He'd say, "We don't preach anything here but the gospel." He took the time to chastise people who made him angry during the week. Then, he collected thousands of dollars to keep his members under the blessings of God. His congregation starved spiritually. Sadly, there are tens-of-thousands of such ministries. The problem is that many members do not care if the truth is not preached. The preacher does not preach the truth outside the walls of the church. The problem with most Christians is that they are at ease on Zion and complacent in their salvation. And many are receiving "kick backs" from the ministries.

God saved us to do more than fill up 18 inches of pew. However, often time if this is what the leadership is subscribing of its membership, then this is what they will do. Many follow the leadership because it is the order of the day. There is a song entitled "Standing on the Promises of God." All of His promises are yeah and amen in Christ Jesus. But, many are not standing on the promises. Instead, they are "sitting on the premises." The world needs to hear the truth. The church needs to act on the truth. The world will not be aped to follow Jesus when churches open their doors a few hours a week and the leadership dish out so called "entertaining motivational pimping erroneous sermons."

WHERE IS GOD'S TRUE CHURCH?

Jesus Christ declared, *"I will build My Church"* (Matt. 16:18). No matter how men interpret it, this passage speaks of a single church! Christ continued, *"and the gates of hell [the grave] shall not prevail against it."* He promised that *His* Church could never be destroyed. Over 2,000 different professing Christian church organizations have been "built" by men in the United States. Another is started every three days. It is estimated that the number of professing Christians are more than two billion. Church attendance as I write is decreasing. The question of finding the right church is being asked more than ever. There is a lot of confusion surrounding the question of which is the *right* church. Now, it can be safely said that "they all can not be wrong." We can also say "that they all can not be right."

Christ built His Church as He said, then we ought to be able to be find it somewhere on earth today. After all these years serving the Lord, I can not help from asking: How do we find it—what do we look for—how do we identify it—how do we know it if we see it? There is a culture war going on in the church.

TRADITIONS OF MEN

Christ said, *"But in vain they do worship Me, teaching for doctrines the commandments of men"* (Matt. 15:9). In Mark's parallel account of this statement, He continued, *"Full well you reject the commandment of God, that you may keep your own TRADITION"* (7:9).

The world's Christianity is filled with traditions. One of the largest is the traditional view of the New Testament Church. Most ministers, theologians and religionists typically define the church in this way: "are those who sincerely believe in Jesus Christ as their Savior comprise Church." Many say that "there is one heaven and one hell." It is generally accepted in the pews that people can believe what they want, or be a part of any group that they choose, and still be Christians—still their reward is heaven. Just because people may sincerely believe these ideas, *they are sincerely wrong!*

My research led me to the Church that Christ promised to build. This Church can be carefully traced through almost 2,000 years of New Testament history. I was shocked. I could not believe the Bible was so clear on a subject that confuses so many. "God is not the author of *confusion*, but of peace, as in all churches of the saints [the context shows this refers to all *congregations* of the true Church, not all organizations of men]" (I Cor. 14:33).

God's Church is composed of *many* congregations of saints was to reflect *peace*—not confusion. We are not to be confused about the identity of the true Church. God commands, *"Prove all things; hold fast that which is good"* (I Thessalonian 5:21). While this certainly refers to scriptural matters God would not exclude something of such magnitude—such as where His true Church is found. He would never emphatically tell people to prove things that *cannot be proven!* It was to find direct, clear, undeniable proof that even the most popular traditions of the big denominations were not based on the Bible—*at all! There* had to be a church that correctly believed and practiced all the doctrines of the Bible.

A PERSECUTED LITTLE FLOCK

When speaking to His disciples about the importance of seeking the kingdom of God, Christ said, "Fear not, *little flock*; for it is your Father's good pleasure to give you the kingdom" (Luke 12:32). By no stretch can churches comprised of millions, let alone over 2 billion, be considered a "little flock." Christ understood that *His* Church—His *little* flock—would be persecuted and despised by the world. Just before His crucifixion, He warned, "Remember the word that I said unto you, the servant is not greater than his lord. If they have *persecuted Me*, they will also *persecute you*" (John 15:20). Jesus had reminded His disciples that "I have chosen you *out of the world*, therefore the world *hates* you." Christ *was* persecuted, to the point of horrible crucifixion after a night of brutal torture. Therefore, the true Church could also expect to be persecuted—and hated! Those in it are not "of the world." The world senses this and hates them for it (Rom. 8:7). Christ used Paul to record, "Yes, and *all* that will live godly *in Christ Jesus* shall suffer *persecution*" (II Tim. 3:12). The word "all" means what it says!

How many churches can you name that are small, persecuted, not of this world? How many churches are hated because it exists? I had three churches that fit this description, and was released because of my Godly views. Other than those, I can not name any. Perhaps, you may know some. Surely not many!

THE IMPORTANCE OF THE NAME OF THE CHURCH

The world's churches have many different names. They are derived in various ways. These include the particular *doctrines* they teach, the names of the *men* who founded them, the humanly-devised type of *church government* that they espouse, their *location*, or their intended scope and size, such as *universal* or *catholic*—in order to be thought of as all-encompassing.

On the night of His betrayal, Christ prayed for His Church. Here is what He said: "*Holy Father, keep through YOUR OWN NAME those whom You have given Me that they may be one, as We are. While I was with them in the world, I kept them IN YOUR NAME ... I have given them Your word; and the world has hated them, because they are not of the world, even as I am not of the world. I pray not that You should take them out of the world, but that You should keep them from the evil. They are not of the world, even as I am not of the world. Sanctify them through your truth: Your word is truth*" (John 17:11-12, 14-17).

There are twelve separate places where the New Testament records that the true church has been kept in the name of the Father—*God*. The first five refer to the entire Church, or Body of Christ, as a whole. The next four speak of a specific local congregation, while using the same term "Church of God." This may refer to the Church of God at Judea or Corinth, etc. The final three references speak collectively of all the individual local congregations combined. All these references use the term "Churches of God." There are twelve churches recorded with the name of God in it.

(1) Acts 20:28: This verse is instruction to the elders to "feed THE CHURCH OF GOD."

(2) I Corinthians 10:32: "Give none offense, neither to the Jews, nor to the Gentiles, nor to THE CHURCH OF GOD."

(3) I Corinthians 11:22: "...or despise you-the CHURCH OF GOD, and shame them that have not?"

(4) I Corinthians 15:9: Paul wrote the same thing to two congregations: "For ... I persecuted THE CHURCH OF GOD."

(5) Galatians 1:13: "I persecuted THE CHURCH OF GOD."

(6) I Corinthians 1:2: "THE CHURCH OF GOD which is at Corinth."

(7) II Corinthians 1:1: "THE CHURCH OF GOD which is at Corinth."

(8) I Timothy 3:5: Paul references any elder in a local congregation: "For if a man know not how to rule his own house, how shall he take care of THE CHURCH OF GOD?"

(9) I Timothy 3:15: "...behave yourself in the house of God, which is THE CHURCH OF THE LIVING GOD." This verse adds a descriptive word to God by using the term "living."

(10) I Corinthians 11:16: "...We have no such custom, neither THE CHURCHES OF GOD."

(11) I Thessalonians 2:14: "For you ... became followers of THE CHURCHES OF GOD which in Judea are in Christ Jesus."

(12) II Thessalonians 1:4: "So that we ourselves glory in you in THE CHURCHES OF GOD."

In the modern age, for corporate reasons, the Church may use an additional descriptive name to distinguish itself from other churches. The name does not make it a church. They must obey His commandments, believing His true doctrines or doing His Work.

Some appropriate to themselves the name of God's Church. They may have a significant amount of truth, but choose to accept a variety of false doctrines. Only one church on the face of the earth has the correct name and teaches all the additional many true doctrines that the Bible teaches! Recall that Christ prayed, "Sanctify them through Your TRUTH: Your word is TRUTH." The Church that Christ works through directs and guides is sanctified—set apart—by its belief of the *plain truth* of God's Word!

UNIFIED THROUGH GOD'S WORD

Men have their own differing definitions of what the Church actually *is*, but only the Bible definition—*God's* definition—matters. Paul wrote to Timothy, "…that you may know how you ought to behave yourself in the *house of God*, which is the *Church of the living God*, the pillar and ground of the TRUTH" (I Tim. 3:15). In the end, no other definition, devised by men, is acceptable. This definition of the Church *Christ* built will guide us throughout the remainder of this "Personal." God's Church has and teaches "the truth." Amos 3:3 asks, "Can two *walk together*, except they be *agreed*?" The answer is NO!

This world's churches do not practice the principle of *"Man shall not live by bread alone, but by every word of God"* (Luke 4:4), exactly as written. Instead, since they follow the many differing traditions of men, endless disagreements separate, divide and create more and more churches of men. They generally do not "walk together," because they do not "agree"—either with each other or God!

An important point, demonstrating the unity of the true Church, emerges from Christ's same prayer in John 17, on the night of His betrayal. He prayed, *"And for their sakes I sanctify Myself, that they also might be sanctified [set apart] through the truth … That they all may be* ONE; *as You, Father, are in Me, and I in You, that they also may be* ONE IN US: *that the world may believe that You have sent Me. And the glory which You gave Me I have given them; that they may be* ONE, *even as We are* ONE: *I in them, and You in Me, that they may be made perfect in* ONE; *and that the world may know that You have sent Me, and have loved them, as You have loved Me"* (vs. 19,21-23). Christ intended that His Church be unified— "one" —*no less than were He and His Father*! There is no room for disagreement in a Church that is *this* unified. This is this kind of unity that allows true Christians to be "in" them—be *in* Christ and the Father (vs. 21). Even in the Old Testament, David was inspired to record, *"Behold, how good and how pleasant it is for brethren to dwell together in* UNITY*"* (Psa. 133:1).

On the day of Pentecost, gathered in "one accord" (Acts 2:1), when the New Testament Church came into existence, 3,000 converts were baptized. They formed the very beginning of Christ's building of His Church. The initial description given was "...and they *continued steadfastly* in the APOSTLES' DOCTRINE and FELLOWSHIP" (vs. 42), "...*all* that believed were *together*" (vs. 44) and "...they, continuing daily with *one accord* ... did eat their meat [food] with gladness and *singleness of heart*" (vs. 46). From these verses, we clearly see that the Church Christ built was unified—in agreement—over doctrine, and together. Notice verse 47: *"And the Lord added to the Church daily such as should be saved."* In the Church Christ guides and directs, He is the One who adds to it, building it!

CHAPTER TEN

ONLY ONE BODY

THE NEW TESTAMENT speaks of the Church of God as the Body of Christ. Paul stated in his letter to the Corinthians that the Church had many separate members. Yet, he said it was like the various parts of the human body. All of the members are connected. First Corinthian 12: 12-14 states, *"For as the body is one, and hath many members, and all the members of that one body, being many, are one body: so also is Christ. For by one Spirit are we all baptized into one body, whether we be Jews or Gentiles, whether we be bond or free; and have been all made to drink into one Spirit. For the body is not one member, but many."* The church is not separate, it is one body.

The process goes like this. When an individual is converted—has repented, been baptized and received the Holy Spirit—then they are placed into the Body of Christ. They are placed into the Church of God. They have been baptized into the church and the Body of Christ. The church becomes one.

Paul uses the analogy of hands, feet, eyes, ears and the mouth to show how different parts of a *human* body are connected within the same person. Paul continues, *"But now has God set the members every one of them in the BODY, as it has pleased Him. And if they were all one member, where were the BODY? But now are they many members, yet but ONE BODY"* 1 Corinthian 12:18-20).

Most of the world believes that the Body of Christ consists of many denominations, fellowships or "communities of believers." In fact some think that interfaith is the way to explain the Church of God. But this is contrary to what the Word of God teaches. This substitute—counterfeit

—idea asserts that Christ and His Body are divided among many groups, organizations, and denominations. This is very far from the truth.

First Corinthians 12 cannot be compromised and changed by human reasoning. The Church of God is not an amorphous, disconnected, body of disagreeing people in an organization that confess Christianity. If a major organ of a body is taken away then it will surely die. A severed part of a human body can not live for very long without blood supply and the connective tissue needed to sustain life. God created the human body. God knows what keeps His church alive and functioning. The church is to be One Body. Colossian 1:18 states: *"And He [Christ] is the head of THE BODY, the Church."* Paul wrote in Ephesians 1:22-23, *"…and gave Him [Christ] to be the Head over all things to the Church, which is HIS BODY."* The Biblical definition of the *Body of Christ* is *the Church.*

In chapter 4:3-6 of Ephesians, Paul admonished the brethren to be "Endeavoring to keep the *unity* of the Spirit in the bond of peace. There is ONE BODY [Church], and ONE *SPIRIT,* even as you are called IN ONE *HOPE* of your calling; ONE *LORD,* ONE *FAITH,* ONE *BAPTISM,* ONE *GOD AND FATHER."* The church is not to be confused about how God organized His church. Jesus, the Christ prayed this kind of Church of oneness and unity. He prayed in John 17:20-23 *"Neither pray I for these alone, but for them also which shall believe on me through their word; That they all may be one; as thou, Father, art in me, and I in thee, that they also may be one in us: that the world may believe that thou hast sent me. And the glory which thou gavest me I have given them; that they may be one, even as we are one: I in them, and thou in me, that they may be made perfect in one; and that the world may know that thou hast sent me, and hast loved them, as thou hast loved me."*

Paul wrote so divinely about the importance of a faithful ministry that follows the guidelines and teaching of God's Church. Paul pointed out in Ephesians 4: 11-16 *"And He gave some, apostles; and some, prophets; and some, evangelists; and some, pastors and teachers; for the perfecting of the saints, for the work of the ministry, for the edifying of the BODY OF CHRIST: till we all come in the unity of the faith, and of the knowledge of the Son of God, unto a perfect man, unto the measure of the stature of the fullness of Christ: that we henceforth be no more children, tossed to and fro, and carried about with every wind of doctrine, by the sleight of men, and cunning craftiness, whereby they lie in wait to deceive; but speaking the TRUTH IN LOVE, may grow up into Him* in all things, which is the Head, even Christ: from whom the WHOLE BODY fitly joined together and compacted by that which every joint supplies, according to the effectual working in the measure of every part, makes increase of THE BODY unto the edifying of itself in love."

The Church is the body of Christ, and He is Head of the church. He governs, directs and builds it, and adds to it daily. God's church is UNIFIED in both *doctrinal truth* and *love*. The Church ("*whole* body" and "every part") are to walk together in *complete* doctrinal agreement under Christ's authority. Jesus, the Christ works through His *true* ministers to keep the Church from drifting into "every wind of doctrine."

PAUL STRESSED UNITY

The Word of God stress unity in His church. The 21st century church is to demonstrate unity and the world should witness this as they observe this in all facets of life. Historical, the CORINTHIAN congregation had many problems—including terrible division and disunity. Paul strongly admonished them to stop entertaining other doctrines and to quit playing favorites with ministers. Paul under the unction of God spoke that to the congregation: "*Now I beseech you, brethren … that you all speak the same thing, and that there be no divisions among you; but that you be perfectly joined together in the same mind and in the same judgment … Now this I say, that every one of you says, I am of Paul; and I of Apollos; and I of Cephas [Peter]; and I of Christ*" (I Cor. 1:10, 12-13). God's Word has not changed and the 21st century church is to obey God's command. We as the body of Christ do not have the luxury of changing His Word to suit the occasion and to be politically correct. Do not miss the intent of this passage. Paul was inspired to describe, in *five* different ways, how completely all of God's people in every age should be unified and in agreement. These verses also cannot be "spiritualistic away" by deceptive human reasoning.

Jesus, the Christ did not give the command for believers to have multiple organizations and individual doctrines for each organization. He did not give instructions for hundreds, even thousands, of divided, competing groups, in disagreement over teachings to represent His church. What we witness in this 21st century are organizations that are diminishing the impact that the gospel message could have on the world. We are to announce that the kingdom of God is at hand. Matthew 24:14 states *"And this gospel of the kingdom shall be preached in all the world for a witness unto all nations; and then shall the end come.* Matthew 28:19-20 states *"Go ye therefore, and teach all nations, baptizing them in the name of the Father, and of the Son, and of the Holy Ghost: Teaching them to observe all things whatsoever I have commanded you: and, lo, I am with you always, even unto the end of the world. Amen."*

1 Corinthians 1:13 ask a question. "Is Christ divided?" The only answer to this question is "no." This is equivalent to asking, "Is grass pink?" or "Is the sky golden?" The answer is obvious. In Amos 3:3, even the question "Can two walk together except they are agreed?" The answer is "no." One would love one and hate the other. Christ is not divided and so the church is not to be divided.

First Corinthians 14:33 Paul tells us that *"For God is not the author of confusion, but of peace, as in all churches of the saints."* Furthermore verse 40 states; *"Let all things be done decently and in order."* Of course we understand that "decency" and "order" are impossible if God's Church is divided into many organizations, denominations, and so on.

Paul's admonition to the PHILIPPIANS congregation: in Philippians 1:27-28 *"...stand fast in ONE SPIRIT, with one mind striving together for the faith of the gospel; And in nothing terrified by your adversaries."* And, In Philippians 2:2 he writes: *"Fulfill ye my joy, that ye be like minded, having the same love, being of one accord, of one mind."* God commands that His church is to have complete unity. This is the only condition that is acceptable to God!

Paul admonished the Colossians to be "knit *together* in love, and ... the *full assurance of understanding,*" and "rooted and built up in Him, and established in the faith, *as you have been taught."* Colossians 2:2, 7). Paul continues to describe unity by saying: B*rethren walk "together," assured of the right "understanding" that they "have been taught."*

The local ROMAN CONGREGATION was experiencing a problem with false doctrines entering the Church. Paul instructed them in this way: Romans 16:17-18, *"Now I beseech you, brethren, mark them which cause divisions and offenses contrary to the doctrine which ye have learned; and avoid them. For they that are such serve not our Lord Jesus Christ, but their own belly; and by good words and fair speeches deceive the hearts of the simple."*

THE TWO TREES

The author asks himself this question. How did humankind get into the state of confusion, division, war, competition and disagreement that *exists in our churches all over the earth? It has be traced back to God's original command to Adam was, "But of the tree of the knowledge of good and evil, you shall not eat of it: for in the day that you eat thereof you shall surely die"* (Gen. 2:17). In Genesis 3:6, Eve, with Adam following, rebelled and ate of this wrong tree. The tree bearing the fruit represented *knowledge* that both "good *and* evil." The tree was not evil—it contained a *mixture* of true and false knowledge. It is the same with the churches of this world. Some have small amounts of true doctrinal "knowledge," mixed with much false doctrinal "knowledge." For 6,000 years, God has told His true servants to avoid mixing truth with error. He warned Adam that eating of the wrong tree would result in death. It did.

THE WARNING IS THE SAME FOR US TODAY!

When I was attending Fayetteville State University, I learned a simple truth from my chemistry instructor. I heard something that I will not forget. Dr. Dix was teaching a lesson on how certain ingredients will cause a compound to loose its usefulness and may even cause death. Her famous words were to "watch what you mix together." For this illustration, think of a delicious cake laced with arsenic, cyanide, rican or strychnine in it, however, all the other ingredients are correct and healthy for the body. While the other ingredients are good and healthy, eating the cake will always result in causing your death.

The good ingredients the cake will not be sufficient to overcome the poison hidden in the cake. Likewise, God's Church does not and cannot mix truth with error. As with the cake, the result for those who do is deadly! The church can not compromise God's Word and expect to live. The church can not use its own man made manipulations to orchestrate God's church. Sooner or later it will cease to exist.

This author has explained the major doctrines taught by God for His church. This is the way the 21st century is to be built. This is not all the ways the list of God commands concerning His church. It was not my desire to cover all of them and to explain all the scriptures. The simple message is that way that was taught them so that His church will be what He intended it to be. Of course, we know why God gave the church its marching orders. He is coming back for His church.

WHAT IS THE CHRISTIAN CHURCH SUPPOSED TO BE?

The Christian church is to be a reflection of Jesus' love, words, and deeds. Its goal should be to glorify God, and make Jesus known to the world. The Christian church is to develop Godly people, and make disciples of every nation. The church is to be a group of believers, on the whole and in part, who live and teach the saving words of Jesus, the Christ. We are to live the truth in incarnated in His Word. The Christian in the church is to live the truth just as Jesus lived it. Jesus is our example.

The church is not a building or a structure. It is not a headquarters at Salt Lake City, Utah, or Brooklyn, New York, or Rome, or Jerusalem, or any other city. The bishop, the pastor, deacons, and so on is not the Head of the Church. Jesus is the head of the Church.

The church is the living Body of Christ comprised of the redeemed in Christ. The external trappings of celebrations, rituals, buildings, robes, hymn books, organs, pianos, chairs, pews, windows, etc. are those are used to assist the Christian to give praise to God. They are not substitutes for the praise of God. Humankind is to give praise to the almighty God.

The visible Christian church is the collection of believers who are saved by the blood of Jesus and God lives in them. (John 14:23). God's church is equipped by God with teachers, pastors, and so on. 1 Cor. 12:28 states that Christians grow by the relationship they have with Jesus through prayer and the study of God's word. They actively seek to expand God's kingdom through preaching and living the Gospel. The Christian church is supposed to be a light to the world. It is supposed to fight against wickedness, oppression, poverty, sin, rebellion, adultery, homosexuality, fornication, abortion, and so on. They are to sit idly by and watch the unbelievers go to hell.

CONDUCT YOURSELVES WITH WISDOM

The church is to be wise but harmless as a dove. They are to "conduct themselves with wisdom toward the unsaved, and witness to them as sincere as possible" (Col. 4:5). The true born again, Holy Ghost filled Christians will not parade themselves on television as incessant beggars of money for their own purpose. They will not be so proud as to over dress expensively and sit in gold chairs and pretend to be the king of kings and Lord of Lords. They will not pretend to weep for others at the drop of a hat. They will not misuse the charismatic gift given to them to take advantage of the less fortunate. They will not speak of Jesus in one breath and then tell dirty jokes in the next breathe. They will not pray in unknown tongues in public and suddenly burst in uncontrollable laughter and start barking like wild dogs in the next breathe as if the Holy Spirit commanded them to do so. The real Christian will not be seen as a person hungry for money, desirous of possessions, an addicted to pornography, addicted to prostitutes, addicted to alcohol, and addicted to drugs. The real Christian will not take the Lord's name in vain. These kinds of sin bring mockery to the name of Christ. Christians are to be holy as God is holy.

The Christian church is to be an example of propriety, decency, self-sacrifice and servitude. The church that is mostly placed on television demonstrates that they are hungry for money, hypocritical, and whining entity that is out of touch with reality. Many churches are out of order.

The Christian church has great liberty to ask for financial assistance. This author is not condemning the right to let their financial needs be known. But, I am discouraging by the expression used to extract monies from the tender heart unsaved trying to be introduced to Jesus. There are thousands of people who are looking to be saved. The Christian knows the plight of the people. The begging, the charismatic chaos, and the chicanery that permeates the high-profile, public church today needs to be eliminated. We true Christians are to speak out and stand on the Word of God.

We need to pray for guidance from God that we can clean the fakeness out of the so called churches before we can start pointing fingers. Those in leadership ought to ask themselves this question: "How will what I do and say appear to the unbeliever? "Will it stump them?" Paul in 1 Cor. 14 wrote that he did not want the church in its freedom to stumble the unbeliever. Some of the leaders consider themselves to be giants. But, remember giants do fall.

The real Christian are mindful of what they do and say in the workforce. Many unbelievers will only see the Christian in the marketplace and make the decision as to rather they will repent. The true Christian represents Christ in the marketplace. Therefore, the Christian ought to live their life representing God in love and with a pure heart, a good conscience, and a sincere faith. (1 Tim. 1:5). The world knows that we are supposed to be followers of Christ. But too often they get the picture that some are only interested in money, buildings, and what they can extract from the public. This is not what the church is to represent. This is not the reason for the churches existence. The church is to demonstrate that their security is wrapped up and tangled in God.

The early believers of Jesus Christ knew that they were not just members of an organization. They realized that they were not just an extension of Old Testament Judaism. They knew they were called followers of Jesus, the Christ. They were members of His church. Throughout the centuries, His church has been the most powerful transforming force in history.

Yet in America the news commentator recently said that the church is losing its credibility and many so-called Christians has abandoned the church. The church in America is said to be anemic and powerless. This author contends that there is good news. There so many things that is still right with the Christian church. All the church has to do is let God transform it to the kind of forces that can be used to openly defeat the satanic forces of the evil ones. This book is not a defense for the traditional church, nor does it run to embrace all new forms of worship. Rather this book examines the biblical nature of church allowing the best to come forth. It is not a book about old churches, new churches or home churches. It is a book about what is right about every true church, no matter the expression, history or culture. A growing number of people are not aware of the enduring strengths of the church. The author contends that if believers in Christ are to effectively move forward with healthy communities and a vibrant faith in this new century, they must be established on foundation, biblical truths and core values. And when this happens, the church thrives as a transforming force.

This author had the opportunity to speak with many people who were junkies to the night club life. Even when he was preaching, he heard nightclub music outside the church door. There were those who brought the nightclub mentality at the steps of the church. They had children serving them beers and wine on the church property. The music got so loud that he had to stop preaching and go outside to minister to the crowd. They were playing cards, drinking wine, listening to nightclub music, smoking, cursing and telling lies. Dressed in his sanctified white robe, he confronted the crowd. One of the people offered him a beer and asked him to take a seat. The author of this book took a seat and told them about the love of God. The congregation prayed while he was ministering outside to the so created nightclub on church property. Months later, the author had the opportunity to baptize each one of them including the children, the wives, and husbands. They became members of the body of Christ.

Years ago, the author remembered that he asked his sainted parents for permission to go to nightclubs. But, his parents gave him the golden nuggets as to why he should not do so. This author used all the bible verses and reasons to put those on the church property that God had a plan and purpose for their lives. His conversations proved that this group was waiting for a disciple to make them disciples. They wanted someone to point them to a better way of life.

Now, I heard many comments about some of what we call the fastest growing mega-churches in the country. Some the comments were very upsetting. Several people say that after attending these mega-churches, the only thing different from the night club experience was that they did not serve whiskey and drugs. These comments gave me a very clear picture of what some of the churches have become. Yes, we have many ideas of what church is to look like. Many people have found a church where they can sin and not be preached to. They are made to feel comfortable in their sins. They have found like-minded people to socialize with and enjoy their company. The question is: Is this the type of church that Jesus shed His blood for?

There are so many options and so many different styles of churches. It is easy to bounce from church to church for a lifetime and never really find what you're looking for. I do not believe that there is no such thing as a perfect church. Each church has its positive and negative aspects. The attendee can be hurt and leave without being missed from the congregation. This author sternly urge his readers to pray, meditate, and ask certain questions to ascertain if a particular church is where God has sent you. The decision to commit to a church may have many different factors. Here are a few questions to ask as you work through the decision:

1. Is This Church Fostering True Spiritual Growth?

Whatever you may be looking for make sure that worship, evangelism, community outreach, and God is the author and finisher of the faith. Prayerfully ask God to make sure you will get help as you grow in your relationship with Him. The sermons preached are to be unadulterated and the Gospel message is practiced in the church. The sermons are to challenge its congregants to grow and help provide spiritual resources for people to grow. The spirit of God is to be present in their praise and they are to worship God in Spirit and truth. They are not to quench the spirit.

2. Are There Opportunities to Serve and Use My God-Given Abilities?

God calls us to serve Him with the special gifts and talents He has given us. Some people are natural-born leaders and teachers, which are vital to any church. However, not every church needs sound engineers and videographers. Finding a place where your spiritual gifts are needed and valued in the operation of the church means that you truly become a part of the body. Finding opportunities to initiate new opportunities and growth in a church is important.

3. Does This Church Value Community?

A church is supposed to be a body, and community is the place where real growth, change and reaching the world truly take place. Outreach ministry is to be a part of the church mission objectives.

WHICH CHURCH IS DOING CHURCH RIGHT?

This author has visited many churches over the sixty nine years of his life. He has been in worship with what is called a church flourishing with an abundance of fruit-bearing and Christ-loving disciples. He has been to mega-churches with thousands of members. He has visited new church-plants where having seven people was something to give God praise. He has visited churches wherein the audio sound systems cost more than eight million dollars. He has preached in churches that met in a school auditorium without a proper sound system. He preached in Europe wherein the church met in the open streets on a regular basis. He has preached in church wherein the pastor wore a under shirt and short pants because it was the kind of clothes most of the congregations could afford. The one church that the author was puzzled was the church wherein the people stood for the entire service without any instrumentation and the woman could not take a part in the worship service.

This author recall witnessing in churches that had soft padded pews throughout the building. He witnessed in churches that had hard metal chairs throughout the building. Many churches where he preached were in the homes of fellow pastors. On one occasion he was called to preach in the garage of a pastor. As a revivalist, he has preached in tents, in the middle of farm land, and on plantations equipped with irrigation ponds suitable for baptizing converts.

Each congregation had their own personality. Some of the congregations had a warm and loving atmosphere. And on the beginning of greeting the congregation that were extremely cold and unfriendly. But before the end of a service, the congregants were loving and turned to be new creations in Christ. There were churches with the spirit of being demons possessed. Demons were attacking the little children and they were screaming for help. The demons were admonished to leave in the name of Jesus, the Christ. The demons did leave and the children were comfortable knowing that at the name of Jesus demons had to flee.

This author has preached in all denominations and all races of Christians. He remembers preaching in a church wherein the temperature was so cold that the entire congregation had to keep on their hats, coats, and gloves on for the entire worship service. Then there were churches wherein the Spirit of God was so rich that everyone of faith were healed. Those that were healed testified and shared papers from their doctors indicating that they were free of whatever malady that was ailing them. On a very serious occasion, a pastor told a bold face lie in the pulpit that seriously hurt the selected pastor. This hurt pastor had been called by God to be the pastor of this particular church. However, within one week the liar who caused much harm was pronounced dead from a sudden heart attack. Also, there were churches wherein the Holy Spirit was so pronounced that some of the congregants seem to float in the air from seat to seat. God made His presence truly known in many of the churches in which this author bore witness. So the question must be asked: Which church is doing "church" right? God knows all about His churches. He is more than able to lead us to the right church. God wants to lead us.

CHAPTER ELEVEN

A VIRTUAL LOOK AT THE CHURCH

I N THESE UNITED States thousand of people stream into America's churches each Sunday. Are these people members of organizations or disciplines of Jesus, the Christ? What is the appearance of a virtual 21st century church? The doors swing open wide. People rush into the sanctuary to find their ideal place to sit. The greeters and the ushers stand ready to point out a vacant seat for the attendee. The praise teams are more than ready to perform as the choir director dictates. There are impersonation personalities standing ready to perform for the masses. The lights and smoke attract the attention of the onlookers. The praise team and professional season entertainers begin their entertainment segment. This is all to be done to the glory of God.

The atmosphere is ready. The congregation is waiting with abated breathe for the glorious experience of worship. The band leader signals that all things are ready. The technicians are ready to use their update media and audio sound system to enhance the performance. The lights are flashing and the signal to perform is given. An animated song leader impersonating a star like the deceased Elvis Presley rushes out with the other performers following. The congregations stand and scream to the top of their voices whatever the artist suggest. The sanctuary is filled to capacity and often time some have to be escorted to the overflow rooms. The lights are flashing, the performers are beautifully dressed in star like clothing, and the music is "off the hook." The upbeat R & B so called Christian music has energized the attendees and they are moving to the beat. They can dance and gyrate as if they were in the top secular club of their day. The performers put on a great show. The mime dancers and other dancers get the opportunity to perform as well. They satisfy the appetites of the fleshy attendees who love to see exotic dancing. At some point the pastor takes the stage and the congregation will give him or her a king's greeting. This is a simplified description of a virtual look at the upcoming and present 21st century church as of this moment in history. A virtual look lets the attendees get the thrill of their lives.

The preachers of these kinds of churches are mostly the best dressed. They are wearing designer and tailor made outfits. He or she preaches a feel good entertaining sermon. The preachers never challenge the balance between truth and a lie. The hot potato sermons are never addressed in this kind of church. The doctrine of heaven and hell, sin, holiness, righteousness, salvation, repentance, justification, resurrection, and others of this type are never addressed. There are a lot of prosperity sermons launched from the pulpit. Before the preachers began to preach a talented soloist sets the tone for the message. Years may past and the preacher will not mention the consequences of sin or the realness of heaven and hell.

Whatever the form of worship they use all of them declare that they are a success. These kind of churches can be found in nearly every large city. They declare themselves a success because they have a large congregation, much capital, and assess to secular power. They have declared that they have reached the presumed level of success and attainment.

While church glamour is in their success mode, outside their walls the sins of the world are on the increase. The same sex marriage act has been confirmed by the Supreme Court. The traditional marriage that God calls for is being abandoned. Many of these churches have not taken a stand on the truth of God's Word. Sin is much more abounding while the so called church is entertaining the congregations. Leadership in America does not look to the church for guidance in integrity. Sin is running wild in the streets as well as in the churches. The percentage of divorces and single-parent homes are steadily increasing. Families are being torn apart because holiness is not practiced as a way of life for these churches. The jails are filled with people who have not obeyed the commands of God. The murder rates in cities are the highest recorded in the history of America. The youth can not easily find Christian leadership. The numbers of young people that have joined gangs and violent organizations have multiplied.

The morals of the United States have continued to degenerate. Yet, the churches appear to be growing larger and more successful, but society and members are separating themselves further from God. We have a problem that must be addressed.

Are these churches really successful? How do we measure the success of a church? Will using a business formula give us the correct conclusion for determining whether a church is a success? Is it true that the church that has the most members, the largest financial income, and the best known church in town is the most successful? Is this the correct formula to use? We submit that this formula is not the formula that God intended for His church to use.

If we have the desire to know if a church is successful, then we ought to ask the originator of the church. We must consult God for the correct answer. God tells us exactly what He wants to take place in His church. When churches follow His model, then they are successful. Until then, they are operating out of order. They might as well hang up a sign on the entrance, "Out of Order." The desire to use God's formula has been abandoned for the most part and many have done it their way.

Jesus gave His apostles their commission and their final instructions to follow in regard of operating His church. He summed up what He desired for them to do in Matthew 28:18-20: *"Then Jesus came to them and said, 'All authority in heaven and earth has been given to me. Therefore, go and make disciples of all nations, baptizing them in the name of the Father and of the Son and of the Holy Spirit and teaching them to obey everything I have commanded you. And surely I am with you always, to the very end of the age."* His highest priority ought to be the churches highest priority. His highest priority was making disciples. Our highest priority is to make disciples. These disciples are to follow Him in a lifestyle that is opposite of the world's lifestyle. The disciples lifestyle is not striving to be politically correct. A disciple's lifestyle is to be holy as God is holy. Holiness is still the order of the day.

The church of Antioch characterized a successful church. They had Godly qualified leadership. Godly leadership speaks on how to live according to God, and they live the life they speak and preach. The Antioch church proved to be the most influential and illustrious of all the churches of their age. The bible studies point to the fact that if you want a successful church, then pattern your church after the church in Antioch. We are to pray for God's blessings, leadership, and guidance through the Holy Spirit for a church that God approves of and will constantly bless.

The church at Antioch was an exciting church, an effective church and an entrepreneurial church. The following dimensions characterized the Antioch church.

1. **EVANGELISM: The Preaching of the Good News (Acts 11:19-21).**
2. **MULTI-RACIAL: Cross-cultural Community (Acts 11:19-20).**
3. **COMMUNITY: Every Member Participation and Discipleship (Acts 11:20).**
4. **COMPASSION: A Sense of Compassion and Caring Generosity (Acts 11:23, 30; 4:32-37; Acts 13:2).**
5. **Radical Identification with Christ (Acts 11:19-26, 13:2).**
6. **TEACHING: Prophetic Preaching and Thoughtful Teaching (Acts 11:26; 13:1; 15:35).**
7. **WORSHIP: Expressive Dynamic Worship (Acts 13:2-3).**
8. **PROPHETIC: Spirit–Anointed Openness to the Spirit's Leading (Acts 11:27-30; 13:2).**
9. **EQUIPPING: Multiplying Disciples and Leadership (Acts 11:26; 13:1-2).**
10. **PLURALITY: Shared Leadership and Word Ministry (Acts 11:25; 13:1-3; 14:28).**
11. **APOSTOLIC: Antioch Was an Apostolic Base Church (Acts 13:1-3; 15:32).**
12. **LEADERSHIP: Lead Person Leadership (Acts 15:13-19).**

There are scriptures that teach this lesson recorded in the book of Acts.

Scripture: Acts 13:1-13:16

Acts 13:1 *"Now there were in the church that was at Antioch certain prophets and teachers; as Barnabas, and Simeon that was called Niger, and Lucius of Cyrene, and Manaen, which had been brought up with Herod the tetrarch, and Saul."*

There was a very active church in Antioch. Prophets and teachers had different duties. The prophets foretold future events. The teachers spoke of things that needed to be learned that had already happened. This church at Antioch was operating in the fullness of the five fold ministry. A successful church is operating in the fullness of the five fold ministry.

Acts 13:2 *"As they ministered to the Lord, and fasted, the Holy Ghost said, separate me Barnabas and Saul for the work whereunto have called them."*

The Lord will speak to us when we have set ourselves aside from all the earthly things for a few days and pray. Turn off your computers, televisions, Ipads and so on. Let the Lord speak to you. Leaders who are called of God must make time for God to speak to them.

Acts 13:3 *"And when they had fasted and prayed, and laid [their] hands on them, they sent [them] away."*

Saul and Barnabas needed extra power from God to undertake this missionary journey. We need to earnestly pray and fast and act as agents of God. The strength comes from God and not man.

Acts 13:4 *"So they, being sent forth by the Holy Ghost, departed unto Seleucia; and from thence they sailed to Cyprus."*

This is truly a missionary journey, because they are sent forth by the Holy Ghost.

Acts 13:5 *"And when they were at Salamis, they preached the word of God in the synagogues of the Jews: and they had also John to [their] minister."*

The early Christians here were Jewish believers. We are to be believers regardless of our origin or background.

Acts 13:6 *"And when they had gone through the isle unto Patmos they found a certain sorcerer, a false prophet, a Jew, whose name [was] Bar-Jesus:"*

Sorcerer had great power. Their power comes from an evil source. We still have sorcerers today. They use astrology, magic, dark arts to convince the people that they have power over God. This has never changed. People are still consulting their horoscope, going to palm readers and practicing all sorts of sorcery. Sorcery is not of God, but is of Satan. Satan has some limited power on this earth, but is not like Jesus Christ who is the source of all power. Sorcerers will deceived many in these last days. Even during this time many thought that they were prophets, because of the miracles he did. They were false prophets. We have false prophets calling themselves leaders of churches. These churches have been listed as successful churches in 2015.

Acts 13:7 *"Which was with the deputy of the country, Sergius Paulus, a prudent man; who called for Barnabas and Saul, and desired to hear the word of God."*

God will accept the wealthy and famous the same as He will the poor. The requirement is the same. They must repent and earnestly seek the Truth.

Acts 13:8 *"But Elymas the sorcerer (for so is his name by interpretation) withstood them, seeking to turn away the deputy from the faith."*

To work against God is a very dangerous thing to do, as this sorcerer will find out.

Acts 13:9 *"Then Saul, (who also [is called] Paul,) filled with the Holy Ghost, set his eyes on him,"* Acts 13:10 *"And said, O full of all subtlety and all mischief, [thou] child of the devil, [thou] enemy of all righteousness, wilt thou not cease to pervert the right ways of the Lord?"*

Being filled with the Holy Ghost was more than what the ordinary had. This was an extra portion of the Spirit. This gave Saul great boldness in the Lord. The words which came from Saul were really not his own, but words the Holy Ghost spoke through him. The Holy Ghost came against Elymas. He called him who he was, the son of the devil. Elymas' power was devil power. Saul was saying to him, you have now come against Almighty God. Elymas was not opposing Saul, but God.

Acts 13:11 *"And now, behold, the hand of the Lord [is] upon thee, and thou shalt be blind, not seeing the sun for a season. And immediately there fell on him a mist and darkness; and he went about seeking some to lead him by the hand."*

The judgment of God is swift when it comes. Those who oppose the Lord today can expect a like fate. The blindness is not a permanent situation, but is for a season. The blindness was so drastic that he could not even see how to walk. This man had already been blind to the Spirit and now he is physically blind, as well.

Acts 13:12 *"Then the deputy, when he saw what was done, believed, being astonished at the doctrine of the Lord."*

This deputy believed what Saul and Barnabas had been saying. The sorcerer had tried to cause him not to believe. When the great power of God was manifest against the sorcerer, the deputy knew who was God. This miracle with the sorcerer erased any doubt he might have had. In Romans 10:9-10, we are told that salvation is to believe. We are not told whether he was baptized or not, but true believers want to be baptized as a show to the world that they have truly believed.

The scripture says in Acts 13:13 *"Now when Paul and his company loosed from Paphos, they came to Perga in Pamphylia: and John departing from them returned to Jerusalem."*

We find that Saul (Paul) left and went for the first time to Asia Minor. Perga was the capitol of Pamphylia. This area was inhabited by the Jewish people. The worship of the false goddess Diana had been prevalent. There was even a temple built right out of town in Perga to this false goddess. John went back to Jerusalem, instead of coming with them to Perga.

Acts 13:16 *"Then Paul stood up, and beckoning with [his] hand said, Men of Israel, and ye that fear God, give audience."*

A person would not be in the temple unless they feared God. His beckoning with his hand was so that they would come close enough to hear what he said. To put it simply he was saying, gather around, I have something to tell you. We summarize that Paul is telling the church of today the following.

The church is successful based on their Godly quality leaders. You can determine the quality of the church by character of their leadership. Unless a church has the ability to attract and develop quality leaders it is merely surviving. We are to ask the Lord to help us draw quality leaders who are committed to the great commandment to love and the great commission to make disciples.

A successful church must produce quality multipliers. A successful church will bear the fruit of having a spirit-filled missionary, a writer or an evangelist. These persons will make a great contribution to the building of the kingdom of God. These disciples outweigh the production a so-called successful membership of onlookers by ten times. We are to ask God to help your church produce multipliers not spectators.

A successful must have prophets and teachers who are in close communion with the Spirit and the Word of God. The preaching and teaching elders of the church must be able to hear what the Holy Spirit says. **We are to ask God to** help our church to work through mature, wise, and courageous men and women who are dedicated to enlarging the kingdom of God in quantity and quality.

A successful church will continue to mobilize leaders for as long as God allows it to assemble. The church will have a considerable number of leaders to teach. (Acts 11:26) The work of evangelism, disciple-making and edification will consistently take place. We ought to ask the Lord to help your fellowship to have a healthy variety of teaching, disciple-making and edification ministries for disciples to grow in all aspects of Christ-like ministries.

A successful church encourages diligence in personal devotions. This church will minister and often fast and pray. God speaks to His churches. God will speak to the church while they are busy worshiping, studying and praying. God will equip the church with the essential spiritual needs. We are to ask the Lord to help us find people who are faithful in little things before they are given responsibility over much. (Luke 16:10) Trust the Lord to convince your disciples to develop an example of thirty minute private devotions every morning.

A successful church under God's guidance will take up their cross in sacrificial service and persecution. The Disciples of Christ are willing to endure great shame, humiliation and hardship for the sake of Christ. Not only do the disciplines fast, but they will welcome those who were persecuted for their faith in Christ. A successful church will ask the Lord to help their disciples to practice self-denial to the world's worries, riches and pleasures of this life. They are encouraged to walk by faith and not by sight.

A successful church will not question the reasons why God has called it to sacrifice even though they may never get the favor returned. A disciple does not have to be publicly rewarded or acknowledged for their service rendered for the Kingdom of God.

A successful church will not dwell on the adversities but the opportunities. It will not become timid in the face of stiff opposition to their cross-cultural evangelizing of the world. Despite all of the difficult people they had to deal with, the successful church will set a pattern of outreach ministries that serves as a model for thousands of years. The successful church will pray that when the odds are stacked against them, they will move ahead with God's purposes regardless of the world's conditions.

When is a church truly successful? It is quite evident that Jesus used a different method for measuring success and failure than we use today. The widow's mite or few pennies held more value to Him than the rich gifts of the wealthy (Luke 21:1-4). He said, *"Blessed are the poor in spirit, for theirs is the kingdom of heaven"* (Matthew 5:3). *He told us that he who is the greatest is he who is the greatest servant* (Matthew 21:25-27). *And He said that the last will be first and that the first will be last.* Because the church was bought by His blood and because He is the Head of the church, we need to be concerned above all with His standards of success (rather than the world's standards) when we measure the success and failure of a church.

Did this commission to make disciples stop with the apostles? No, it is clear that it is His commission to us as well, for He said *"to the very end of the age."* We are not at the end of the age yet, and it has been a long time since the apostles have been with us. Who, then, are to make disciples today? There is only one possible answer —*the twenty first century church is to be busy at the very same task that the first century church made its highest priority!* When is a church successful? We are only truly successful, when we are successful at fulfilling Jesus' commission to the church and are making disciples who will follow in the footsteps of Jesus Christ.

How are we doing today? The majority of the churches are striving to become mega churches. The pattern for getting a successful church is not the same as it was in the early church. If we would take off our American cultural glasses and look through the spiritual eyes of Jesus, we will discover that the success most churches seek is quite different from what Jesus describes for His church.

Our local churches are not focused on building disciples. Our local churches are not focused on making disciples. Instead they are focused on building its attendance. Church attendance is most often the driving goal in American churches.

I have attended the Hampton Conference and many other national become mega churches. The pattern for getting a successful church is not the same electives were geared around membership and prosperity. They attract people who are called "noted experts" on church growth. The vast majority at conferences obviously believe that church growth is what is most important. The vast numbers of people who attend national conferences go with the idea of finding out how to create the largest attendance for their churches. They would have their largest attendance at the elective on church growth.

Sadly, though, our churches are often content as long as the attendance is doing well, even if there is very little effectiveness at building disciples. As long as the attendees keep attending, the church is all too typically looked upon as being a successful church. But, Jesus' mandate to the apostles was not for them to go and build churches with large attendances, but He commissioned them to go and *make disciples of all nations ... teaching them to obey everything I have commanded you.*

These churches full of attendees are very ineffectual at penetrating our society with God's love, truth, and righteousness. They are not effective in warring with our relentless enemy. The church has become a meeting, conferencing, and networking place. They have become entertainment centers for many people who hardly even know each other.

What we need in these perilous times are churches that are truly making disciple centers. Jesus and the apostles reached out to everyone, as we should. The preachers did not adjust their message or methods to pander to and placate the multitudes. Their focus was clearly on reaching and building disciples. Their emphasis was on building disciples who would be able to face Satan's best forces. They were dedicated and determined to build God's church in God's way. God desires disciples to be much more than Sunday morning attendees. His disciples are to follow in the footsteps of Jesus. Peter, Paul, John, and all the others raised a standard for following the example of Jesus, the Christ. They had one primary purpose in life, to further God's kingdom on earth no matter what the cost.

It is recognized that no church is fully perfect. It is also recognized that no church has fully arrived. The church in this sinful world must have a determined action to make disciples and be like Christ. Each church in these last days must have a divine goal dictated by God.

But, what should be the goal of *each* of our churches? This goal must be the key factor for its existence. Every disciple ought to be able to understand the objective for this is what we seek after. The pastor must believe it as well as the congregation of believers. This measures the success of the church. If this is what they believe, then this will become their highest priority. This highest priority should be to make disciples in the same way that Jesus and the apostles made disciples. True success in a church, then, is the success that God alone can enable us to do, and that is the growth in that church of real disciples and real growth in those disciples!

When are we successful in the God's Kingdom? This is a perfect question. People may say that a church or a person is successful. But, this does not make it true. God is the only divinity that assures us of success. It is His Kingdom and He alone makes the guidelines for being successful. The church can not afford to make up their rules. If they do, then they will find that God will say depart from me, I never knew you.

It is easier to answer the question, "When is someone successful in the world's kingdom?" Success in our society is usually measured by that which is *outward* and easily observable. Who are the successful people in our society? They are typically those who have some type of outward and obvious signs of success. They may have elevated positions in our society. Some of them own expensive cars, and live in lavish houses. They have power over others and make it obvious by using money to become their dictator. They usually show some outward signs of success.

This is not the type of success that we should seek after in our churches? Success in God's kingdom may have nothing to do with any of these measuring sticks. In the Beatitudes, Jesus said blessed are the poor, mourning, meek, and hungry. To be successful in God's kingdom, we will have to go in the very opposite direction from those who use the world's definition for success.

Those who are successful in God's kingdom are those who have humbled themselves and become servants. Jesus' disciples thought that following Jesus would result in them being served by many. Many false prophets are in the pulpit because they want to be served by the congregation. But, Jesus taught His discipline the real meaning of a servant. Jesus washed their feet. He taught them that success in His kingdom meant that they would need to learn how to become the servants of many.

The pastors of our time must learn that success in God's kingdom must start with humbling ourselves. It may seem that a person who uses the secular marketing plan for his church is successful, but this is not God's church. It is a church that has been organized by man for man's purposes. Not only does God lift up those who humble themselves. He lifts them even higher in the ways of His kingdom. God knows who is successful. He rewards those who are of His type. He gives them a success that lasts forever. Jesus said that the first will be last and the last will be first. He also said that no man can serve two masters. Which success are we going to seek? Are we going to seek the success of a non-believer? Are you going to seek the success of doing what Jesus commanded the church to follow?

I am reminded of a story about a young man. This young man was endowed with the ability and personality to be successful in many areas in our society. He was determined to spend his life following the guidance of God for his ministry. He was called to pastor three churches. Each of those churches refused to follow him as he followed Jesus. His priority was God's priority and make disciples. Many years were spent trying to educate his congregation of the merits of following the plan of God. After many years in these churches, he found himself as God dictated not a pastor anymore. He was determined and prayerful that God would eventually give him an explanation of what happen to him over those thirty seven years. Was the churches that he led with God as his guide successful? He was educated in the finest schools, set under the tutorage of one of the greatest pastors, earned degrees in finance, accounting, marketing, and so on. He had meaningful networks and many God given talents. But, he refused to use marketing schemes and misinterpret the Word of God to gain attendees and exhort monies from congregants and/or business people through trickery. The question remains on the table, was he successful? Really, this pastor has assisted entrepreneurs in writing marketing plans for secular business adventurers. He was serious about building a church only in the way God has commanded. He said, "He is no fool who gives up what he cannot keep to gain what he cannot lose." There are different views of how the church ought to be built. The view that one takes will lead to God's approval or disapproval.

DIFFERENT VIEWS OF SUCCESS WILL LEAD TO TWO VERY DIFFERENT TYPES OF CHURCHES

If pastors and church leaders believe that success in the Christian world is to take on the formula of the business world, then they will direct their efforts in this matter. They will strive to build larger, and richer; more attendance, larger buildings, and richer possessions for their church. They will promote and treat the church as a business venture. Their marketing message will be "Come to our church and get what you want in a church—total excitement, the greatest speakers, the best and talented musicians, and the best elaborate programs for you and your family."

There is nothing wrong with this model. The problem is that they are calling it a church and stealing the glory from God. They are seeking to entice people to come and attend their church, rather than attend God's church. They are seeking to market their church on a competitive level. God wants the church to be united. All types of people are to be the church. They encourage people to leave one church to attend their church which is devoid of the priority goal of making disciples. They are seeking to gain customers rather than seeking to build disciples. This church is built on competitiveness with other churches. This is the same with big businesses. Their goal is to get people to choose their product instead of another product. They act as if they are successful when people leave one church for another. This model confuses the people who are seeking the Lord for salvation. The churches who practice this model believe they have reached the ultimate success when they have become the largest church in town in the state, and so on. This is an attendee driven church.

The discipleship-focused church has very different goals. Their goal is to promote obedience to Jesus Christ, even if it does not help their own church to grow in attendance. They are praying to God to send laborers. They are successful in God's sight according to His Word. They encourage those in the church and those who join to become disciples. They are teaching and preaching holiest. This type of church does not have as a goal the desire to promote itself or seek to build its church at the expense of other local churches. Its goal is to promote God's work throughout its community and abroad.

This church puts its efforts into ventures differently from those who used a well thought out marketing business plan void of the Word of God. They will not use a calculated business formula to entice people to their church. They will preach the unadulterated gospel even though their hearers may leave and go to another church. Churches with this mission as their priority focus on sharing the gospel message with as many as possible. They realize that seeds of the gospel are being planted and that may not bear fruit until God deems it to be so. They are what God calls a remnant church.

They are willing to spend time and money on efforts that further the gospel. This will not divert their efforts because they desire to have a larger congregation and/or a larger building. This church will pray, fast, preach, and work directly with family members in an effort to help them become disciples. They are not trying to be a movie star, but to be God's servant. It is their desire to build up the Kingdom of God. The goal is not to seek attendees, but to seek those who are willing to become Christ's disciples. Their goal is to seek after more growth among those who are already His disciples.

WHO ARE THE *"ATTENDERS?"*

Attenders or attendees have been used to describe those in our churches who are like the "multitudes" who followed Jesus. Jesus had a large number who followed Him. But, they did not become His disciples. Many of them turned away when they learned that He was not offering them an earthly kingdom with earthly wealth. Jesus was offering a heavenly and spiritual kingdom with spiritual wealth. God sent Jesus so that we might have abundant life. They were those who loved Jesus' miracles, but had no interest in following Him to the cross. Also, there were those who seemed to be disinterested later became Jesus' true followers. Thousands came to believe in Him after His resurrection from the dead. The church has not been called to build up multitudes.

It is clear, however, that Jesus did not build His church with the disinterested multitudes. He did not build His church with the superficial and selfish interest people who were interested in what He could do for them. Jesus built His church with those who really became His disciples. Jesus built his church with those who recognized their sinfulness. He built His church with those who genuinely appreciated what He did for them on the cross. He built His church with those who were willing to follow Him on the path to the cross.

Many churches today are focused on adding attendees to their churches. If the idea is to seek attendees and not to make them disciples, then we are missing the priority. This is not a judgmental accounting of the churches. We do agree that the world is not attracted to the gospel. The church is called out to set the stage for Christ-like living. The voice of the church should not be shut up and saying nothing as the adversary attempt to destroy the purpose of the church. The world hates the church. God's church can not please the world. The church has to pay the cost of being the church.

Jesus turned away the rich young ruler and others who were not willing to pay the cost that was necessary in order to follow Him. We ought to have the boldness to say to the world today that God demands that we obey His commands. We are either a disciple of Jesus, the Christ or we are not. If we are not willing to do it God's way, then we are not His disciple. Yes, we can attend church regular and still not be one of Jesus' disciples.

There is a time and place in the Christian ministry for being correct. The author of Hebrews calls those to whom he is writing "slow to learn" (Hebrews 5:11-14), James calls those in his audience "double-minded" (James 1:4-8, 4:4-8), and Paul calls the Christians at Corinth "worldly" (I Corinthians 3:1-3). This is not being arrogantly judgmental. The truth will set you free. We can be an inspector of the fruit of the church. God said that judgment will began at the House of the Lord. Paul tells us that, among other purposes, God's Word was given to us for correction (II Timothy 3:16-17).

Many of our churches have been bragging that building large attendances is the measurement of a church's success. It has been repetitively said that the building of large attendances has become more important in many of our churches than building disciples. Yes, it is appropriate for there to be correction given for this misstatement of facts. We can not afford to draw a dividing line of demarcation in the Christian church. We need growing communities of growing disciples of Jesus Christ.

Then, who are the attendees? They are those who do little more than attend our churches. Some attendees can at some time in the future become Disciples of Jesus Christ, but at the moment they are spectators and not participants. They must be trained by other disciples.

People come to church buildings on Sunday mornings for a variety of reasons. Many attend for less than pure motives. I grew up believing that people came to church on Sunday mornings because they love the Lord, His word, and His people. Later, I learned that young men and young women came primarily to find a mate. Then, I found out that a businessman's primary goal was to use the church to make business contacts. Now, I realize that some parent's main desire is to put their children in youth programs, to help keep their children out of trouble, or even for the church to baby-sit their children. But, when the churches have God's priority in prospective, the attendees can learn about their sinfulness and God's grace toward them and choose to turn whole-heatedly to Jesus Christ. But, now many of these churches have refused to preach the doctrines of Christianity?

Many of the attendees have not yet become Christians. Some of them will continue to attend church as long as the program is interesting and not boring. But, they may have little interest in becoming disciples. Others come to churches hoping to find something great in the huge building. They may later become Christians if the Word of God is preached. Again, the motive of the church should be put in the hearts and minds of the people.

Still other attendees can be people who have mixed motives. They have not decided what is most important to them. Some may come looking for a girlfriend, but have vowed to themselves not to get married. James says they are "double-minded." They are not willing to give their lives to Jesus as He has given His life for them. They attend because they are confused.

It is not unusual for the attendees to want to be served and not to be servants. They love to follow a popular figure. They love to be entertained. When Jesus performed miracles the attendees loved to be in His company. Attendees' who have not yet become disciples can attend for years without making a commitment to disciples. They can attend for years and not go to a single bible study.

In general, the attendees during Jesus' day were unwilling to give up some part of his or her life to follow Jesus. They were unwilling to give up personal priorities. They placed Jesus on their secondary list. Many do not want change their lifestyles to follow Jesus. They want to be a part without being a part. They are trying to prove that "they can have their cake and eat it to". This is the modern day approach. They will attend these marketing churches for entertainment and do not want to be a disciple.

Having attendees can create a serious problem. After many years of having attendees, they will eventually gain influence over others. They will gain a position that will influence the departments in the church, such as the choir, youth ministry, usher, and so on. They will become involved in the decision making process of the church service. When there is a shortage of volunteers they will take up the lack. Without a spiritual commitment to build up the kingdom of God they will work until they get an important position in the church. They will have a half-hearted and begrudging attitudes when others try to assist them to complete a job. They will began to love the prestige of being seen in the church doing a specific task. They will become heavily involved in the church governmental task. They will bring the secular attitudes into the church. These attendees will not have any biblical knowledge of how the church should work according to Jesus. They will not have any idea of what the church priorities ought to be. They will divide the church and create strife in the church. Not only are attendees not a measure of a church's success, they hinder a church from being successful in making disciples. But Disciples of Christ are bold and are filled with the Holy Spirit. An attendee is not bold in the Spirit of God and is not interested in building up the Kingdom of God.

Years ago, a mega church wanted to launch a Bible Study Class to teach the biblical art of evangelism. Each time the church tried, it was met with opposition. Each time there was an attempt to generate enthusiasm for a bible study class, many so-called leaders would argue against the class being started. They considered it a waste of time. The next year, several preachers within the congregation were allowed to teach out of any book they wished. These preachers began to teach on the mission of evangelism. There was a great movement in the church. Many members of the church signed up for the classes. The efforts to stop the movement was unsuccessful. Why? God has a way for moving His plan forward even when there is much opposition. God calls us to be obedient to His Word and make disciples.

WHO ARE THE *"DISCIPLES?"*

Who, then, are the disciples? When Jesus asked His early disciples to follow Him, Peter and the other fishermen left their fishing nets enterprise. Matthew left his financially rewarding tax-collecting job. Others left their occupations behind and to follow Him. It was a "Pearl of Great Price," but they were willing to give up everything to follow Him. By contrast, John chapter six said they the multitudes who had been His followers left Jesus. They began to realize that the kingdom Jesus was offering would require many changes in their lifestyle. They were not willing to make these changes. But, Peter and the other disciples stayed. They knew that Jesus could fill their spiritual hunger and needs.

As we are living in the 21ˢᵗ century, there are many who still believe that real life is found in Jesus Christ alone. This country needs God. It will will not be too long that people will have to make a choice in America. America is traveling in the wrong direction. They are moving farther and farther away from the creator. The church is to assist people in making their lives richer in Jesus, the Christ. We believe to follow Jesus Christ is not just a small part of our lives; we believe that He alone gives meaning and fulfillment to our lives. It is a lifestyle for us.

The Word of God is absolutely clear about who are disciples. God sent Jesus to further clarify the requirements for discipleship. This is one way to measure church success. We ought to know who is a disciple and who is not. Let us consider the characteristics of disciples.

1. Disciples know the Bible is the book of life. Jesus said, *"If you hold to my teaching, you are really my disciples. Then you will know the truth and the truth will set you free." John 8:31, 32 2*

2. Disciples have an insatiable hunger to understand God's book of life. *Yes, they* are imperfect and flawed just like Jesus' early disciples. However, they are eager to understand the bible and make it their way of life. Peter said *they long for God's Word like a new baby longs for milk.* (I Peter 2:2) *Disciples will study to show themselves approved to rightfully divide the Word of God.* They do not teach their opinions.

3. Disciples long to be with other Godly leaders. Jesus chose twelve to be *"with* Him." (Mark 3:14) Paul chose Timothy to be with him. Paul had a number of disciples like this who traveled with him. Barnabas, Silas, Aristarchus, Tychicus, Trophimus, Sopater, Secundus, and Gaius were only some of those who wanted to be with Paul and who traveled with him. To be a disciple in 2016 and in the future is God's command.

4. Disciples are those who have left their goals to be worldly successful and strive to focus on following the plan of Jesus, the Christ for their lives. In Luke 14:25-33, Jesus told the crowds or multitudes that they would need to love Him more than their families regardless of the cost. The rich young ruler was not willing to give up his riches. Disciples will have only one master. The Word says that they can not serve two masters. We are commanded to build a successful church using the Word of God and not the lies of the enemy. Disciples will not be divided between the world and the kingdom of God.

Years ago I help organized the "Teens for Christ, in a city high school. One of the things I told them was that they were called in this school to be F.A.T. one of the "Teens for Christ," asked what does this mean? When I first met him, he was in his junior year. He was a troubled teen. Lately, I was told that he did not have the the nurturing of a mother nor the model of a good father. It was the plan of the principal to expel him from school. Of course, the principal was abiding by the rules. However, being the business manager, I did not have a teaching assignment. I pleaded his case and promised that I would act as his guardian angel as I did many students.

This troubled teen was given a choice. He could either be expelled from school as sanctioned by the officials or he could accept my tutorship. He accepted to allow me to help him get focused. I literally begged his teachers to accept him back into their classes. This was not easy, but each agreed only if he was a model student and achieved a passing grade. Having worked with him for months, I invited him to join the Teens for Christ. He accepted the invitation and was introduced the plan of Christ for his life.

Having joined the "Teens, I explained to him what "F.A.T." meant. I told him that the disciples of Jesus, the Christ were called to be **F**aithful, **A**vailable, and **T**eachable. With much prayer and supplication, guidance, , sacrificial offerings, and so on, he graduated and went to Harvard University. Little did I know that at times he was sleeping in school buses at night. Little did I know that he was attending almost every Christian revival in the city and at times Christian parents were demanding that he spend nights with them.

Since his graduation I was privileged to be present at an assembly held in his honor. Of course, he was gracious and told the audience that he was successful in making God's vision come into fruition in his life because he was "F.A.T." Today, he is a prominent Pastor and finishing up his last year at Harvard Law School. It was he who wanted to be "F.A.T.", thus being a disciple of Christ. A church is not successful just because they have thousand of attendees. Jesus primarily focused on making disciples.

Many churches today brag on church attendees. The idea is to make disciples and let disciples make more disciples. We are not to parade our church leaders who entirely use secular business plans as Disciples of Christ. Disciples enjoy personal Bible study. They love to preach and teach God's Word. Disciples love to study the Word of God individually. They are not solely working in the kingdom for fame, fortune, power, and money. *Fellowshipping with other disciples is the highlight of their lives.* They only enjoy church services and meetings that are Christ-like and require obedience to the Word of God. Disciples enjoy talking about spiritual things and serving God.

There is much to be said about disciples as it relates to letting the wheat and tare grow together. Many have the incorrect interpretation of this scripture as recorded in Matthew 13. This parable which Jesus taught relates to the fact that wheat and the weeds look alike. They look so much alike that if you try to pull out the weeds, you will also pull up the wheat. I am not suggesting that we pull out the attendees from the church. Instead, I am giving a new formula for determining when a church is to be considered successful. The formula to be used is simple. We are to focus our attention on building disciples. The primary focus is not growing attendees. We must not lower God's standards and pass these lower standards to next generation as the formula for success. We must keep our attention on growing wheat and not tare.

The fact is that even Jesus chose a disciple that betrayed Him. His name was Judas. We can not be perfect when we make disciples, however, this must be our primary objective. Every church attendee ought to be tracked to be a disciple of Christ. The work of making disciples is never completed. It is to be the lifelong pursuit of every church. It is to start within the home. A parent's goal should be that their children will become a disciple. When church attendees arrive at church, they will have been groomed for discipleship.

It is true that those who want to be just attendees will leave the church. We do not read in the bible that Jesus chased after them, but Jesus does look for His lost sheep. The church should not design programs to chase after attendees. We are not to water down the gospel just to fill seats. We are not to compromise the gospel for the sake of calling our churches successful. Preachers have been called to preach, teach, and show people the error of their ways. They are to sound the alarm.

INSTITUTIONALIZE CHURCH VERSUS GODLY CHURCH

The primary goal of the attendance-focused church is to keep the attendee coming. Those who are attendees will openly complain when the preacher preaches too long. They are constantly watching their watches and are highly upset when the clock strikes pass the common hour for adjournment. Their attention span is very short when it comes to the Word of God. The message must be simple and not profound. They will complain when the messages are too heavy or too deep. They do not want to think or mediate on any given subject. They want to be served milk and not meat. Meaty messages for them are difficult and boring.

Simply, they have itching ears and like ear itching messages. They like "ear tickling" messages. They want the sermon to be positive and not pointing any fingers at them. They will reject any message that has a negative connotation. The message must be interesting to them and emotionally inspiring. The attendees are impressed with a pastor who uses a lot of humor when preaching. They look for a charismatic entertaining person to preach to them. Sadly to say, many false prophets are in the church preaching watered down messages that can not be found in the bible.

The church meetings in the attendance-focused church are also designed to keep the attendees coming. The meeting will house an agenda of low-commitment and much entertainment. Usually, they will have entertaining speakers, talented musicians, fast-paced movies, and no chance for interaction of serious subject matters. The meeting will not ask for commitment, sacrifice, a change of life-style, or personal vulnerability. If the meetings schedule prayer meetings, help for the needy or fostering growth in the communities, then the attendees will not come. The attendees will dwindle. There is also a problem if the meetings discuss the moral wrong in our society (like abortion or pornography).

The primary goal of the discipleship-focused church is "to keep the disciples growing." To make disciples, the Sunday morning message must be designed to keep them growing. The pastor and teachers must be dedicated to make disciples. They must be taught to understand and apply God's plan for their lives. The pastor must be dedicated to teach and to preach the whole Bible. They must not pick and choose what to preach, but allow the spirit of God to lead them on what the congregation needs to hear from the Lord.

True disciples desire more than short messages. In fact, they are not clock watchers. In Acts 19:8-10 the disciples at Ephesus sat for hours, probably in the hottest part of the day, learning from Paul's teaching. They were not in a hurry to get home. They were eager to learn all they could from him. They were not lukewarm Christians. They were "hot" in their desire to understand God's book.

True disciples enjoy challenging messages. Disciples desire to move from spiritual milk to meat. They are eager to understand the easy parts of the Bible as well as the difficult parts of the Bible. They want to hear the unadulterated Word of God. Disciples are primarily interested in Biblical sound messages. They are interested in how to grow as a Christian. They are not particularly interested whether the sermon is humorous or entertaining. Of course, humor and a dynamic personality can be a plus, but it is not a requirement. Disciples are primarily interested in hearing from a Godly preacher who has received a Word from the Lord. They prefer a spiritual diet and not a diet of spiritual cotton candy.

Disciples desire high-commitment meetings that will help them grow as Christians. They desire to have an opportunity to be effective in their Christian service. They want to be active disciples and believe that the Bible is the final authority for how God wants them to live. They love Bible studies. In bible studies they have the freedom to be real and vulnerable about their needs, doubts, failures, and sins. They desire prayer meetings where they pray for each other and for the world. They want their meetings to lead to Godly actions. Disciples have a strong desire to encourage and care for one another, to share the gospel, to reach out to the needy, or to confront some type of moral problem in society.

Jesus did not focus on the multitudes. He focused on His disciples. He started out with only a few. In Judges seven, God whittled Gideon's army down to a very few. God's pattern in the Bible is to do His work through the few who are wholehearted rather than through the multitudes that are halfhearted.

How DO *Disciples Act When They Find* Himself Or Herself In An Attendance-Focused Church?

In America, there are churches where the common belief is that it is more important to keep the attendees coming. They believe that Disciples of Christ have no place in the 21st century. What is it like for disciples in these churches? Simply, they are dissatisfied. They are weary when the day of worship comes. They are discontent with the short, ear-tickling, entertaining, and milk messages. They constantly pray for God to take control. Their pray life increases because they are in search for God's church. When they have the opportunity to be in the company of other disciples they express their discontent. They hold back the tears as they look for God to take control of the situation.

They are not satisfied with the low-commitment meetings. They seek and pray for higher commitment meetings. They are discouraged and frustrated by lack of enthusiasm, and even show bold opposition for watered down sermons.

However, in these churches disciples are usually the most responsible and willing workers. They realized that they are overworked and are doing what the attendees will not do. It is true that only a few are doing most of the work. It is difficult for them to resent those who want to do nothing. They have to keep praying about the attendee's lack of dedication to the work of the Lord. The disciples are nominated frequently for the positions that many are not interested in doing.

Disciples will usually carry more of the load in these churches. They are on the building committees, church building clean-up, leading the youth group, teaching Sunday school, working with Vacation Bible School, singing in the choir, visiting new comers, serving on committees, and so on. They have little time for their spiritual growth. They have little time for spending time with God, Bible studies, and Christian fellowship.

Due to their heavy involvement, they have little time for the highest priority of Christian life, a relationship with Christ. They have little quality time to spend with their families. They have little time to become involved in the life of the community in which they live. Because of so many responsibilities, they have little time for fellowship, encouragement, and edification. The disciples' life usually grows weaker rather than stronger.

Finally, a disciple in this kind of church is looked upon as a malcontent. Firstly, there is an attempt to ignore them. The church will say "do not say anything and maybe they will go away." Many in the church will tell them "not to rock the boat." Sometimes, they will take a leave of absence hoping things will change upon their return. Then, they may become a faithful worker and express discontent in private to those who are also disciples. However, if they continue to speak out about the inconsistency between what the Bible teaches and what the church does, they will meet opposition. Jesus, Paul, Stephen, and others in the early church met this same type of opposition.

How Do Attendees Act *When They Find* Himself Or Herself In A Discipleship Focused Church?

Attendees who are really not disciples on Sunday morning will soon find it uncomfortable in a church that is primarily intent on building disciples. They will ultimately respond to the discipleship-focused church in the same way as the multitudes responded to Jesus' message in John six. Jesus said that He is the Bread of Life. Aware that His disciples were grumbling, Jesus said to them, 'Does this offend you?'

The attendees will grumble when the messages are about spiritual things. They are not interested in spiritual things. In Jesus' day, many of his followers turned back. Many found that type of message offensive to them. They will grumble and will threaten to leave the church. Too often, many pastors will not do what Jesus did. The pastors chase them, change their message to please them, and eventually degenerate into an attendance-focused church. *(John 6:25-70)*

The attendees in a discipleship-focused church will tend to cater to, and direct their adulation to those who are dynamic, charismatic and humorous. They will even idolize them. This pattern of behavior is recorded at the church at Corinth. Some idolized Paul, others Peter, and others Apollo's. *(I Corinthians 1:12) Many preachers today ought to realize that even Paul was not dynamic enough speaker for those who were not disciples at Corinth: "When I came to you, brothers, I did not come with eloquence or superior (impressive) wisdom as I proclaimed to you the testimony about God. For I resolved to know nothing while I was with you except Jesus Christ and him crucified. I came to you in weakness and fear, and with much trembling. My message and my preaching were not with wise and persuasive words, but with a demonstration of the Spirit's power. I may not be a trained speaker, but I do have knowledge." I Corinthians 2:1-5 and II Corinthians 11:5)* Paul did not come to them with the eloquence that impressed the Greeks, but he came to them with the message that Jesus Christ was crucified for their sins.

Attendees in a discipleship-focused church will not have any interest in the high-commitment meetings. They will only become interested when they become Disciples of Christ. Churches with thousands in attendance will have small attendance at their prayer meetings. Though thousands followed Jesus, only a few left all and followed Him. Attendees will not be interested in doing anything that cost them anything. In Paul's last letter, II Timothy, he encourages Timothy to be willing to endure hardship. Jesus suffered; should we expect anything less?

Ed Stezer, an executive director of Life Way Research expressed his views on the Pew Research Center as their report has some Americans behaving as if the Christian church is all but dead. He said that "the decline of nominal Christianity is not the only thing happening, but it's a big part of the real story." This author agrees with his assessment. He clarifies the Christian walk in three categories. He calls them cultural, congregational, and convectional. The Cultural Christians identify themselves with the being a Christian, but do not practice the lifestyle. The Congregational Christian has some content of being a Christian, but rarely attends church. The Convectional Christian regularly attends and lives their lives around their faith. This author indicates that if the church is to be successful then they need to be about the business of making disciples.

About 70%-75% of the U.S. population calls itself Christians. However, the **Pew Research** study in 2015 indicates that only 25% of the U.S. population practices their faith in the matter that God commands. This survey includes the evangelicals, Catholics, mainline Protestants, and others. The questions remains, what does the future hold? Are all these denominations what God intended for the church model of growth? Is the internet and business marketing plans killing the church? Is this possible to be a "Cultural Christian, a Congregational Christian, or even a Convictional Christian, according to the Pew categories?" The fact is that regardless of secularism taking up the manipulation of numbers to paint the church in decline, this author contends that we are seeing an outburst of truth as we fight the cultural war that is taking place in the church.

CHAPTER TWELVE

AN ATTENDEE VS DISCIPLESHIP

TOO MANY PASTORS in our American church culture take on the characteristics of a CEO in a business corporation. Many of the church leaders act very much like the corporation's Board of Directors. However, many of them need to realize that they are the head of a religious church of God. Society and for the most part, have accepted the church of God as a corporation. The church is operating on a 501 (c) (3) filed with the IRS. But, the Word of God never called any church a corporation.

The pastor in the attendance-focused church (or the customer-focused) church is paid a professional salary. They are given the charge to keep the church buildings full to capacity and the financial offerings high enough to meet all expenses. They are hired to maximize profit and growth. In the attendance-focused church, the prestige of the church is more important than the needs of the people. For example, this type of church is like a professional ball team. The primary goal of the team is to win the championship. Coaches and players are only important to the team if they can help the team to win. When the coach is unable to lead his team to victory, then he is replaced by another coach. In the middle of a season a coach will be replaced so that the team can win the championship. The team and its success are more important than the coaches and the players. So it is corporate success is more important than the individual people. The church-attendees mode of operation is more important than the individual people. Some may debate whether this is an acceptable state for professional ball teams. Winning and being better than other teams may be most important in professional sports, but is this what God desires for His church?

The attendance-focused church's primary goal is to be successful in their sight. To the pastor the people's primary purpose in the church is to build up the organization. As a church grows in success those who were important parts of the church's success can become expendable. They are replaced by the new and more accomplished members who join the church.

This is so much different from God's plan for the church. God's goals were not church success. His goal was impartiality, genuine love, and unconditional commitment to those that Jesus died for. The church is meant to be a place where those who accept Jesus as their personal savior can find love and acceptance within His church. In the church people are to find love. In the church they are to be encouraged to have a personal relationship with Jesus, the Christ. It is not a place where people are unimportant unless they can in some way help the Pastor, the church or the denomination to be successful. Paul said to Timothy in I Timothy 1:5. "The goal of this command is love which comes from a pure heart and good conscience and a sincere faith." Love is to be the goal of a church, **not** corporate success.

The typical characteristics of the pastor in the attendance-focused churches are interesting. The pastors of these churches carry most of the load. The whole church takes its command from the pastor.

(1) He is looked upon as a church professional. He is looked upon as being distinguished from other church members. He carries the title of being called "Pastor," "Reverend, or Doctor. "As a result, he is often tempted to feel that he is an elitist. He is tempted to place himself in a class alone with the doctors, lawyers, and others. Some place themselves above them and the President of the United States. Many do not look to God, but to themselves.

(2) He assumes that he has the sole right to lead religious ceremonies in the church. He is constantly in the way of the spotlight and hardly anyone has the opportunity to work out their sole salvation without his permission. It is interesting that Paul's disciples did most of the baptizing rather than Paul (I Corinthians 1:14-17).

(3) The Pastor believes that he alone has the role of being the polished salesman in all entities. He has the gift of keeping the attendees

coming back. It is his religious responsibility to make attendees feel comfortable. He is the only one that can keep the attendees attending.

(4) *This Pastor is totally responsible* to get the attendees to do the extra-credit-type of duties in the church. He is the sole recruiter. He is the only called out person to keep the church on key and growing. I believe some think that they are the electric that keeps the wheel spinning. If he slows down, everything in the church slows down, stops spinning, and falls apart.

(5) The pastor believes that he is responsible to keep people happy in the church. He can not afford to make waves. He can not do anything that would discourage anyone from coming. He must meet everyone's expectations. It is his professional job to keep the church running smoothly. He puts this pressure on himself. Jesus did not try to meet these entire requirements placed on this kind of pastor. Jesus words and lifestyle often angered and divided people. Jesus made waves. Jesus discouraged some from following Him.

(6) This pastor has determined that he is expected to be the master of everything. He has determined that he is the best teacher, counselor, administrator, financial wizard, evangelist, song leader, salesman, friend of all, comforter, charismatic speaker, polished master of ceremonies, janitor, maintenance man, and bus driver, and musician, helper of the needy, preacher man, and a man without human weakness. He knows that he is able to get along with children, the elderly, able to be on the level with the wealthiest and the poorest in the church, a master of each moment, a stand-up comic, an intervene in crises, to be always available, an expert on alcoholism and drug addiction, to be responsible to meet every emotional and economic need in the church. The pastor believes himself to be adept at resolving conflicts, a visionary, an architect, a fund raiser, an accomplished politician, and give seminars on how to do all of this. Not one within the church or outside of the church can come close to doing this kind of work for the Lord.

I wonder if this type of pastor is able to do all aforementioned who will get the glory. Attendance-focused churches are referred to as the pastor's church. The pastor of this type of church is called a "successful" church. Many if not all the other churches are trying to emulate the business style of this church. The pastor is often put on a pedestal as that of a movie and/or sports star. The tragedy is of this is the fact that he is just a man. Man is not perfect. Man's will is prone to fall just like the rest of us. I have lived long enough to see those who have been raised to the level of a super star in the church have tumbled down the ladder and crashed like a falling star. The fall was great and great was the fall. Why? They were raised up so high. Only Jesus Christ deserves to be raised up and to be worshiped. Only Jesus lived a perfect life. Only Jesus deserves the praise of the people. But, the attendance-focused churches tend to create these types of stars. I wonder if some of the pastors are false prophets.

A DESCRIPTION OF A DISCIPLESHIP-FOCUSED PASTOR

Again, there were not any corporations in Jesus' or Paul's day. Based on the description and business plan of the attended church many would call Jesus' church unsuccessful. Yes, they would say that the church Jesus Christ and Paul led was not successful. A church that focuses primarily on discipleship is strikingly different from a successful business corporation. Also, the Pastor's function would also be strikingly different. Of course there will not be a CEO in the discipleship-focused church.

Ephesians 4:11-12, commands the Pastor's to equip or prepare (disciple) God's people for the work of the ministry: "It was he who gave some to be ... pastors and teachers, to prepare God's people for works of service so that the Body of Christ may be built up." But, the title "minister" gives the impression that he is to do all the work of the ministry. The attendee's church gives the impression that the church is to be ministered to or served by him. This perception is the very opposite of what the Bible teaches.

The ministry is to be performed by each Christian. The pastor is to make disciples. The pastor's job is to see that they are trained for this work of ministry. He is not to even attempt to do all the work. He is not to try to be the sole person in the spotlight. Also, the Pastor is to emulate Jesus and Paul. He is to choose some to be **with** him. He is to work knowing that he will pass on the leadership of the church to the next generation. Paul chose Timothy. In his last letter to him, he said these words, *"And the things you have heard me say in the presence of many witnesses, entrust to reliable men who will also be qualified to teach others."*

We do not see the corporation style churches with their Pastors and church leaders following the model of Jesus. In fact they are too busy to spend time making disciples of younger Christians for the future generation. If their primary goal is discipleship, then they will do as Peter, James, and John. Jesus and Paul proved their methods to be of God's plan for the church.

Finally, the Pastor is to be a shepherd or pastor over the church. God said He would send the church pastors after His own heart. The shepherd is to watch over and guide his sheep. The Pastor is to do the same for the membership of the kingdom. They are to care for and guide the members along the right path. What if one member of the church begins to fall away from the church? Typical for many pastors hardly even a member is slipping away from the corporate church. This is not what God desires for His church. Like a good shepherd, the pastor is to be attentive and find ways to assist the one slipping away. So a good shepherd will direct his primary concern toward reaching and bringing that church member back into the fold!

Paul made an illustration of what is to be done. "You know how I lived with you the whole time I was with you ... *I served the Lord with humility and tears, ... I have taught you publicly and from house to house ... For I have not hesitated to proclaim to you the whole will of God."* He warned them that there would be false shepherds that would come out of the very middle of them who would twist God's Word and try to draw disciples to follow them. *(Acts 20:18-31)* Is this the heart of a corporation CEO or the heart of a pastor?

The pastor of a discipleship-focused church will be very different from a pastor in the attendance-focused corporation:

(1) There is not a scripture that calls the pastor a "Reverend." Pastor Timothy Ball, of Timothy Baptist Church, Baltimore- first brought this to my attention. In fact, he would not allow his congregation to refer to him as "Reverend." In the Bible "pastor" is a function.

It is not a title. Pastors are not different from other men. They should have been called by God. They have a leadership-servant role in the church. But, the fact is that they are human men. God chose them because they meet the requirements for leadership in God's church by God. Therefore, they are to be respected as leaders and appreciated for the work they do. They are not to be viewed as gods. They are not to be viewed as professional elites or movie stars. They are men of God who carry a Godly gospel that is to witness to a dying and sinful world. They are not elite in the society nor are they to be worshiped as a god.

Paul said that we are not to elevate any man to a position above other men: *"As for those who seemed to be important—whatever they were makes no difference to me."* (Galatians 2:6) "James, Peter, and John, are reputed to be pillars." (Galatians 2:9) Paul was not being disrespecting the apostles. He was frank and clearly stated Jesus position on the matter. Christ (and not any man) is the only One who should be looked upon as the Pillar of the church. James, Peter, and John were simple fishermen and they were special because of what God had done in their lives!

Jesus also said that men should not seek to be elevated above other men: "Everything they do is done for men to see … … they love the place of honor at banquets and the most important seats in the synagogues; they love to be greeted in the marketplaces and to have men call them 'Rabbi.' But you are not to be called 'Rabbi' for you have only one Master and *you are all brothers* … Nor are you to be called 'teacher' for you have one Teacher, the Christ." *(Matthew 23:5-12)*

(2) The Bible does not declare that pastors are "clergy" who alone can perform sacred roles such as performing funerals. Paul was not the only one that performed baptisms at the church of Corinth: *"I am thankful that I did not baptize any of you except Crispus."* (I Corinthians 1:14) Paul was glad that he did not baptize every Christian at Corinth. He did not give the impression that he was, somehow, a ceremonial representative for God.

The High Priest in the Old Testament was referred to as Jesus Christ. The ceremonial priests were each a picture of the individual Christian. There are not any ceremonial positions in the New Testament. All Christians are priests. *"But you are a chosen people, a royal priesthood, a holy nation, a people belonging to God, that you may declare the praises of him who called you out of darkness into his wonderful light."* (I Peter 2:9) Pastors are not a one-man welcoming committee for people being saved. The church is not a building. The church is the people. Putting all the pressure on the pastor to represent God's church is not taught in the Bible. The pastor-teacher is to train and prepare the whole church to minister to each other. We are the Body of Christ. We are to represent God in our lifestyle everyday in and outside of the church.

TWO TYPES OF CHURCHES WITH TWO TYPES OF MINISTRIES!

The goal of the attendance-focused church is corporate success. The ministry and service is primarily directed toward increasing the church's attendance. Most of the service takes place within the walls of the church building. Any type of service that does not help the church to grow in attendance is considered a waste of time.

The signs of a church that is attendance-focused:

(1) There is little or no cooperation with other churches in town.
(2) There is little or no ministry sanctioned and encouraged outside the church.
(3) There is little or no concern for Christians outside of the church.
(4) Time spent discipline young or eager Christians is seen as a waste of time by the pastor.
(5) Little or no money is spent that do not directly benefit the church (such as evangelistic efforts or helping the needy outside of the church.

This type of church reminds me of an old cliché, "us four and no more." They are concerned with their home and what is within their walls. They invite in only those whom they can reciprocate and do not threaten the pastor position. Their primary goal is to grow in numbers and be successful. They prefer that only those whom they enjoy being with socially, come to their church. They are not really interested in a bunch of needy people attending the church. They do not want their attendees to be uncomfortable.

Service in a discipleship-focused church is quite different. The focus of service is directed toward individuals and not toward numbers of people. There service is concerned for each person in the church and for individuals outside of the church. They are concerned with growth toward Jesus Christ in individuals' lives rather than corporate success. They are concerned with what is happening in the hearts of people, rather than how many people are coming to a building.

In a discipleship-focused church, the church members will bloom where they are planted. The pastor and the elders will encourage them to grow in their relationship with God. They are encouraged to fulfill God's purposes in their lives. God will motivate them to serve Him. God will give them every opportunity to serve Him in this present age.

Many of us have been blessed to have been associated with a discipline church. Christ-like people reached out to us and encouraged us in our Christian lives without a pastor encouraging them to do so. The early church was not a self-directed ministry. It was spontaneous. It had a courageous outreach emphasis for the needy. They were ripe for God's harvest, but the laborers were few.

The early churches in Asia—such as Colossae, Thyatira, and others were started by the disciples of Paul. He instructed them for long hours while he was in Ephesus. They left Ephesus and bloomed all over Asia (what is now Turkey). The bible does not say that Paul started these churches. Paul's letters to Colossae and Philemon indicates that his disciples were the leadership in charge. A discipleship-focused church will begin to see ministries develop wherever disciples are located. The pastoral leadership does not have to be involved, but the leader knows it is happening. The pastor will support all the efforts of the ministry.

Most of the service in the discipleship-focused church will be directed toward reaching out in love to those in need. They will share the gospel; build up fellow Christians in the faith; even if it does not help the church to grow in numbers.

What are the ways the church can reach out and touch our world? The church can help single parents and children who have poor home lives. The church can provide an after-school programs for latch-key children. The church can become big-brothers or big-sisters to lonely young people. The church can visit lonely and elderly people at home or in the nursing homes. The list can go on and on.

Attendance-focused churches usually do not go outside the walls of the church to witness to the lost. A church whose primary focus is discipleship will reach out to anyone. They will witness to those on the church corner as well as those who come to church. They do want more people to attend church, but they are more interested in seeing people repent to join their congregations.

There are many that will disagree with this way of thinking. They will openly say that there is no church that is totally like this attendance-focused church. There is not any church that is self-centered. Of course, there is not a church that is perfect. Even Jesus talked about only one church that meets His idea of working for the kingdom. Many He said, *I know your works.* We may not in our lifetime see a perfect church like this discipleship-focused church. But, this does not mean that we ought not to focus all attention on striving to be a discipleship-focus church. The early churches also were far from perfect. But, we should not be content with a lukewarm, self-centered, and worldly church.

Does this mean that church will never be perfect? Does it mean that church will never be perfect until we go and live with the Lord? Does it mean that we should be satisfied with the way churches are operating? I believe that answer to all these questions are no. The bible does not teach that we can be perfect nor does it teach that the church will operate in a perfect operant. The Bible teaches that we will never be perfect in our lifetime. We are told to work out our soul salvation. We are to be transformed by the renewing of our minds. We are to seek after holiness. We are to continually and wholeheartedly seek what God commands the church to be in this century. God does not want us to operate churches in His name with the primary purpose of getting people in the seats and begging for monies. Instead, we are to perform the "Great Commission." We are to make disciples. We need God's spirit in our churches to make this possible. We are not a church if the spirit of God is not freely moving upon the congregants. We are to pray and welcome the spirit of God in our churches. We are to be encouraged to obey God and do everything He calls us to do. We are to make sure that we are doing God's will in our churches.

Two Types Of Body-Life

What is body-life? Body-life describes the type of spiritual fellowship, biblical unity, and cooperative service that God desires a church to experience. It is somewhat like the personality of the church. The Body-life in a discipleship-focused church and in an attendance-focused church are opposites.

The fellowship in an attendance-focused is somewhat superficial. People can sit in an attendees focus church for years and not know each other names. Sunday after Sunday, they will not know over five people who attend the same church. There are no incentives for people to get to know one another. The interaction is akin to riding on the subway, buses, train and airplane. The fellowship can be called *"Christianity subway ride," "Christianity bus deport," and/or "Christianity airplay travel."*

A church that practices discipleship will be committed to building relationships. They are determined to build relationships between Christians and God. They will foster relationships between Christians and other Christians. The Word of God commands us to build each other up. Even the disciples were to go out two by two. We are to grow as mutual disciples of the body of Christ. This can not be accomplished if we are not seeking to get to know one another.

When we get to know one another, then we will know their needs and short comings. The Word of God commands us to love one another. Knowing them and their needs will help us to be more responsive. We will demonstrate our love not only in words but in deeds. We will show our love in "actions and in truth." (I John 4:16-18). This means that we will comfort them in the good times and when times are challenging. As Christians, we will be able to show our love by giving up our time as well as our resources. The Word of God will be demonstrated, *"Bread caste on the water shall soon return."* Our lives will become more comfortable and less stressful. We as Christians should want to get to know our fellow Christians and fellow human beings.

In this century, it becomes more difficult to get along with new people we meet. It is not easy to get a good response from people we want to meet. But, this should not be the case with discipleship Christians. Jesus reached out to the quick-spoken Peter. Jesus reached out to the quick-tempered James and John. We are to follow the examples of Jesus. We are to reach out to our fellow congregants. Jesus left His comfortable home in heaven to enter this sinful world. We are to do the same. We are to leave our home, our seat of comfort, and place of complacency and reach out to people. We are to make disciples.

Another quality of fellowship that is missing from the attendance-focused church is authenticity. They do not have an idea of what the lifestyle of the person sitting next to them is like. In church they usually put on their best character and go to church. They act as if they do not have any problems or concerns. They are somewhat like a movie star acting out a strip. They act as if they are a clown on a stage. They are not really themselves. The church is mostly very artificial in character and deed. Really, simply put, they are phony. Who are these people? They are the attendees of the twenty first century we see each Sunday.

The tragedy is we as church goers need to be loved and accepted. They can not truly be loved fully because of their superficial character. This superficiality prevents them from knowing one another. Therefore, we do not know their failings, weakness, and short comings. We need to love them for who they are. We need to extend the same love and grace to them as Christ extends to us. It is the duty of every Christian to love, extend grace and mercy between each other. We are to have faith in God that He will look beyond our faults and see our need.

Christians are to support, encourage, and love one another. However, this is not often found in the typical attendance-focused churches. Why? Many of the attendees will not take off their masks. They are not authentic with each other. Instead many will pay professional counselors when it ought to be given within the church congregation between one another. The monies wasted could be used to build up the Kingdom of God.

Churches that are dedicated to discipleship will be committed to authenticity. The Bible is very clear about authenticity. It tells about the sins of the biblical heroes. It does not soft pedal their sins or their failures. We can help each other if we trust, love, and care, pair, and grow in Christian love. We can help others in all levels. The disciples were needy and so are we. In a church that is committed to discipleship, fellow Christians are willing and able to strengthen the weak in love. Authenticity and removing the masks to genuine Christian is essential for discipleship. It is very helpful when used to the glory of God.

Body-life in a church that has been effective in discipleship will grow as Christians that will be motivation to minister to others' needs. They will grow in the areas wherein God has gifted them. The church will grow stronger and stronger in the area of giving. They will ultimately grow and become an expression of every dimension of God through Jesus, the Christ. The church is functioning according to God when every member is showing love inside and outside of the church. They practice love as a way of life.

Paul wrote to the Ephesians and said, "God gave gifted men to the church to prepare God's people for works of service, so that the Body of Christ may be built up until we all reach unity in the faith and in the knowledge of the Son of God and become mature, attaining the whole measure of the fullness of Christ. Then we will no longer be infants tossed back and forth by the waves, and blown here and there by every wind of teaching. Instead, speaking the truth in love, we will in all things grow up into him who is the Head that is Christ. From him the whole body joined and held together by every supporting ligament, grows and builds itself up in love as each part does its work." (Ephesians 4:11-16) "And I pray that you, being rooted and established in love, may have power, together with all the saints, to grasp how wide. The churches of the 21st Century does not resemble the historical church as recorded in the New Testament. For instance, the list of the Protestant churches in the United States is a non-exhaustive list. Many of these Protestant churches has more than 2,000 members. Most of these churches are mega churches and some fall outside this definition.

Paul wrote that *"long and high and deep is the love of Christ, and to know this love that surpasses knowledge... ... that you may be filled to the measure of all the fullness of God."* (Ephesians 3:17-19) These two passages in Ephesians describe what most disciples of Jesus Christ have come to desire for the church. But, those who are attendees do not understand these scriptures. They have a list of personal goals that they are trying to meet. It is not on their list of things to do to direct their efforts toward helping anyone. God's commands for the His church are of little or no interest to them. These passages are looked upon as being idealistic and impractical. The have brought the worlds view into the church. However, for disciples God's goals become what God desires for His church and it becomes their highest goal. Christ died for the church. We called the church a blood washed and bought church!

What does God desire for His church? He wants us to grow as Jesus' disciple. (1) We are to *agree in unity the truth of His Word and* share wisdom and understanding about who Jesus, the Christ is. (2) We are to continually build *each other* up in the things of Jesus, the Christ. (3) We are to work tirelessly in cooperative works of the commands of God for our lives, (4) We are to continue to grow closer in fellowship with God and one another. (5) We are to be in unity and experience every dimension of Jesus, the Christ His love and His love within each other. (6) We are to experience His fullness of His love together. We can not possibly do this by just being an attendee with our mask on. It is in church where we can grow in disciple-making while we are together as a community of believers. God is calling for all Christians to be disciple driven. He is not calling for segregated congregations. We are all to make disciples and be unified in His objectives for building up the Kingdom of God.

This is not a "Pie-in-the-sky" dream. All things are possible if we pray and believe. However, it is a "pie-in-the-sky" dream if a church is determined to be an attendee church. It is a "Pie-in-the – sky if the church is determined to change God's Word and does it their way. With God's power in a disciple church, it is a "Divine Certainty." The Word of God says, *"Now to him who is able to do immeasurably more than all we ask or imagine, according to His power that is at work within us".*

CHURCHES WITH DIFFERENT TYPES OF OUTREACH

The way these different types of churches handle their outreach is entirely different and distinct. The attendee churches are confident that attendance is the absolute sign of success, so they reach out to the outsider.

Every new person that attends the church becomes a success symbol and a new offering symbol.

I take no pleasure in saying this, but it is the truth of the matter. A new attendee becomes the object of success for the church to pamper. They become one more leg on the chair of success in the minds of the attendee's church formula for growth.

The audience can observe that pastor to determine if they are attending an attendee church. The pastor will get overally excited about a newcomer. But, when the newcomer becomes a part of the church, then the pastor is no longer excited. A stable member of an attendee church is lost in the congregation. What we witness is a competitive race for numbers. It saddens my heart to think that this spiritual leader sees a newcomer as nothing more than another number in the congregation.

But, the discipleship pastor sees the newcomer as a potential Disciple of Christ. This pastor realizes that this newcomer will need his or her time, commitment, and hard work for making him or her a Disciple of Christ. The whole church understands the commitment that must be made in behalf of the newly acquired member. They are excited about the task of making the newcomer a disciple of Christ, even if the person does not stay for a long period of time. They are happy that they had the opportunity to work out their soul salvation in behalf of the newcomer. They believe that if the newcomer should leave the church, then they would have sowed a productive seed in the heart and mind of a new disciple for Christ. The world would be a better place because of the steadfast work and determination to build up the kingdom of God. Even if they leave the church, the discipleship church will take care of their newcomer when requested.

The primary goal of an attendee church is to make people come to church regardless of what it takes. This type of church will pay overly large sums of money to bring in a world renounced speaker in order to fill the seats. They will bring in entertainers, comedians, advertise free give always, and even give chances to win a car in order to fill seats. Their primary goal is to bring in the number. They will tell lies to fill seats. However, it must be clear that every church that bring in special speakers and so on are not attendee churches. What makes a church different is the purpose of these speakers and special guest. The discipleship church has a lifetime commitment of evangelism and discipleship. To think vice versal demonstrates that they are interested in numbers and not followers of Christ. It will be obvious that they are attendance focused.

The outreach of a discipleship-focused church is to lead individuals to trust and obey God. They will constantly meet the needs of their disciples and encourage them to build up the Kingdom of God. They are not concerned about the cost, because they know that God will meet their every need.

There is not anything wrong with bringing a selected group of speakers to encourage God's servants to build up His Kingdom on earth. However, these individuals must be genuine, loving, and determined individuals filled with the power of God that are willing, ready, and able to equip the saints of God. What happens too often is that many churches allow what is called "quick pro recycling." They make a business plan to scam the people in order to get a healthy stipend.

So, in the 21st century only a few are reaching out in this circle. Therefore, the circle flow of wealth is concentrating on a few pastors who are trafficking the gospel for a livelihood. So these churches have their leader making excessive fees for preaching a watered down message to many functionally ignorant people. The bible tells us to study to show ourselves approved in handling the Word of God.

These churches may have so-called famous speakers, preachers, and musicians attending their services, but the spirit of God is absent. They are not feeding the people with the Word of God. Instead they are trained professional entertainers used for the task of gaining people to become attendees. Of course, they are not equipped to handle these numbers of people and teach them the way of the Lord.

But, the discipleship church is committed to lead each person down the road of becoming a disciple of Christ. They will have in place all things needed to lead the newcomer to the next level in Christianity. Special meetings will be scheduled, bible study sessions will be ready, prayer partners will be eager to start praying, sufficient number of disciples will be ready to train and encourage. All will be ready for the newcomer to grow in the discipleship church.

The discipleship-focused church will have programs ready that will allow each newcomer to be comfortable regardless of their station in life. This is what God does for His new disciples. So it is that the discipleship-focused church will have everything in place for their arriving disciples. I would like to make it clear that our goal should not be to recruit people to fill the seats. God said pray for the harvest for the laborers are few. Our goal ought to be to teach them, love them, and care for them and disciple them. We are to be the salt and light in the world. When God sends them to His church, then we are to share with them the gospel of Jesus, the Christ. We are to preach and teach the unadulterated Word of God without fail. We are to preach and teach in season and out of season. We are to tell them about the love of Jesus, the Christ. We are to emulate what God says in our everyday Christian walk. We are to walk with the Lord in spirit and truth, each and every day.

This is the word of God concerning the outreach of God's ministry to the Christian church. For Jesus said *on this rock I will build my church and the gates of hell will not prevail.* Jesus, sacrificed His life for the Church. He has not given anyone the right to change its purpose or to change His Word to be politically correct and for the sake of Civil Rights. His outreach formula is the same. God is not interested in large numbers that fill buildings. God is interested in saving our souls to be fitted for Heaven. His love for us and His sacrificial gift is where our discipleship imitative ought to begin.

CHURCHES WITH TWO DIFFERENT TYPES OF SPIRITUAL LIFE

A church which is not dedicated to discipleship will have a false spiritual life among its members. This type of church will give the appearance of a miracle vibrant spiritual life. The leadership will create a smoke screen and an illusion that genuine spirituality is occurring each worship service. The churches will have an artificial presentation that they are spiritual but they are not required to be obedient to every Word that proceeds out of the mouth of God. This type of church does not require that their membership be obedient and trust God to deliver on His promises. Jesus commissioned His churches to make disciples. These disciples are to obey Him each and everyday. It is important to realize that there are churches that are intentionally falling short of what Jesus commanded them to do in order to be called successful. Beautiful music coming out the mouths of sinners does not make a spiritual church. They are not honoring the commandment to make disciples when knowing they are just entertaining the congregation. Having a school of biblical scholarship that does not intend to rightly divide the Word of God does not make the church a spiritual church. Jesus commissioned the church to go and make disciples.

Making music is a beautiful gift of God. The bible says make a joyful noise unto the Lord. Music does usher individuals in a state of worship. However, music is used in churches to create an artificial replacement for true spirituality. The Word of God says they that worship Him must worship Him in spirit and truth. Talented musicians have long known that they can create an atmosphere of emotional control on the congregation through effective rhythm and sound bites. Music has the ability to soothe the savage breast. Many talented musicians have mastered their music so that they can give the false impression that God is present and moving in the church. But, the congregants are only having an emotional experience through the patterns of emotionally driven musical patterns made by talented musicians.

A church congregation can have a mixture of people that have hatred for one another. Child molesters can be present, liars, the unsaved, and many immature people, but a talented musician has the gift to make it seem like there is a spiritual stirring in the worship service. All of them can be drawn into an emotional mood of self made so called "spirituality." The attendee church may use this methodology every service so that the newcomer sees the crowd of worshipers and believes that they are Disciples of Christ. The newcomers believe that they are witnessing a spirituality that takes place only in this particular church. This is not a discipleship church, but an attendee church. There may be a total absent of the power of God working in the church. There may not be a discipleship class and there is not a real drawing of God's spirit that is moving from heart to heart. Yet, a talented musician is talented enough to make a false presentation of the working of the spirit of God. The church must beware of false and talented musicians who represent themselves as God's musicians.

In a discipleship church the disciple is obedient to God in everything they do for the building up of the Kingdom of God. This type of commitment from the Disciples of Christ is the only way true spirituality will take place in the churches. Some of the churches will have an emotional moving service with music, but there is not any true spirituality taking place. God's spirit will not dwell in any unclean place.

Our churches need lively, beautiful and moving worship services. But, God is not pleased when His spirit is being counterfeited to give a false impression of His presence and approval. The Word says deep called unto deep. Music should never sought to be used as a replacement for the real spirituality that only comes from prayer, meditation, obedience, holiness, and through a daily walk with Jesus, the Christ.

There are churches that foster the idea that there is a sacred and secular divide in people who attend the church. The church allows their members to entertain the idea that when they are in the world they can behave as the world behaves. But when they enter into the sanctuary they are to leave the secular world outside the door.

The membership in the attendee church is allowed to believe that when they walk into the church, a light comes on that transforms them to Christians. The sacred building and the obvious sacred stained glass windows sends a signal that they are walking on holy ground. The pews in which they sit are sacred. The Allen organ they listen to peels out the very sound that comes from heaven. The pastor speaks in a sacred tone with a voice that sounds as if God is speaking. They continue to come every week to be led into the sacredness of holiness in this building. On communion Sunday's they come wearing sacred clothes and take sacrament. But, when the benediction is given, they leave the "holy" world to go back into the real world. They do not live as a Christian ought and set an example for the world. They have pulled off the church uniform and have put on their secular clothes and ready to live a secular life as soon as their feet strike the street. In fact, before they leave the parking lot, they are ready for the secular world to consume them until the next so called worship service.

To the attendee church the idea is to make money off those who attend. There is not a need to teach to the people that they are to be holy as God is holy. Their lives do not have to be different from the way the world acts. They will allow the people to be politically correct. It will not be mentioned from the pulpit that God's Word describes real historic events. Why? They are direct differences between the sacred world and the secular world. The differences are demonstrated in the attendee church. It is important to the attendee leader to foster the idea that the congregants enter into a sacred religious mood and or experience when they attend church each Sunday. They constantly tell them that God loves you.

The fact of the matter is that the attendee church places music, language, clothes, and so on as the sacred artificial replacement for God's spirituality. So it is that they have designed a place that replaces the Holy Spirit for those who are not educated in the characteristics of the Holy Spirit. They have the organized marketing scheme to convince that all attendees have to do is go to the sacred church building. Of course, this is only the design of the marketing tool to make the attendee church feel they are successful.

To live a true spiritual life is the command of God on every believer. *"Be filled with the Spirit."* (Ephesians 5:18) *"So I say, live by the Spirit."* (Galatians 5:16) Jesus declared, *"Believe me, woman, a time is coming when you will worship the Father neither on this mountain nor in Jerusalem ... Yet a time is coming and has now come when true worshipers will worship the Father in spirit and in truth." (John 4:19-26)* For the discipleship churches, there is no split personality in the mind of the believer. Sacred and secular has no place in the mind of the disciple. For example, the Bible is not a religious book to be read only on Sundays, but it is the incarnated Word of God. The bible is the Creator's instruction manual for His sons and daughters in the faith. Disciples use the bible to find answers to every question concerning how to live their lives in a Christ-like matter. It allows them to speak truth to power and the secular world. When the disciples come to church nothing changes other than they have walked into another building. God is already with them and they are ready to fellowship with other disciples and worship together. A real disciple remains focused on God throughout their life's journey. Going in and out of buildings does not change their commitment to live holy lives.

Another artificial form of spirituality is the depth of knowledge of the Bible. The churches that place most attention to the numbers of scriptures their congregants quote can be a form artificial spirituality. The devil can and will quote scripture. Bible knowledge and quoting is good, but like music it can become false form spirituality. The knowledge of the bible ought to be a part of the congregant's lifestyle. To quote and admonish congregants to do what God says and the person does the opposite is hypocritical. Instead of this scholarship being a true spiritual building for the kingdom of God, it becomes a hindrance. For as Paul says in I Corinthians 8:1: *"Knowledge puffs up, but love builds up."* If the individual truly loves God, then they will keep His Commandments and obey Him.

Jesus said in John 8:31, 32: *"If you hold to my teaching, you are really my disciples. Then you will know the truth and the truth will set you free."* Discipleship training will admonish congregants to obey God's will and purpose for their lives. Churches that pride itself in being a classroom for learning the bible or a biblical institutionalized church are no more than a classroom for learning. A discipleship church requires personal accountability. They grant opportunities for the disciples to obey what is taught in the Bible. If they are teaching the art of preaching the gospel, then opportunities are available to practice and affect this skill in love. Jesus chose disciples to work in the marketplace. He did not choose them to sit in a classroom and listen to Him teach. He did not put them in an incubator for life. He taught them by being with them as their master teacher. Jesus held His disciples accountable for their sins and failings. He helped them to become obedient to Him as He was obedient to His Father.

Another form of spirituality is determined on how well congregants obey a list of religious rules within a church setting. These rules may not agree with the sound doctrines of the tenants of the Bible. But, spirituality is measured by how congregants keep them. This is exactly what the Pharisees did in the scripture. They developed a list of rules and regulations that others had to obey for them to be spiritually acceptable.

Also, doctrinal purity is used to determine if a person's spiritual state is acceptable. But, obeying a set of rules and having the right doctrine is not the same thing as spiritual maturity. Knowledge of doctrine can lead to a prideful life. We are to have a humble spirit and spiritual walk with God.

The Pharisee in Jesus' parable in Luke 18 was quite proud that he did not have the sins of a tax-collector. This is a form of artificial spirituality. Congregants are still using this artificial spirituality in churches today. True spirituality involves a humble and loving obedience to Jesus Christ.

Artificial spirituality is counterfeits of true spirituality: emotionalism, creating a religious and sacred world, building settings for academic knowledge about God, and a list of proper doctrines and practices. They are important, but they must be used to the glory of God. God is calling and has set in motion the need for discipleship churches that operates in the spirit of Holiness. We are to obey Jesus' teachings at all times as a way of life.

In the discipleship-focused church there is not a need to create an artificial form of spirituality. Why? Christ is already there, and the spirit of God is evermore present. There will be obvious evidences of God's presence. His spirit will move from person to person. True spirituality will be seen in the growth in the fruit of the Spirit. There will be growth in agape love, peace, and joy. There will also be growth in righteousness, purity, faith, and sacrificial Christian service. There will be evidence of growth in real spiritual life. The discipleship church will not have any type of spiritual counterfeit in the church.

The discipleship-focused church will be filled with Jesus joy. There will be a divine fellowship that will become the personality of the church. The topics of the church will be based on spiritual pursuits, victories, and testimonies. But in the attendance-focused church, it would rarely be about spirituality based matters.

The attendee church discusses the same topics that non-churchgoers talk about. Therefore, it is apparent that the spiritual life in these different types of churches is as different as apples and oranges. They do not even resemble each other in fashion or form. The attendance-focused church has a form of godliness. They do not have the presence of God's Spirit. They like God's power. The disciple-focused church is obeying God and pursuing His will and purpose so that they can experience God's power and are seeking to trust and obey all that Jesus has commanded them to do. God bless them with true spirituality.

CHANGE AND TRADITIONS

Years ago, Heraclitus of Ephesus, (535 BC–475 BC) a Greek philosopher, was known for his doctrine of change being central to the universe, and for establishing the term Logos in Western philosophy as meaning both the source and fundamental order of the Cosmos. He stated "everything changes and nothing stands still." This author believes change is as important. We learned as teenagers that change in the church can be controversial. Pastors have been voted out for trying to bring about change in the church. The 21st century church look upon change in a different way. There is the attendee's way of change and there is the Discipleship way of change. Of course the change is distinctively separable and sometimes a controversial issue in churches.

The institutionalize church is known for its traditions. Traditions have been a stabilizing and foundation grounding for the church. There is a traditional time for having church services. If the church broke with the time tradition week after week, there would be an outbreak in the ranks. To break with the time tradition, would cause chaos into the church. Many members would discontinue attending a church if it posted varying times week after week. But, there must change in church to breathe in new life for the congregation. For a church to institute a new youth program, a new choir, a new bible study class, and/or a new musical program will be stimulating to the life of the church.

Neither tradition nor changes are bad. The question is not if the church should break with tradition and/or institute change. The church will have do both in its lifetime of existence. The real question is when should the churches do things in a traditional way and when should they make changes to usher in productivity? The attendee church has its way. And the discipleship focused church has its way.

The fact is that what has become traditional is not always found to be biblical. For many churches, it is not even known how certain things became traditional. Rituals are different in some churches, yet they are traditional. The traditional rituals may have been written by an elderly pastor who did not take its meaning from the bible. The mission statement could be out of sink with biblical teaching. Yet, it is a traditional experience for the congregation.

There is a question asked in the bible about the use of tradition in the churches. Matthew 15:3: *"And why do you break the command of God for the sake of your tradition?"* The answer came back saying, "this is how we always did it." Sometimes traditions are out of step with the direct Word of God. It could be that the tradition is moving in the wrong direction in which God intended the church to go. However, tradition is important to churches in this 21st century.

Many in the pews look upon change as a threat to the existence of the church. Church members will fight change if they believe a portion of their life is threatened. Sad to say, if Blacks start joining a White church in record numbers, this change would cause many members to become upset. This also will happen vice versa. Also a middle class church will become uncomfortable when low-income children and/or families began to attend the church in great numbers. It is also true that older members will get upset if they think their church is being over ran by younger and college students. The research reflects that many churches like the church just as it was. They cherish the thought that the church would remain the same.

If new comers join a church and postulates change, they will be looked upon as an enemy or a villain. They will be antagonized and feel a force upon them as if they are being asked to leave. Anxiety will be launched on them, and if they do not get spiritual guidance they will eventually leave. The problem is that the lifestyle that is being forced upon them produces a change in their character and/or position of thought concerning biblical meanings. This change challenges their perspectives of kingdom building and kingdom living. It occurred when Jesus was living in the midst of the Pharisees. They resented Jesus coming and changing the religious system that they had established for their people. It profited them and made their lives complete in their sight. This kind of writings today will also make readers uncomfortable with these findings. Many would put up a fight and others will see through God's revelation the error of their ways.

How does the discipleship-focused church handle traditions? The discipleship-focused church looks upon tradition and determines if they are in sink with biblical teachings. If God's purposes can be better fulfilled and helpful in a different way that warrants a change, the change is in order. A new way that overtakes a non- functioning and out of date function will be institutionalize to more effectively accomplish God's purpose and will for the church. In the same matter if a tradition is no longer serving God's purpose and causes a conflict will quickly set aside. For instance, if bible study will assist a great number of people on Sunday morning, rather than Saturday evening, then change in tradition will take place without confusion. The time will need to meet the need of these participates rather than a teacher. God will have many teachers to accommodate the need for instructions. However, this type of change must be done with sensitivity, love, patience, and prayerfully. The discipleship-focused church always emphasizes the Word of God as important and deem it to have priority over traditions held by men and women in a church.

Hymns are traditions in the church. Hymns that are rich in the word of God and bathed in the Holy Spirit should remain in the church. Hymns like Amazing Grace, Precious Lord Take My Hand, Yes, Jesus Loves Me, and so on should always be a part of the church's tradition. Prayer meetings, biblical based testimonies, healing services, deliverance services, revivals, baptism services, communion services, and praise services, to mention a few should always be a part of tradition for the church. Services wherein God alone gets the glory should remain a tradition of the church. But, none of these traditions are the best that God has for His church. Eyes have not seen nor have ears heard what God has in store for those who have been called to usher in the church His desires. A discipleship-focused church will seek out God's best for every situation. The Pastor of the church realizes that God will and can speak to any saved and born again disciple to enhance His church. Regardless of how it was done in the past, God is still speaking. And we still need God in our churches. There will always be those who will try to stop change by saying, "we have not done it this way before." They will not say, "We tried it that way before, and we found out it will never work that way. What we need to hear is that they are willing to try new innovations based on God's Word to bring about the most effective ways to do Kingdom building.

The discipleship-focused church does not avoid change at all cost. In this type of church, change is exciting in the life of the church. The discipleship-focused church will not bring in secular change into a church for the sake of getting more members in the seats. They will not allow changes that go against God's plan for the church. What are some of the changes that a discipleship-focused church would like to see in this 21st century? I believe that they would agree on these changes if God deems it necessary for the church.

(1) A change that obviously shows a spiritual growth in the disciple's spiritual attitude and thereby be a greater asset to Kingdom building.

(2) A change in the congregants that matures them into better disciples of Christ as they attend church services. This will mean that as new comers visit the church, the membership would welcome them as Christ welcomes us when we give our lives freely and

unconditionally to Him. The new comers will be welcomed to become loved and honored trophies in the Kingdom of God.

(3) A change wherein the church will witness and discern more biblical and effective ways to accomplish God's purpose and will for the church.

(4) A change wherein the will of God will be obvious that as new comers come into knowing Christ as their personal savior, new leadership has arrived, new ministries has formed, and new social arrangements has been made, and a new fellowship has transformed.

The only sought change in an attendee-focused church is a change that involves church growth. They are looking for people to fill the seats. These generally take place by the use of deft political marketing tools, political maneuvering, secular reasoning, secular musical productions, R & B capitalistic, prosperity syndromes, reversal heroism, and so on. The bible tells us from such beware.

The honest new comer seeking Christ would flea from an attendee church because their needs are not met. Some may go and seek a smaller church wherein they may get more attention from the pastor, and perhaps find out what discipleship really means. Sam Cooke sung a song, "A change will come." Yes, a change will come, but will it be a change for the better.

We are living in a time in the history of the church wherein there is a trend to observe other churches. In this modern growth church era, many pastors and congregant leaders are seeking guidance from what is referred to as mega churches for guidance. They are attempting to copy their strategies and patterns to advance their churches. Many of these mega churches are not biblically sound. In fact, they are out of order as it pertains to the things of God. They have questionable doctrinal beliefs and have institutionalized secularism within the churches as being biblical. Many of their leaders are known as false prophets and are prostituting the gospel for self aggrandizement. Yet, many start up churches and others are trying to pattern after these kinds of churches. There are those churches that are following their advice more are less than of being successful churches in the sight of God.

There are many churches in the United States and in Korea who many so called church leaders have patterned themselves after that teach pagan doctrines to grow their church to a super church. They have become more concerned with being successful in assets, attendances, and buildings than the Word of God. They are no longer interested in being successful in the eyes of God. They are not interested in a biblical pattern for building and overseeing God's church. I submit that God is not interested in this type of church. Many have created so called successful churches that do not have any relevance for the tenants of faith exposed by the Word of God. They have created successful secular churches and have abandoned the ways of God. The question has been asked, what shall the righteous do if the foundation is destroyed?

A disciple-focused church is characterized by ushering in changes that will help the church to more effectively build disciples for the kingdom of God. But, the attendee-focused church will change that and will signal an effective change in the number of people that will come to their church. The attendee- focused church will stay away from any change that will cause discomfort among those that are already attending. The attendee- focused church will continue to keep their services exciting and entertaining. They will not raddle the cage and cause any person to leave because of what the Bible says is a sin. They treat it as a home. They do no mind change in their homes if it brings a greater sanctification and comfort. So, this is the same formula they use in their church services. They do not resent a little change if it will lead to a more pleasurable experience. If change will create more excitement, then they welcome the change.

Discipleship-focused churches love the change that moves them to a life of change that brings them closer to God. They welcome the change that brings them to a closer walk with God. They are constantly praying for a deeper relationship with Jesus, the Christ. A discipleship-focused church encourages any change that gives them a deeper faith in God. A new ministry can come on board that reaches out and touch some of the greatest and most painful sores in our society, the discipleship-focused church welcomes this change. A program could be initiated that brings people to become more open to each other and reaching out to others; they welcome this change. A ministry could implement a total marital counseling initiative class bringing a methodology to fix problems in marriages; they will welcome this change. These changes may occur in a discipleship-focused church, but will rarely happen in a church that is seeking success through a worldly success formula.

THE CHURCH BUILDING

The church we reference in this 21st century is not the church during 1st century biblical times. It is not the early church referenced by Jesus. The church during first century biblical times was the people. Today, as quiet as it is kept, the church is still the people. The church is the temple of God. *Do you not know that your bodies are temples of the Holy Spirit, who is in you, whom you have received from God? You are not your own; you were bought at a price. Therefore honor God with your bodies. Corinthians 6:19-20).*

There is a difference in the role of the attendee-focused church and the discipleship-focused church. The attendance-focused church places more attention on the building. The church for the most part is seen as a "sacred" building. The pulpit has a special sacredness about it. Only preachers, clergy, and special called can set foot in the pulpit. Then everything else is sacred. The stained glass window, pews, pulpit, organ, piano, hymnals, crosses inside the building and on top of the building are seen as being sacred. It is tantamount as walking into the holiest of holiest when entering the church. When people enter it seems that they are expected to walk differently, talk differently, look differently, and smell differently. The pastors look differently, do things differently, talk differently, and expect certain people to do likewise. But, the problem is that when they go back to their homes, many take on a different countenance.

The Discipleship-focused churches realize that the building is where the church meets. What makes it different is that this is the building that is man-made and God meets His people in this building. The church is a meeting place where two or three gather together, they touch and agree and God commands a blessing. We believe that God blesses the church because of His promises to the saints of God for being obedient to His assembly as called obediently. God honors His promises. All His promises are yes and amen in Christ Jesus. The scripture references these ideas clearly.

In Isaiah 44:15-20,

15 *Then shall it be for a man to burn: for he will take thereof, and warm himself; yea, he kindleth it, and baketh bread; yea, he maketh a god, and worshippeth it; he maketh it a graven image, and falleth down thereto.*

16. He burneth part thereof in the fire; with part thereof he eateth flesh; he roasteth roast, and is satisfied: yea, he warmeth himself, and saith, Aha, I am warm, I have seen the fire:

17. *And the residue thereof he maketh a god, even his graven image: he falleth down unto it, and worshippeth it, and prayeth unto it, and saith; Deliver me; for thou art my god.*

18. *They have not known nor understood: for he hath shut their eyes, that they cannot see; and their hearts, that they cannot understand.*

19. *And none considereth in his heart, neither is there knowledge nor understanding to say, I have burned part of it in the fire; yea, also I have baked bread upon the coals thereof; I have roasted flesh, and eaten it: and shall I make the residue thereof an abomination? shall I fall down to the stock of a tree?*

20. *He feedeth on ashes: a deceived heart hath turned him aside, that he cannot deliver his soul, nor say, Is there not a lie in my right hand?*

God speaks about people taking a tree to make an idol. Then, they have the audacity to call it their god. They take the rest of the tree and burn as a fire to get warm. God is the deity that can turn wood into a sacred object. If God has not ordained it to be so, then it is not a sacred object. We can not turn a building into a sacred object unless God has made it so. The Word of God in the Old Testament reveals that the temples were sacred because He designed them. He has explicit orders on how to design and building the temple. God gave us a picture of how we were to approach God through the blood of Jesus Christ. We do not find a perfect description written by God on how to build a church building in the New Testament.

The bible tells us that the early church met in homes, in halls, and in wherever a building was available. Many Christians are comfortable thinking that we have made tremendous progress because we have a church building. We have called some buildings "store front churches, small churches, remnant churches, medium size churches, and mega churches." There is a competitive spirit among churches based on size. We submit that the opposite has occurred. In many ways we have gone backwards. Not only has church attendance decreased, the respect for the church as leaders has diminished. Because the early church did not have buildings, they saw themselves as churches wherever they met. They did not have to think about going to church. They saw themselves as being with God where they found themselves to be at a present time. In this 21st century, many think that in order to be with God, they have to meet Him every Sunday in the church building. They do not have the day to day relationship with God. Surveys indicate that many go to church buildings to meet with God. Some denominations leave their doors open that people may have the opportunities during the week to have a little talk with God.

The attendee-focused church has its primary focus on securing numbers of attendees to be successful and with the emphasis in this 21st century on the building itself being sacred and what happens in this so-called sacred building takes the focus off what the people are doing on a daily basis. We do not offer apologies for what is happening. God is giving us the truth and the truth will set us free.

The attendee-focused church has issued the proclamation that if you have a big building with a lot of people, then you are successful. The church that has a small building with a small number of disciples is not successful if we use their formula. This formula is flawed and the Kingdom of God is suffering because of it. One can have a big building with a lot of people attending and have an extremely weak church. In fact many of these so called churches can be considered an organization. God is not concerned with numbers and buildings. God's word says He is concerned with what is taking place in the hearts of the people. God said to Samuel: "*The Lord does not look at the things man looks at. Man looks on the outward appearance, but the Lord looks at the heart.*"

The size of the building is very important in the attendance-focused church. The size of buildings has become important within our society. The size of a person's house is a primary indicator of the wealth and success of a person. We have bought into the measurement of success. It has become the primary indicator of the success or failure of a church.

So, it has become the primary way that an attendance-focused church displays its success in the hearts of many. They used the cost of the building and the size of its church building to make a statement about its success. They copied the way an expensive house and car have come to be status symbols of success within our society. We do realize that an expensive house can give one more trouble than a modest home. We do realize that an expensive car can be more troublesome than a car that gives great transportation. We should not be doped by the formula that attendee-focused churches use a formula for success. Yes, the expensive building with many people has become the status symbol that a church is successful.

Surely few would disagree that a large, costly building signals to the world that the church is successful, and a small church building signals church failure. The world will continue to believe this. However, the Christ-like world ought to know the truth. The Disciples of Christ ought to know that this definition is not true. The Christian world should not accept this definition without an examination of fruits that come from these attendee focused churches. This may be the society's and the world's evaluation of success. But, truly it is not God's standard of measurement.

Does this book point out that it is ungodly to make a large church building? Are you saying that God can not be pleased with a large church building filled with many people? The answer to both questions is no! We are saying that God should and must be the purpose for such buildings. The real question is what is the purpose of the building? God may allow these churches to build these buildings. We do have free will. Why are we building it?" Is the primary reason so that we as a Christian society can more effectively build more disciples for the advancement of the Kingdom of God? Will we be better equipped to reach the down trodden in love? Will we be better equipped to leave a legacy of Christian love to the future generation? Will we be able to restore economic wealth to future generations? Is the building going to be a more effective way to minister to the sick, widows, orphans, and sinners? The church building can not become a symbol for idol worship. Of course, all Christians know that this will be a stink in the nostril of God if the church was not built to glorify Him.

I wonder if this newly acquired wealth housed in the building could be used effectively in another way. Of course, most of it has come from the tithes and offerings of the "have not's." They brought their tithes and offerings to the store house for centuries. Could not God be expecting the disciples of Christ to open up the storehouse and build banks, credit unions, manufacturing plants, and create job opportunities for the less fortunate? If the attendee churches does not get a bail out, how will they care and pay for their building?

Really, is it biblically sound for smaller functioning churches to loose its place in the kingdom of God as they support attendee-focused churches, and strive off the functionally ignorant attendee's attempt to find God? Some of these buildings are designed to magnify the worldly success of the church. Other buildings are designed so that they can become 7-day-a-week ministry centers where Jesus' servant heart will be expressed and magnified. Prayerfully, these buildings will shine the light on the world and they will see God's hand orchestrating His spirituality throughout the history of the Christianity.

Make no mistake in your evaluations, a large building, packed to the rafters with people, is not a concrete sign that a church is working for the advancement of the Kingdom of God. We have seen some large churches that mesmerize people with manipulative "name-it-claim-it", a "positive thinking" secular orators, talented musicians, circus type atmosphere, club mentality atmosphere, and Las Vegas propaganda approaches. Overnight they seem to draw large numbers of people to a church building. But, we have noticed that many of these types of large churches and ministries have come crashing down in recent years. And so-called small churches have fallen by the waist side.

God's Word demonstrates that the smallness of a church is not a direct sign of failure. Jesus did not have a large building. He had large crowds of people following Him expecting a miracle and/or a blessing. The bible says that Jesus seated 5,000 on the ground, feed them, and taught them how to become a disciple. However, Jesus' ministry dwindled to only a few when He was being crucified. Only a few was at the foot of the cross when He was dying for the sins of the world. He did not have a large church building. He did not have thousands of people witnessing His crucifixion. Using the 21st century definition of success, Jesus would be considered a failure. Off course, only a person who has said there is no God would call Jesus a failure.

Can we consider Paul's ministry as a ruler indicating as success or failure? When Paul was at the verge of death, he uttered these words to Timothy. *"You know that everyone in the province of Asia has deserted me, including Phygelus and Hermogenes." "At my first defense, no one came to my support but everyone deserted me."* (II Timothy 1:15 and 4:16) Paul did not have a large building and congregation. Does the Christian world consider Paul a failure? Paul wrote two thirds of the bible in which all Christians have studied. Does his writing sound like a disciple who has failed to satisfy and obey God? Did his work go for nothing? Was Paul a failure? No, Paul was not a failure. His ministry is still being shared.

The size of a church building and the size of your congregations is not a signal of the success of your ministry. Jesus made reference to this as He spoke about the size of the widow's offering. Jesus said she gave more for the advancement of the kingdom than the affluent was willing to give. The size of the building and the congregations is not a good basis for judging the success or failure of a church before God!

As the church continues to think on this issue, some may come to the conclusion that this book is to attack large churches. There are those who might think that there is an animosity against large churches that has motivated the writing of this book. Certainly, this is not the case at all. This author has experienced the working of the smallest church, the medium church, and the largest church. The experience received from various sizes of churches has placed this author in the position to see ministry from all perspectives. In fact, I have benefited from all denominations large and small. I have preached and taught in most denominations regardless of race and creed. I have gotten excited in being in the presence of those whose intention was the primary goal of making disciples. Some of my most enjoyable, satisfying, and heart wrenching experiences have come in extremely large churches. There is nothing more satisfying and rewarding in the Christian walk than seeing a very large church use their facilities to make disciples for the Kingdom of God according to the scriptures. Still, only God knows if even a large disciple-focused church is more successful than a small discipline church. God can use a very small church to disciple a few people. But within the small church, only He knows who will be used in a mighty way to His glory. God can also use large churches to make more disciples than a small church. So, it is that this book is to encourage the readers given the chance, you ought to have as your primary focus to make disciples. Be encouraged regardless where God has placed you. We are to forget about success according to man and let God lead and guide your ministry. Stay focused on the command of God. The book's message is to stay focused on making disciples, regardless of the size of the church God has called you to pastor.

Of course, we are to understand that there are too many large churches that do fit the description of an attendee-focused church. A friend asked me to write a book entitled, "Pimps in the Pulpit." This is not my intention to expose churches or names of church leaders. As Christians we are to watch and pray. The fact remains that we do have attendee-focused churches. Within these churches the majority is not being nurtured and they are really only attendees. Together in prayer, we can make changes, be it traditional or otherwise to make the Kingdom of God advancement in the hearts of attendee's by spreading the word to be careful why they attend church in the building in this 21st century.

It is important that the Christian communities have the use of church buildings. Christians need church buildings to have fellowship gatherings, funerals, weddings, and other Christian services. However, these building should be used to glorify God. The Christians need church buildings to have regular meetings to schedule pertinent events. But, when they become places to make idol worship, then they are not following God's plan for the church.

When people come to a church building because they have the desire to be a part of what is named successful in the eyes of man, then the building is tainted with secular agendas. We are not to worship the leader or the building because they are viewed as successful. The building is to be a place to worship a holy and sovereign God of the universe.

CHARACTERTICS OF THE ATTENDEE-FOCUSED CHURCH

1. They have as their primary goal to build a successful church by attracting numbers regardless of the Word of God and cost.
2. The disciples are burned out and resentful because only a few are doing the work.
3. The pastor is the primary worker.
4. Everything revolves around the pastor.
5. Disciple-making is usually a low priority.
6. Discipleship meetings are offered if the participants have extra time.
7. Bible studies are an opportunity to share opinions, not biblical based study of the bible.
8. Membership rarely talks spiritually about life and the Word of God outside the meeting place.
9. Many people attend worship service that is not Disciples of Christ.
10. Many of the worshipers do not know each other.
11. Many worshipers do not agree with the basic teachings of the church.
12. Many of the worshipers attend solely to make business contacts.
13. Some are attending for the sake of their children so they can obtain a discount rate to their schools.
14. Some attend worship service and use the service as a social network to get a date or to find a spouse.
15. Some attend because of family tradition.
16. The pastor makes a point to give a message that will not offend his audience.
17. Most of the pastor's strong messages can be easily ignored.
18. The people are held accountable for what is being taught.
19. The pastor makes sure that he does not do anything to drive the people away.
20. The pastor has the skill of a successful politician.
21. The atmosphere of the church is that of a politician's setting.

CHARACTERISTICS OF THE DICIPLESHIP-FOCUSED CHURCH

1. The primary focus of the church is to aide the congregations to be disciples for the Kingdom of God.
2. There are a growing number of disciples that are walking with God.
3. There is an obvious and growing love between members of the church.
4. Migration of members to different locations continues and members remain in contact with each other in a loving bond.
5. Leadership keeps growing and constant development takes place.
6. The leadership needs can be easily found and tapped within the church population.
7. Leadership is primarily used within the church; therefore recruiting outside the church is not needed.
8. There is a genuine desire for discipleship training and fellowship within the church.
9. The body of the church is constantly growing in record numbers.
10. Those who are not interested in discipleship are comfortable and can be easily detected.
11. The pastor's messages are biblically sound and helpful in developing healthy Christian lives.
12. The pastor preaches the unadulterated Word of God and will not sugar coat God's Word.
13. The pastor preaches the whole counsel of God.
14. Sinners are confronted within the church.
15. There will be waves and turbulence in the church because sin will not be tolerated.
16. The church will focus on living holy lives before Christ.
17. The church will not compromise God's Word for the sake of growth.
18. The church will not adjust for those who do not like a discipleship-focused church.
19. The type of meeting held will lend itself to those of toward prayer, edification, worship, compassion, and outreach.
20. This type of church is not competitive with other churches or memberships.
21. This type of church will seek ways to cooperate with other churches with the same Godly goals.

Each potential worshiper ought to have the summary before them that describes the actual church organization. They are to have in writing the kind of church it is seeking to become. The church ought to know if they are seeking to become an attendee-focused church or a discipleship-focused church. Of course, as I emphasized earlier no church is fully one or the other. The question is which type are they committed to becoming? What is their primary focus and doctrinal approach?

The fact is that the church is primarily seeking after one type or the other. Jesus said in, Matthew 6:24 "*No one can serve two masters. Either you will hate the one and love the other, or you will be devoted to the one and despise the other. You cannot serve both God and money.* If we are serving the wrong master, we need to change masters!

THE END PRODUCT OF THE ATTENDEE-FOCUSED CHURCH

Is there any good that comes from this type of church? Many churches can be in the developmental stage and can serve a purpose in the mind of God. I do not want to give the false impression that a church is either attendee focused or discipleship-focused.

There are Christians that are a mixture of self centered at one point and presses to become more committed to God's purpose for their lives. Some churches are the same way. They are determined to live for Christ and have a driving force to increase numbers and a holy desire to build millions of disciples for Christ. The late Sister Mary Frazier, told me years ago to always look for the good in everything and emulate it.

So as I focus on the attendee-focused church, there is good that springs forth.

1. Large crowds draw big bucks. Monies can be give to missions, and many can hear the gospel if preached.
2. These churches can reach many that others may not be able to do.
3. Small group fellowships are often formed within this large church and provide a discipleship atmosphere. The opportunities present themselves if the focus is placed on discipleship.

This is the good I see, but there is a bad side.

1. The pastors of super churches can become idolized as super-stars.
2. The super-star pastors can devastate those inside of the church and have a destructive impact on those outside of the church.
3. Other members who are not super-stars are looked upon as second-class members of the church, rather than equal members of the church.
4. The rich and successful are praised and those in lower social classes are hardly even missed when they stop attending.
5. The decisions are made by those who have opposite goals for the church.
6. Committees are usually made up of disciples and attendees.
7. The elders, deacons, board, or whoever leads the church consist of a mixture of attendees and disciples.

In Proverbs 3:5-6, Solomon says, *"Trust in the Lord with all your heart and lean not on your own understanding; in all your ways acknowledge him, and he will make your paths straight."* The attendees want to lean on their own understanding and the disciples want to trust in the Lord with all their hearts. Therefore, there is much confusion in the church. Disciples know the frustration is tantamount to drawing a line in the sand.

The procedures to select the church's leaders are as follows:

1. Leaders may be voted upon (can be a popularity contest).
2. The church may choose those who have been successful outside of the church such as businessmen, lawyers, teachers, principals, administrators, etc.).
3. The church may choose leaders based on longevity of the person.
4. The church may choose those who would be offended if they are not chosen.
5. The church may choose anyone who is willing to take the office.
6. The church may choose those who are dignitaries.

America is filled with churches that experience disagreement among the church leadership. Attendees-focused churches usually do not make much progress in accomplishing God's goals, unless of course, the Disciples of Christ take control of the entire process. God gave us the formula for winning the battle against our enemy in the book of Judges.

God described the kind of soldiers needed to win a battle against the adversary. The attendee-focused church with a mixture of Christians, nominal Christians, and new comers I do not believe are the type of soldiers God is calling to do battle against Satan. This type of church has not been a threat to Satan's strongholds. In fact, Satan has entered the church and is making his impact on the church. It should be vice-versa.

This is another reason why this book is sorely needed. God is giving the churches a wake up call. Satan is making a radical impact on the church doctrines and core beliefs. Instead of the church influencing morality on the world's morality, the world's morality is influencing the church. As someone has said, "We need to get the world out of the church before we can get the church out into the world."

CHAPTER THIRTEEN

THE FINAL PRODUCT

It Is Not All Good:

T HERE IS A negative side of the discipleship-focused church. The negative side is that there is tremendous opposition from many congregants against making discipleship the highest priority focus point. Many of these opposes are selfish and do not want others to take part in the decision making opportunities in the church and Christendom.

The bible teaches us a lesson. There was strong opposition against Jesus as He made disciples. Paul says that there will be strong opposition of us as well. The ruler of darkness fights day and night to destroy the notion of churches making effective disciples. The adversary is not concerned about the singing, praising, and fellowship. He directly attacks all who has as its top priority discipleship training.

The strongest opposition to make discipleship will come from the religious community. So, there was strong opposition for Jesus and Paul that came from the religious Jews; so there will be strong opposition to those who are effective at making disciples. The so-called religious communities did not have any desire to obey the "Great Commission."

This author has a strong desire to declare that the strongest opposition the churches face are those who oppose discipleship as the primary focus of the church. In this 21st century, if the church is to survive the onslaught of negatives of the world of not being the church that God intended, then they must get about the business of building and making disciples. The Word of God records that it was the religious people who set the stage for Jesus to be crucified. It was the religious who chased Paul from city to city. It was the religious people who took part in stoning Stephen to death.

In retrospect, it was the religious people who stood in opposition to this author making disciples in the churches God assigned him to pastor. And it should not shock you to find out that there are some religious people in your church that are against making disciples. Many will say it is a waste of time. They would say that you can not change people. There will be those who will say based on the previous lifestyles; they do not deserve a chance to serve in the Kingdom of God. Do not be surprised, then, if there would be a wave of opposition to come forth and make an earnest effort to stop people from reading this book. Some people will be convinced that it is not worth the cost to make disciples. They will argue that the funds would be better spent in building a larger sanctuary. The fact of the matter is that the entire congregation will not rejoice when the church makes discipleship the highest priority in their church. Jesus made the Great Commission the highest priority. We are to trust and obey His Word. Facing the opposition is the cost we pay to trust, obey, and follow Jesus. Jesus told us to count the cost. The Dr. Eugene Peterson, one of my instructors at the Saint Mary's Seminary University recorded the Great Commission statement this way; Matthew 28:16-20 The Message (MSG).

16-17 Meanwhile, the eleven disciples were on their way to Galilee, headed for the mountain Jesus had set for their reunion. The moment they saw him they worshiped him. Some, though, held back, not sure about worship, about risking themselves totally.

18-20 Jesus, undeterred, went right ahead and gave his charge: "God authorized and commanded me to commission you: Go out and train everyone you meet, far and near, in this way of life, marking them by baptism in the threefold name: Father, Son, and Holy Spirit. Then instruct them in the practice of all I have commanded you. I'll be with you as you do this, day after day after day, right up to the end of the age."

The King James Version stated; Matthew 28:16-20 King James Version (KJV)

16. Then the eleven disciples went away into Galilee, into a mountain where Jesus had appointed them.

17. And when they saw him, they worshiped him: but some doubted.

18. And Jesus came and spake unto them, saying, all power is given unto me in heaven and in earth.

19. Go ye therefore, and teach all nations, baptizing them in the name of the Father, and of the Son, and of the Holy Ghost:

20. Teaching them to observe all things whatsoever I have commanded you: and, lo, I am with you always, even unto the end of the world. Amen.

The emphasis on making disciples comes from within your own church. Will the church obey God and listen to the words of the congregants who are in opposition?

But, there is a great deal of good in the discipleship-focused church. They will witness the love of Jesus in a way that can not be described in this book. There is a blessing on the church wherein the people will receive that makes their heart glad and will rejoice regardless to whatever state they find themselves facing. Paul's prayer for the church: *"I pray that out of his glorious riches he may strengthen you with power through his Spirit in your inner being so that Christ may dwell in your hearts through faith. And I pray that you being rooted and established in love, may have power, together with all the saints, to grasp how wide and long and high and deep is the love of Christ, and to know this love that surpasses knowledge that you may be filled to all the fullness of God."* (Ephesians 3:16-19) Jesus prayed for the church:

John 17:20-23King James Version (KJV)

20. Neither pray I for these alone, but for them also which shall believe on me through their word;

21. That they all may be one; as thou, Father, art in me, and I in thee, that they also may be one in us: that the world may believe that thou hast sent me.

22. And the glory which thou gavest me I have given them; that they may be one, even as we are one:

23. I in them, and thou in me, that they may be made perfect in one; and that the world may know that thou hast sent me, and hast loved them, as thou hast loved me.

The church that is effective in making disciples will know the love of Jesus and will be filled to the beam with His precious Holy Spirit. Paul said:

Ephesians 3:19-20 King James Version (KJV)

19. And to know the love of Christ, which passeth knowledge, that ye might be filled with all the fullness of God.

20. Now unto him that is able to do exceeding abundantly above all that we ask or think, according to the power that worketh in us,

The process of making disciples has a great by product. The newly made believers will have the experience of forgiving, the experience of God's grace on his or her life, learn to be an encourager, learn patience, kindness, the thrill of being accepted by Jesus, and being able to accept corrective criticism in love. Because of the acquired traits, the discipline will have a deeper and a greater understanding of the love of Jesus for them. They will experience the goodness of the God Head. They will know Jesus for themselves and realize that God is a *"very present help in the time of trouble."* Paul says in the verses above, *He is able to do way beyond what we think He can do in our lives and in His church! (Ephesians 3:19, 20)*

This type of church will develop an internal stability. The church at Corinth was a babe in Christ. They drunk milk and was known to squabble. They were a divided church. Paul says: *"Brothers, I could not address you as spiritual, but as worldly—mere infants in Christ .... For since there is jealousy and quarreling among you, are you not worldly? Are you not acting like mere men?"* (I Corinthians 3:1, 3) A church full of baby

Christians is a baby church and a quarreling church. A church full of matured Christians are a peace-loving, grace-giving, stable and unified church. This is the kind of church we sought to seek to be a part of.

This type of church is going to have a stable doctrine. Paul says, *"Then you will no longer be infants tossed back and forth by the waves and blown here and there by every wind of teaching and by the cunning and craftiness of men in their deceitful scheming."* This type of church is full of maturing disciples. They will grow in agreement and discernment. They will know the truth from a lie. The membership will not be easily fooled by false teachers. They will be on the watch for false prophets. God told them to watch and pray.

Matthew 7:15-20 The Message (MSG)

15-20 *"Be wary of false preachers who smile a lot, dripping with practiced sincerity. Chances are they are out to rip you off some way or other. Don't be impressed with charisma; look for character. Who preachers are is the main thing, not what they say. A genuine leader will never exploit your emotions or your pocketbook. These diseased trees with their bad apples are going to be chopped down and burned.*

Matthew 7:15-20 King James Version (KJV)

15. Beware of false prophets, which come to you in sheep's clothing, but inwardly they are ravening wolves.

16. Ye shall know them by their fruits. Do men gather grapes of thorns, or figs of thistles?

17. Even so every good tree bringeth forth good fruit; but a corrupt tree bringeth forth evil fruit.

18. A good tree cannot bring forth evil fruit; neither can a corrupt tree bring forth good fruit.

19. Every tree that bringeth not forth good fruit is hewn down, and cast into the fire.

20. Wherefore by their fruits ye shall know them.

The discipleship-focused church is stable in their doctrines.

The discipleship-focused church is filled with teachers. The book of Hebrews gives a strong reprimand to the Hebrew Christians because they were not growing in the faith. The author says, "*that they should be teachers, but instead they still needed someone to teach them*" the "*elementary truths of God's word all over again.*" (Hebrews 5:12) But, when disciples are being made, teachers will come forth. There will be many in the church, but God will identify those who are to teach His people. These teachers are not to be hand picked by leadership so that they can control what the congregants learn. They are filled with the Holy Spirit and God imparts the words of learning to their souls. It was said that one church had so many teachers that those attending a seminar knew that the pastor believes in discipleship because each of the teachers had sound doctrines and excellent training. This is a good reflection and complement to the pastor. The brand new disciples were recorded as saying he came to the seminar unlearned and left a brand new servant of God.

In a discipleship-focus church many will mature to the level of being committed to God. They will have spiritual maturity, experience in ministry, ministerial skills, and a love for the church. Perhaps they will have the same level of efficiency as the pastors and leaders of the church. In a discipleship-focused church there will be many in the community who will be blessed by their qualified and Holy Ghost filled disciples.

The discipleship-focused church will have a productive outreach program. The church that has made discipleship the core of the mission will become the salt and light of the world. For they leave the confines of the building and reach out to the lost and downtrodden. They are building disciples and not just focused on filling seats in the sanctuary. They are determined to make more and more disciples. The discipleship-focused church will have an effective spiritual plan for making disciples in such a way it will be contagious to others who watch them in action. Others will emulate the plan and the church will continue to grow in leaps and bounds.

Are you wondering why more and more people are moving away from God and have stopped attending church? Have you wondered why many churches are closing their doors? The commitment of the Christians to become disciples has been lost in the shuffle to obtain success. In this 21st century there are less committed disciples.

The early church grew tremendously because the disciples and apostles were committed. They were willing, and ready to give their lives for the cause of Christ. The biblical records show that most of them died martyrs' deaths. A church filled with people who are there for self can not expect to have the type of impact that the early church experienced.

Many Christians in America are not willing to give up their lives for the cause of Christ. They do not want to feel uncomfortable for a few moments. Many will not take a stand for the Christian way of life. This is one of the reasons why America will continue to slide downward. The church needs to follow God and so does this nation. A nation who does not have God as its leader will ultimately fall. Psalm 33:12 *Blessed is the nation whose God is the Lord, the people whom he has chosen as his heritage! Isaiah 60:12 For the nation and kingdom that will not serve you shall perish; those nations shall be utterly laid waste.* The church must take on the attitude that it is not too late. We can expect God's grace to be sufficient. We can make disciples. We are living in the last days. However, we are soldiers in God's army and we can do something about the state of our country and our world. God will allow the church to have an impact on the world. We can have a greater impact if we obey His command to make disciples. At least the church ought to be able to say like Paul.

2 Timothy 4:7-10 King James Version (KJV)

7. I have fought a good fight, I have finished my course, I have kept the faith:

8. Henceforth there is laid up for me a crown of righteousness, which the Lord, the righteous judge, shall give me at that day: and not to me only, but unto all them also that love his appearing.

The church must fight to the very end. We can not afford to do any less.

GOD'S PLAN FOR THE DEVELOPMENT OF A DISCIPLESHIP-FOCUSED CHURCH

Obstacles facing the discipleship-focused church

God never told the church it would be easy to follow Him and His precepts for Christianity. We must accept the burden and bear the cost. Jesus paved the way with His blood. The early disciples and apostles were willing to pay their cost. However, there are obstacles to overcome and only then will Jesus deem His church a success without spot or wrinkle. Listed below are a few obstacles that stand in the way of the church making disciples.

There is an invisible and relentless foe. Satan is totally opposed to God's church being successful.

Satan uses the temptations of the world to draw the church from God's plan. He tried to tempt Jesus from doing His Father's will for the church. He tried to destroy the plan for the church. He wanted Jesus to focus on the flesh, the eyes, and pride instead of God's plan for the church. Satan is still using his temptation plan against the church for the 21st century.

1 Peter 5:8 21st Century King James Version (KJ21)

> *8. Be sober, be vigilant, because your adversary the devil walketh about as a roaring lion, seeking whom he may devour.*

GOD GETS THE LAST WORD

1 Peter 5:8 The Message (MSG) by Eugene Peterson

8-11 ***Keep*** *a cool head. Stay alert. The Devil is poised to pounce, and would like nothing better than to catch you napping. Keep your guard up. You're not the only ones plunged into these hard times. It's the same with Christians all over the world. So keep a firm grip on the faith. The suffering won't last forever. It won't be long before this generous God who has great plans for us in Christ—eternal and glorious plans they are!—will have you put together and on your feet for good. He gets the last word; yes, he does.*

1 John 2:15-17 King James Version (KJV)

15. Love not the world, neither the things that are in the world. If any man loves the world, the love of the Father is not in him.

16. For all that is in the world, the lust of the flesh, and the lust of the eyes, and the pride of life, is not of the Father, but is of the world.

17. And the world passeth away, and the lust thereof: but he that doeth the will of God abideth for ever.

1 John 2:15-17 The Message (MSG)

15-17 Don't love the world's ways. Don't love the world's goods. Love of the world squeezes out love for the Father. Practically everything that goes on in the world—wanting your own way, wanting everything for yourself, wanting to appear important—has nothing to do with the Father. It just isolates you from him. The world and all it's wanting, wanting, wanting is on the way out—but whoever does what God wants is set for eternity. Satan is the creator of false teachings.

1 Timothy 4:1-4 King James Version (KJV)

1. Now the Spirit speaketh expressly, that in the latter times some shall depart from the faith, giving heed to seducing spirits, and doctrines of devils;

2. Speaking lies in hypocrisy; having their conscience seared with a hot iron;

3. Forbidding to marry, and commanding to abstain from meats, which God hath created to be received with thanksgiving of them which believe and know the truth.

4 For every creature of God is good, and nothing to be refused, if it be received with thanksgiving:

Jude 1:4 King James Version (KJV)

4. For there are certain men crept in unawares, who were before of old ordained to this condemnation, ungodly men, turning the grace of our God into lasciviousness, and denying the only Lord God, and our Lord Jesus Christ.

TEACH WITH YOUR LIFE

1 Timothy 4:1-5 The Message (MSG)

4: 1-5 The Spirit makes it clear that as time goes on, some are going to give up on the faith and chase after demonic illusions put forth by professional liars. These liars have lied so well and for so long that they've lost their capacity for truth. They will tell you not to get married. They'll tell you not to eat this or that food—perfectly good food God created to be eaten heartily and with thanksgiving by believers who know better! Everything God created is good, and to be received with thanks. Nothing is to be sneered at and thrown out. God's Word and our prayers make every item in creation holy.

Satan is the "accuser of our brothers."

Revelation 12:10 King James Version (KJV)

10. And I heard a loud voice saying in heaven, Now is come salvation, and strength, and the kingdom of our God, and the power of his Christ: for the accuser of our brethren is cast down, which accused them before our God day and night.

Revelation 12:10 The Message (MSG)

7-12 War broke out in Heaven. Michael and his Angels fought the Dragon. The Dragon and his Angels fought back, but was no match for Michael. They were cleared out of Heaven, not a sign of them left. The great Dragon—ancient Serpent, the one called Devil and Satan, the one who led the whole earth astray—thrown out, and all his Angels thrown out with him, thrown down to earth. Then I heard a strong voice out of Heaven saying,

Salvation and power are established!
Kingdom of our God, authority of his Messiah!
The Accuser of our brothers and sisters thrown out,
who accused them day and night before God.
They defeated him through the blood of the Lamb
and the bold word of their witness.
They weren't in love with themselves;
they were willing to die for Christ.
So rejoice, O Heavens, and all who live there,
but doom to earth and sea,
For the Devil's come down on you with both feet;
he's had a great fall;
He's wild and raging with anger;
he hasn't much time and he knows it.

The adversary is determined to get the church off track. He has got the church off focused in many ways. In this 21st century we have witnessed too many ways wherein the adversary has achieved a small part of his plan. The world is bragging and boosting about it in the media. Many churches have given into the ways of sexual temptation and same sex marriages. False prophets and false teaching has invaded the church and many of the congregants do not know it. Satan has ushered in a wave of condemnation and guilt that are crippling many of the churches. Satan is on the march to destroy the church. Can you imagine what will happen if the church is destroyed during our time on earth? Whether the church recognizes it or not, we as the church are being besigned by the power of the satanic. I am sounding the alarm as God is my witness. There is a question that confronts us now recorded in the book of Psalm.

Psalm 11:3 King James Version (KJV)

3 *If the foundations be destroyed, what can the righteous do?*

Psalm 11:3 The Message (MSG)

A David Psalm 11:1-3

I've already run for dear life
straight to the arms of God.
So why would I run away now
when you say,
"Run to the mountains; the evil
bows are bent, the wicked arrows
Aimed to shoot under cover of darkness
at every heart open to God.
The bottom's dropped out of the country;
good people don't have a chance"?

Satan is trying to destroy the very soul of the church.

The discipleship-focused church faces legalism. This is a difficult obstacle to fight. The book of Galatians gives us the formula to overcome legalism. What is legalism? In Christianity, legalism is the excessive and improper use of the law (10 commandments, holiness laws, etc). This legalism can take different forms. The first is where a person attempts to keep the Law in order to attain salvation. The second is where a person keeps the law in order to maintain his salvation. The third is when a Christian judges other Christians for not keeping certain codes of conduct that he thinks need to be observed.

So, we have arrogant men who set up rules and demand that churches must obey to please God. Judaism and the Pharisees were legalistic. Jesus had to overcome this to build the church. The church has to overcome this in order to continue to build successful churches in the 21st century. If we allow legalistic rules to take root in the churches, then it is very hard to get them out. Jesus warned the church about allowing legalism to take root in the church. Jesus gave strong words to the Pharisees about legalism. Matthew 23 points this out clearly. Paul's strong words to the Galatians in Galatia another point of this proof. In each case, they are some of the strongest words of condemnation that are found anywhere in the Bible. Legality is one of the favorite weapons of the enemy. Satan loves to get disciples to be legalistic. When this happen, then he has destroyed the churches enjoyment of the Spirit. He then can use the church to spread havoc among a generation or a company of believers, and ruin a vital, active, and growing Christian group.

In this 21st century, Satan has used clothing styles, length of hair, secular line sexual dancing, mime secular dancing, rewritten R&B songs, and certain demands of ritual observance to destroy the church. He uses it in a legalistic way. The question is not if it is legal, but is it Holy and does it meet God's approval. We are questioning whether these things are legal to be taking place in the House of God.

Satan has changed the intent of the Ten Commandments. There are questions in the church as to whether you may cut your lawn on Sunday or not. Satan has made the church question the kind of foods we are to eat. Satan has opened the church eyes to thinking about the behavior restrictions we are to adhere. Abortion, and use of medication are being questioned as if it is permissible. All these things can become legal when they are legislated by the government. For instance, in some states the government says it is legal to smoke marijuana. Same sex marriage is legal based on the Supreme Court ruling. In the state of Florida there is an organization that will not be allowed to receive USDA food unless they removed portraits of Christ, the Ten Commandments, a banner that reads 'Jesus is Lord' and stop giving Bibles to the needy. Legality is being used in Colorado concerning a baker who refuse to make cakes for gay wedding, but the court has ruled in favor of the baker for now. The Park Service in Missouri legally announced a new policy requiring churches that wish to hold baptisms in public waters must apply for a special permit within 48 hours in advance to baptize a believer. But, in this case the pastor took a stand against this order.

When the church refuses to back down, the church usually wins. What this means is that if enough churches take a Godly stand for their faith, they will get stronger. The world will notice that we are serious about our faith in God. There will be more believers rejoicing on what God will do.

Ray C. Steadman in his book entitled, "Legalism" states "that there are areas in which we are left free to be guided by our conscience, by instructions through His Holy Spirit, by His Word, by trusting in God in faith, and standing up for our convictions." Legality is hypocrisy when we view it through the lens of God and use a theological application to determine its meaning for the 21st century church. Often times legality is used by phony so called Christians in the marketplace. It is a false way to try to appear right, when it is plainly against God's way. This becomes a stench in the nostrils of God. God wants His church to be honest and true.

False teaching and prophets are a major obstacle in the discipleship-focused church. Jesus predicted that prior to His return that many false prophets and false religions would emerge. The disciples came to Jesus privately and said, *"Tell us, when all this will happen? What sign will signal your return and the end of the world?"* (Matthew 24:3) *"Many will come in my name, claiming, 'I am he,' and will deceive many ... For false Christ and false prophets will appear and perform signs and miracles to deceive the elect—if that were possible."*(Mark 13:6, 21) *"and many false prophets will appear and deceive many people."*(Matt 24:11) There were many letters written to the early churches to confront some form of false teaching (Romans, II Corinthians, Galatians, Colossians, I and II Thessalonians, I Timothy and I John). False teaching which presents a false and distorted view of reality is like a cancer eating up the souls and minds of the church. They can weaken and even destroy a church if God does not intervene. The church cannot recognize a false teaching unless they know the truth of the scriptures. If the church does not want to be deceived, the church must spend time studying the Holy Scriptures and know and understand what it says. If the church is not well grounded in the truth, then they will be very vulnerable to falling for any deception.

The church must put God first. Matthew 6:33 King James Version (KJV) 33 *But seek ye first the kingdom of God, and his righteousness; and all these things shall be added unto you.* The song, "I Have Decided to Follow Jesus" was penned by a Maharajah's son. His son wanted to be baptized, but his father said if he died, his son would loose his inheritance and his royal position. The son declared I will follow Jesus! So, his son took flight. This song is sung even today by many churches with a strong affirmation. They sing and declare "I Have Decided to Follow Jesus."

Most of the early Christians martyrs died horrible deaths. They had decided to seek ye first the kingdom of God. They refused to deny God as their savior. Caesar tried to force them to bow down, but they refused. Again, we must take a stand.

Sadly to say, there are many churches that are not willing to stand on their principles. They have refused to put Satan to shame. Other religions in America have refused to adhere to legality and will not compromise their beliefs. Paul said "for Christ I live, and for Christ I die." Even Olympic athletes are willing to sacrifice in pursuit of an Olympic medal.

We are living at a time when the church can no longer hide behind the church building and declare they are successful. Those who have made discipleship their priority will be given the power from God to make a difference in the world. The church that is engulfed in preaching the unadulterated gospel, exhorting Jesus, the Christ, and making Disciples of Christ will be the church that people will be looking for. The church must put God first.

There are churches that are financially strong that will do whatever it takes to get larger. They are determined to make sure that none of their attendees will not be dis-satisfied with what is preached. They are not willing to pay the cost that comes with calling Christians to become disciples of Jesus Christ. They will not jeopardize the cost of losing even a single attendee. They know that these members can become their slaves.

The church must agree to develop a different standard and definition for success. Many of the churches who have announced that they are successful have found that their ladders of success were leaning against a deteriorating wall." Their ladder was not leaning on Jesus and His tenants of faith. The church must stand on the rock of Jesus. Jesus said, "and I say unto thee, that thou art Peter, and upon this rock, I will build my church; and the gates of hell shall not prevail against it." Where is your church? My church is within me.

The apostle Paul was a success while he was in prison. There were elements in Rome who used his imprisonment to try to argue that they were the ones who were successful. Paul was declared a failure. We also need to wholeheartedly pursue God's goals even if it means that at times it appears that we are failures. The 21st century church must agree to develop a different standard and definition for the overall church.

One of the greatest obstacles to building this type of church is that we must realize that only God can build His type of church. He alone deserves and should receive the credit for building this kind of church. Solomon says, *"Except the Lord build the house, they labor in vain that build it: except the Lord keep the city, the watchman waketh but in vain" (Psalm 127:1).* Many have proud tendencies and want to build a church that they can be proud of. But, if we build the church it will be an abomination in God's eyes. When we recognize the fact that it is God who builds the church, then the church is humble. Jesus humbled Peter to see how wretched he was, and to see that good, purity, and love can only come from Him!

Another great obstacle to building this type of church is waiting on God's timing. Sometimes it will appear that God's goals for a church will not be accomplished. Sometimes a church may totally reject, and have no desire, to become a discipleship-focused church. It may appear that all have forsaken and will not embrace God's vision for the church. The pastor and the leaders may think that they are standing alone in this venture. The workers may seem to be released from the building process. But, we have to keep the faith. We can trust God to accomplish whatever He has purposed. God may embrace their vision at a later date.

The church at Corinth was led away from Paul's teachings by false teachers. But, Paul wrote them a strong letter. Again, they were committed to doing it God's way. There may be a time when Christ's ministry goes from being successful to being an apparent failure in the eyes of others. It is difficult for a church to go through times that are similar to what Jesus and His apostles went through. Our heart aches when it appears that everything is falling apart. But, the church must remember that God is a part of it. He is in the midst of it. God never fails.

There is another obstacle that the discipleship-focused church may face. Satan will use people inside and outside of the church to hemp opposition on the church. He uses people who are genuine Christians to deceive others. He will even use preachers and pastors in an effective way to destroy the church. Many preachers have suffered for the cause of Christ because other preachers wanted their position.

I remember hearing about a preacher being used by Satan. This preacher showed up periodically at a church and boldly declared that he coveted this church. Paul gave the church a comforting word about facing the enemies of the church. He said that the church should not let the sun go down on our anger, for if we hold grudges against Christian brothers and sisters we give the devil a foothold so he can use *us* to destroy each other and God's work. The author of the book of Hebrews tells the Jewish Christians of his time not to allow tough times to produce in them a "root of bitterness." Satan seeks after those he can use within the church to get a church off-track. We can be sure that Satan's opposition will increase as a church begins to make effective and fruitful disciples. The Sensational McMillan Singers wrote a song entitled *"Let the Fire Burn."* The lyrics is admonishing the church to let the Holy Spirit burn throughout the church when Satan is on the attack.

THE CHURCH CAN OVERCOME
THESE OBSTACLES.

Consider this list as to what the church can do to overcome the works of Satan against the church. It is not an exhaustive list. This is a list that is relevant for building a successful 21st century church. We need to go back to the old landmark for building a successful church. The churches primary concern should be as to what is God doing in the hearts of individuals. We are not to be concerned with how many people the church can get into the seats of a building at any cost. James' words: *"Listen my dear brothers: Has not God chosen those who are poor in the eyes of the world to be rich in faith."* Paul, who had made it in the world, became poor in the world so he could be rich toward God: *"If anyone thinks he has reasons to put confidence in the flesh, I have more: ... A Hebrew of the Hebrews, a Pharisee, as for legalistic righteousness faultless. But whatever was to my profit I now consider loss for the sake of Christ. What is more I consider everything a loss compared to the surpassing greatness of knowing Christ Jesus my Lord, for whose sake I have lost all things. **I consider them but rubbish,** that I may gain and be found in him ..."* (Philippians 3:4-8) Now, is that not an example of creating a new standard of success?

Philippians 3:4-9 The Message (MSG)

2-6 Steer clear of the barking dogs, those religious busybodies, all bark and no bite. All they're interested in is appearances—knife-happy circumcises, I call them. The real believers are the ones the Spirit of God leads to work away at this ministry, filling the air with Christ's praise as we do it. We couldn't carry this off by our own efforts, and we know it—even though we can list what many might think are impressive credentials. You know my pedigree: a legitimate birth, circumcised on the eighth day; an Israelite from the elite tribe of Benjamin; a strict and devout adherent to God's law; a fiery defender of the purity of my religion, even to the point of persecuting the church; a meticulous observer of everything set down in God's law Book.

7-9 The very credentials these people are waving around as something special, I'm tearing up and throwing out with the trash—along with everything else I used to take credit for. And why? Because of Christ. Yes, all the things I once thought were so important are gone from my life. Compared to the high privilege of knowing Christ Jesus as my Master, firsthand, everything I once thought I had going for me is insignificant—dog dung. I've dumped it all in the trash so that I could embrace Christ and be embraced by him. I didn't want some petty, inferior brand of righteousness that comes from keeping a list of rules when I could get the robust kind that comes from trusting Christ—God's righteousness.

Jesus replaced being served with serving as a sign of greatness. He demonstrated greatness when He washed the disciples' feet. We, in our churches, need to create a new standard of success. And because the world is continually inundating us with its version of success, we can never stop holding God's measurement of success before our people!

The Bible is the Word of God and is the only fully dependable guide to success in His church. If we are seeking to build a successful church business, then we can look in many directions for advice and guidance on how to build a successful business. The people can use the marketing plan of the business world and hire an MBA graduate to implement the principals to build a successful business church. We can seek to build our church in a way very similar to the way in which a business seeks to build success. We can go to seminars throughout the U.S. and the international world using the model we think is successful. Now, there is nothing wrong with benefiting those who have been able to successfully apply biblical principles. But, there has been too much emphasis on duplicating what appears to be successful in eyes of the world, even if it is being done by a church that has very questionable biblical teachings and practices. Please remember that their wall is fallible and has deteriorated. But, if we are seeking to build disciples according to the command of Jesus, then we are seeking to build up the Body of Christ through the power of the Holy Spirit. This is the best advice we can find. The solution is encased in the Bible.

Almost 95% of the people surveyed indicate that the church as it knows it is nothing more than a business. There is nothing wrong with using business principals to run the business side of a church operation. But the church ought to be a sacred business that is as a divinely empowered fellowship of supernaturally born-again believers that is operating in Holiness, and totally governed by the sovereign God of the universe.

If this is not the case, then the Bible's instructions informs us that the church has, by default, been looked upon as being irrelevant and is out of order. The bible for thousands of years has been the private devotional manual for disciples of Christians, rather than a business manual that has been misused by false prophets to extort funds to line their pockets. How do we overcome the difficult obstacles that face the discipleship-focused church? In short, we need to fully follow the pattern of Jesus and the apostles, no matter what the cost.

It is obvious that we have built churches using man-made strategies. Yes, we have built in some ways successful business churches. Now, lets concentrate and prayerfully build churches that make disciples and make use of these disciples to the glory of God. We seek to make use of these buildings to make disciples of those whom God has called. We must recognize that there are those who have been planted in the midst to empower the work of the adversary and to destroy the very works of Christ.

The bible is relevant and this is the time to stand up for Jesus. For we need God's guidance as never before, as we approach what appears to be the very last days of the church. God is coming back for a church without spot or wrinkle. We are ready to do this work. He has put us in the position. Let us work together to build up the branch of Zion. Let us together move to the next higher dimension in Christ to the glory of God.

The church must let Jesus be the model for the church. We need to make "making disciples" the highest priority in our churches. The early church laid the foundation. The spirit of God breathes on the church. Jesus made a promise to the church. There is not a better time than in the 21st century to let God's glory shine in all churches until He comes again. We can not afford to move the ancient landmark.

The early church was commanded to build disciples. It is now time for our blessing to become manifold. God says, *the first shall be last the last shall be first.* This is the day that we are to begin mentioning the fact that our churches have disciples and are ready to speak truth to power. This is the day that God's disciples are to be mentioned from the pulpits that God has empowered them to make more disciples. The church is ready to submit their plan to God and to promote disciples to be used on the battlefield.

God wants each church to move to a higher dimension in the Lord. The main priority in the early church was to train disciples. Somehow, the church missed this opportunity. Only a few remnant churches stayed on course. *Jesus said in Matthew 7:13-14 "Enter by the narrow gate; for wide is the gate and broad is the way that leads to destruction, and there are many who go in by it. 14 Because[a] narrow is the gate and difficult is the way which leads to life, and there are few who find it. Wide is the way to destruction but narrow is the road to righteousness."* This author and pastor has been given the authority to admonish the modern day church to train disciples and to encourage other churches to make discipleship their priority. Tear out the false foundation and replace it with discipleship prioritization. It is time for an examination. Even if the church is on point, an evaluation is always in order.

These are certainly the last days on earth. We are to take note as to what Jesus did on His last days on earth. Jesus chose to devote the last part of His ministry on earth to spending time with His closest followers. For the leadership of the church, our last days ought to be spent devoting our time with our disciples in the concerted effort of making disciples. Some of that time, He spent with only the twelve. There were other times that He was alone with Peter, James, and John. If Jesus devoted the most important days and hours of His life to building a few disciples, should not the most important part of our church's schedule be devoted to building disciples? We need to devote the prime time in our churches to training a group of men and women who will in turn train and build other men and women. Do not try to expel women from the circle. Jesus also spent time with a group of women. Many of these women were with Him when He was on the cross. America and the entire world needs the leadership of the church. America is on a downward path and it is time for the church to take the lead as they follow Jesus.

Our nation is turning from God, the One True God of the Bible, at breakneck speed. The Word of God has never been so rejected in America as it is in this 21st century. We can see the results of filling the seats in church and not making disciples. Christians have not been so shallow, weak, driven by worldly desires, and led to the slaughter by deceptive leaders as now. The church must immediately get on the job and start making disciples. The world is thinking that Christianity is in favor of the course of action that is taken place in America and in our churches.

There are questions that we must ask Christians. How can a believing Christian stand up and vote and openly declare to support politicians who stand against biblical truths? God will hold these individuals accountable. America was at its best when it was truly a God-fearing nation. Even though many say that America was never a Christian nation. We must admit we had more churches confessing and practicing God as their Savior than now. And the more ungodly this nation has become, the weaker this nation has become in every aspect. Things have been happening that history has never recorded. Such as:

1. Pope Francis became the first pope to emerge from Latin America.
2. Two homemade bombs ripped through the crowd of fans and runners at the Boston Marathon finish line, killing three and wounding nearly 300 others.
3. Another legal issue that divided the country this year is gay marriage.
4. The worst storm of the year hit the Philippines on Nov. 8, destroying nearly everything in its path and leaving more than 5,000 people dead.
5. Typhoon Haiyan was one of the strongest storms ever recorded in history.
6. The United States government was forced to shut down in October following Congress's failure to pass spending bills to fund the government.

When a nation honors God great things happen for the nation. The nation is honored and respected by all nations. God will bless a nation who owns Him as their creator. These things will happen.

1. The nation is fruitful in every way and place.
2. The nation has military strength and God will fight their battles.

3. The nation has monetary freedom, they will lend to others and shalt not borrow.
4. The nation will lead not follow.

But when a nation, including America turns from God, all kinds of curses come. America is experiencing some of these now.
1. The nation's food supply is foreign;
2. The nation's financial system is foreign;
3. The nation's military is stretched too tight;
4. The nation's leaders are the tail and not the lead;
5. The nation's will become perverted and corrupt,
6. And God has removed His hand of blessing!

Our only hope is to turn to God, the author and finisher of the Universe. Many of the scholars and leaders say that there is a connection between God and the government. Many of them are disciples of Jesus, the Christ. They believe in the infallible Word of God. "Blessed is the nation whose God is the LORD." PS. 33:12; *"The wicked shall be turned into Hell, and all the nations that forget God."* Psalm 9:17

It is not a secret in America and outside of America that this nation has turned from God, and God has turned from America! Many do not believe that America has ever holy accepted God. But, we know that many churches once diligently made disciples and trusted God. God honored America because of these saints of God. The only way to explain the unusual phenomenon's of this 21st century is to look at them in the light of the Holy Bible! It is the only foundation in which any nation can use as a foundation level. The scriptures are plain and to the point. Psalm 33:12 *Blessed is the nation whose God is the Lord, the people whom he has chosen as his heritage!* Isaiah 60:12 *For the nation and kingdom that will not serve you shall perish; those nations shall be utterly laid waste.*

In the 21st century small groups are important. Also in the early church small were very important parts of the structure of the early church. "Every day they continued to meet together in the temple courts. They broke bread in their homes and ate together with glad and sincere hearts." We have discipleship-focused churches that emulate the actions of the early churches. These churches are being blessed. The author can testify to this scripture as being totally correct. (Acts 2:46) They met as a large group in the temple, but they also met in small groups in homes. We know that the churches that were later started in cities outside of Israel met in homes. Part of the discipleship structure in our churches need to take place in homes or small groups. Jesus' small group emphasis was the twelve.

There needs to be times set apart for instruction. In Acts 19:9-10, we learn that Paul took his followers to a lecture hall and taught them there for two years. This type of instruction may have been similar to our Seminaries, Bible schools, and Sunday school classes. So, there is a place for this type of instruction. We need to promote our instructional classes in the church and seek to involve as many as possible in them.

We need to showcase our living disciples not when they have deceased, but while they are living every opportunity available. The pastor is not the only person whom God is using. The leadership must do more than instruct, the leadership must pass on a lifestyle. The leadership must disciple by becoming involved in each disciple's lives. Many of the leaders refuse to shake hands with other disciples, nevertheless become involved. One would wonder what is the real reason not being involved in other saints lives. Jesus chose twelve to be with Him. Our church leaders and the members of the church also need to be choosing at least twelve to be with them.

The church needs to pray for a vision and together let that vision take place in the church. The book of Acts provides us with a description of God powerfully working in the church and through the church. In the book of Acts, God has given us a vision of what He desires to do in and through the 21st century churches. In the book of Ephesians, Paul describes what God desires for the church. The vision we find in these chapters is as follows: we see him, praying that Jesus Christ would be at home in their lives, that He would fill their lives, that they might live and love as He lived and loved, that they together might become an expression of every dimension of Jesus' love, and that they might together be Christ's Godly disciples through whom He expresses Himself. Today, we need to confidently, and with faith, declare God's vision for our church. Where does God want us to go? And where will God empower us to go, if we fully trust and obey Him? Without this type of vision and faith, it is very much like starting on a trip with no idea at all of where we are going. We do not get anywhere, because we do not have any idea of where to go. Because of lack of vision less churches are not seeking God's vision for their churches in the first place, they do not get to where God wants them to go.

God gave Abraham a vision of what He wanted to do through Him. God gave Moses a vision for what He desired to do through him. We need to pray and ask God what He desires to do through us individually and through our local church. He will give us the power and resources to do what He desires for us to do.

We need to be willing to fail and to learn from our failures. One of the greatest costs that we must be willing to pay if we are going to build God's church God's way is that we need to be willing to fail. God's people through the ages have only been able to be truly successful after they failed. Moses totally failed to deliver the people of Israel from the Egyptians when he killed an Egyptian that was beating a Hebrew. After forty years in the wilderness tending sheep he was ready to be used by God to rescue the nation of Israel from Egypt. Peter failed horribly when He denied Jesus, but he was used by God to preach a message of salvation at the Feast of Pentecost; a message that brought Jesus' church into existence. For us to do God's work, we must first totally fail at doing God's work our way.

Failure played an important role in Paul's life. Paul had been forced out of Ephesus by a mob. Paul said at this time: *"We were under great pressure, far beyond our ability to endure, so that we despaired even of life. Indeed, in our hearts we felt the sentence of death. But this happened that we might not rely on ourselves but on God who raises the dead. We always carry around in our body the death of Jesus, so that the life of Jesus may also be revealed in our body. For we who are alive are always being given over to death for Jesus' sake, so that his life may be revealed in our mortal body. So, then death is at work in us, but life is at work in you."* (II Corinthians 1:8, 9, 4:10-12)

Our natural human tendency is to seek to build the church with our own strength, for our own selfish purposes. That part of us must die, before we can be used by God to build the church with His strength and for His pure reasons. *Real* love and real dedication only comes from God's Spirit. God uses the trials in our lives, His Word, correction by Christian friends, preaching, and His sovereign ordering of events to put to death our old life, so that we can do a new work in the power of His Spirit.

How can we be used by God to build a church that is truly successful? We must be willing to become the last before we can be first. We need to be willing to be poor before we can become rich. We must become a church full of servants before we will be a truly successful church before God.

We need to do our work in the power of the Holy Spirit. Listen to why Paul was able to do the work in the early church because he said, *"we proclaim him, admonishing and teaching everyone with all wisdom, so that we may present everyone perfect in Christ. To this end I labor, struggling with all his energy, which so powerfully works in me."* (Colossians 1:28, 29) When we die to our own goals and desires and are fully committed to what God desires to do in the church and the world, then we begin to experience His power to do His work. We are not going to be empowered by God to build a successful church that will glorify us, but we will be empowered by Him when our motives have been purified by trials and by the word of God. God's work will be tiring, for Paul says in these verses that were quoted that he struggled or agonized. But, we will never be alone or powerless in this struggle. Jesus Himself said He would be in the yoke with us. (Matthew 11:28-30) In God's work, we need to be continually depending on God to lead us and to empower us. As was mentioned earlier, if God does not build the church, we will have labored in vain.

We need to love those we are disciplining with a father's and a mother's love. *For you know we dealt with each of you as a father deals with his own children, encouraging, comforting and urging you to live lives worthy of God, who calls you into his kingdom and glory.* (I Thessalonians 2:11) If making disciples is a work of love then it is a work of God. We care and pray about our children no matter where they go and no matter what they do. There are times, of course, when parents become cold toward their children. We are to passionately care for those we reach out to in the church and seek to disciple them with a parent's love.

We need to seek to obey Jesus' Great Commission in spite of opposition. Listen to the way Paul worked in one church: *"we dared to tell you this gospel in spite of strong opposition"* (I Thessalonians 2:2) A regular part of what Paul faced as he sought to establish churches was opposition. He was stoned, whipped, imprisoned, vilified, and chased, but he never backed off from what he had been called to do. So, we should not back off from what we have been called to do, no matter how much opposition we may face.

Paul was totally focused on what God desired for His church. He pursued that goal even against the strongest opposition. Because he was empowered by God, he was able to persevere in seeking to build God's church God's way right up to his last days on earth. In the last chapter of II Timothy, the last book that Paul wrote before he died, he tells us that he had fought the good fight. Fighting this good fight would soon cost him his life at Nero's hand, but he was confident that there was a crown on the other side of death. Can we expect to build God's church God's way with any less of a commitment to God's work?

We need to use God's armor so we can be victorious over our spiritual enemies. We need to continually remember that our enemies are not men, but invisible spiritual beings who are relentlessly warring against us. Paul lists in Ephesians 6, our spiritual armor. Also, throughout the Bible we are given instructions concerning our enemy and how to be triumphant in our war with him and his forces. We need to know the truth so that we will recognize demon-inspired teaching. We need to resist temptation and pursue what is pure. We need to remember that there is no longer any condemnation because of what Jesus did for us on the cross. We need to flee from anything that is part of the occult. We need to draw near to God, and if we do draw near to Him, we need to be confident that He will draw near to us.

We need to confront false teaching. Paul did not just accept that there will always be false teaching, and then go on with his work of disciplining. He strongly confronted false teaching. In the book of Galatians, he strongly confronts legalism: *"I am astonished that you are so quickly deserting the one who called you by the grace of Christ and are turning to a different gospel—which is really not a different gospel at all."* Evidently some people are throwing you into confusion and are trying to pervert the gospel of Christ. But even if we or an angel from heaven should preach a gospel other than the one we preached to you, let him be eternally condemned!" Should we be softer on false teaching than Paul was? Paul saw it as a destructive cancer that needed radical surgery to keep it from being destructive in Christ's Body and to keep it from spreading. The apostle Paul and the apostle John were continually dealing with false teaching in their letters. Today, some would discourage us from confronting false teachers. It is looked upon as unloving. Is it unloving to expose Satan's lies? Paul obviously did not think so.

Our churches will not be what God desires them to be if we continue to be soft on the cancerous false teaching that seeks to worm its way into our churches. Listen to Paul's words in Acts 20:29-31: *"I know that after I leave, savage wolves will come in among you and will not spare the flock. Even from your own number men will arise and distort the truth in order to draw away disciples after them. So be on your guard!"*

We need to seek out those who will be faithful disciples, so that they can faithfully disciple others. Jesus and Paul also focused on those who wanted to be disciples and who were willing to pay the cost necessary to be disciples. Paul encouraged Timothy to seek out faithful men who would learn from him and then pass on what they had learned from him to still more faithful people. (II Timothy 2:2) We, in our modern world cannot find a better way to build God's Kingdom than the method that was used by Jesus and Paul. They sought out the Peters, Jameses, Johns, Timothys, and they poured their lives into them. We also need to prayerfully seek out those who are poor in spirit and are willing to leave everything else behind to follow Jesus Christ. Then, we need to pour our lives into them.

We need to choose godly leaders. An essential component for developing a discipleship-focused church is that we need to choose those who have been true disciples and who have matured in their faith to be the leaders in our churches. As was mentioned earlier, if we have a mixture of attendees and disciples as leaders, we will bog down; and it is very unlikely that we will make progress toward God's goals for the church. In I Timothy 3 and Titus 1 there is a list of qualifications for elders and deacons. It is essential that we use God's list of qualifications for selecting our leaders, and it is essential that we do not use some other method for choosing our church leaders.

We need to choose leaders in the church who have demonstrated that they are servants in their homes and the church. For the work of being a church leader is not like being on a board of directors of a corporation, but we are to choose those who are committed to serving Christ as a way of life. Leading in the church means they are to be leaders in service. As will be emphasized in the next section, leading by example is an essential part of training the church for its work of ministry. Listen to Paul's final words to the elders at Ephesus: *"In everything I did, I showed you that by this kind of hard work we must help the weak, remembering the words the Lord Jesus himself said: 'It is more blessed to give than to receive.'"* (Acts 20:35) We are not to choose leaders who want to be lords over the church, but leaders who have given themselves to God and who will serve and shepherd the church towards God's goals for His church.

Church leaders are to lead by setting an example for the rest of the church. The two letters to Timothy were Paul's instructions to Timothy about church life, the Christian ministry, and disciple-making. We should not be surprised that there are instructions in these two letters that will be critical and essential in developing discipleship-focused churches. Listen to what Paul says to Timothy about the importance of setting the right example for other Christians to follow: *"Don't let anyone look down on you because you are young, but set an example for the believers in speech, in life, in love, in faith, and in purity … Be diligent in these matters; give yourself wholly to them, so that everyone will see your progress. Watch your life and your doctrine closely. Persevere in them, because if you do, you will save both yourself and your hearers."* (I Timothy 4:12, 15, 16) *"But you, keep your head in all situations, endure hardship, do the work of an evangelist, and discharge all the duties of your ministry."* (II Timothy 4:4) We do not make disciples by just what we say, but it is both by what we say and what we do! It was not just Jesus' words that influenced His apostles, it was His life. A godly example is an essential ingredient in developing discipleship-focused churches.

We need to be continually teaching God's Word: Listen to some more instructions given to Timothy by Paul: *"Until I come, devote yourself to the public reading of the Scripture, to preaching and to teaching."* (I Timothy 4:13) *"All Scripture is God-breathed and is useful for teaching, rebuking, correcting and training in righteousness so that the man of God may be thoroughly equipped for every good work."* God's Word, the truth, must take center-stage in the up-building of Christians. Attempting to summarize each of these subjects in this list is difficult, for a book could easily be written on each of these subjects. In short, the Bible is the spiritual food that is absolutely essential for spiritual growth. Secondly, the Bible is our one map for guidance in the spiritual life. If we do not continually concentrate on its teachings, we will get off course. In our churches, we should continuously be busy feeding our church members with Gods' word to ensure that each member of the church is receiving the spiritual diet that will most help them to grow, be healthy, and flourish as fruitful Christians. We should continuously be busy giving them the spiritual guidelines in the Bible that will help them to stay on God's narrow way, and that will protect them from being enticed down one or more of Satan's many paths that lead away from God.

We need to lovingly correct and rebuke our fellow Christians. Listen to Paul's instructions to Timothy" *"In the presence of God and of Christ Jesus, who will judge the living and the dead, and in view of his appearing and his kingdom, I give you this charge: preach the word; be prepared in season and out of season; correct, rebuke, and encourage with great patience and careful instruction."* In Paul's letter to Titus we are surprised by these strong words: *"Even one of their own prophets has said, 'Cretans are always liars, evil brutes, and lazy gluttons. This testimony is true. Therefore, rebuke them strongly, so that they will be sound in the faith."* (Titus 1:13) *Even elders are to be rebuked when they sin.* (I Timothy 5:20)

The temptation is for us to only tell people what they want to hear. The book of Proverbs is clear: a fool despises correction, but a wise man benefits from it. *"Better is open rebuke than hidden love. Wounds from a friend can be trusted, but an enemy multiplies kisses."* (Proverbs 27:5-6) *(See also Proverbs 9:7-9, 10:17, and 12:1)* Discipleship will not be effective without correction and rebuke. Those in attendance-focused churches do little correcting, for their main goal is to keep their attendees coming. In discipleship-focused churches, rebukes are essential to keep Christians growing. If they turn away from the truth spoken in love, they are foolish and are unwilling to hear the truth about themselves; but if they receive the correction, they will grow and learn from your loving correction.

We need to encourage our fellow Christians. In Paul's instructions to Timothy, he was told to teach and rebuke with perseverance, but he was also told to encourage his fellow Christians. In one of the best known verses in the Bible, the author of Hebrews talks about the importance of encouragement in the church: *"Let us not give up meeting together, as some are in the habit of doing, but let us encourage one another—and all the more as you see the Day approaching.* In most cases, Christians will not become all they can become in their Christian lives without someone encouraging them regularly. And as Paul told Timothy, *we are to encourage others "with great patience."* (II Timothy 4:2)

We need to be continually praying for each other. Paul often mentioned in his letters that he was constantly in prayer for his disciples

(See Philippians 1:3-6,9-11; Colossians 1:3,9; I Thessalonians 1:2; and II Timothy 1:3). He also exhorted those in the churches to be continually in prayer: "and pray in the Spirit on all occasions with all kind of prayers and requests. With this in mind, be alert and always keep on praying for all the saints." (Ephesians 6:18) If Paul found prayer indispensable, can we build a discipleship-focused church without a total commitment to prayer? If prayer was an essential part of Paul's discipleship-building, so prayer must be an essential part of our work!

I have listed and briefly described several essentials that are needed for building a discipleship-focused church. Can we build this type of church without even one or two of them? For example, can we build disciples without correction, without encouragement, or without prayer? Our list is not exhaustive, but everything that has been listed is clearly an essential part of God's program for building His church.

Paul is a prime example for us of what it takes to build disciples and to build the Body of Christ. He loved, he was compassionate, he forgave, he corrected, he spoke the truth, he was humble and he never gave up. He was knocked down, but he was never knocked out. In our modern-day churches, we need Paul's style of leadership, not corporation CEO's. We need those who passionately care for everyone inside the church and outside the church, not those who are seeking to make a name for themselves.

There is no easy way to develop a discipleship-focused church. That is undoubtedly why we are often so willing to be satisfied with something less than what God desires for the church. It is much easier and less costly to develop a church that, as some have said, is a mile wide and an inch deep. Are we in our Twentieth First Century America, with all our riches and conveniences, willing to pay the cost that is necessary to build a church that truly fulfills the Great Commission? This type of church dedicated to prayer and to making disciples in the power of God's Spirit will have an impact on our world. Some will hate the light, but there will also be many who will be drawn to the light.

I will close this chapter with my testimony in the midst of this 21st century to my family, friends, readers, and of my church family New Shiloh Baptist Church, Baltimore, MD. I will give the same closing signature (Looking Unto Christ) as the late Rev. Dr. Harold A. Carter, Sr. of the same church, wherein his son the Rev. Dr. Harold Carter, Jr. is the current pastor. I testify and summarize my training unto my ministries in this statement that keeps me focused on discipleship. The late Dr. Carter would sign his letters, "Looking Unto Christ." He encouraged this author to do the same. He said sign the letter, pray, and think about your testimony.

This author gives this testimony to the saints. I am a part of the fellowship of Jesus, the Christ and I'm not ashamed of the gospel of Jesus the Christ. I know I got the Holy Ghost. The dye has been caste on me through my father, mother, and countless saints of God. I was called by my name by God to preach. I've got to preach this gospel, for it is the power unto salvation. I step over the line. I've seen the rainbow sign while being wet miraculously by the midday dew and rain that no humankind has seen. I've been shown the rainbow sign. The decision has been made. I am a disciple of Jesus, the Christ. I'm not going to look back, let up, slow down, take a back seat, or be quiet. I'm yelling "go ahead" anywhere I can give a witness. My past has been redeemed, my present has been sanctified, and my future has been prophetical. I am redeemed and set free. What I am doing makes sense. My future is secure. I'm done with lowdown living. Praise God my future is secure. I don't need preeminence, position, promotions, plaudits, or popularity to keep me going. I don't need to be recognized, praised, or rewarded by people. I'm walking by faith and not by sight. The Lord is with me. My work is a labor of love. I'm lifted by prayers of the righteousness of God. God has given me much patience to carry on. God has given me comforting power beyond my faintest dream. My goal is heaven. I'm going to see Jesus one day. I know the road is narrow and the way will be rough at times. But still I fight onward. Sometimes the way gets so hard. My companions are few and my friends are fewer. But, I want you to know that my guide is reliable. I am focused and my mission is clear. My call is undeniable. I cannot be bought, compromised, detoured, lured away, turned back, deluded or delayed, because Jesus holds the key. God is leading and guiding me. I will not flinch in the face of sacrifice, hesitate in the presence of the enemy to quote the gospel, pander at the pool of popularity to speak truth to power, or meander in the maze of mediocrity. I won't give up, be shut up or shush up, until I have stayed up, stored up, prayed up, paid up, and preached up for the cause of Christ. If knocked down God will pick me up. I am a disciple of Jesus. I will go and must go until Jesus comes, must give until God stops giving, preach until there is no place to preach, and work until God stops me. And, when God comes for His own, He will have no problem, for I will be somewhere waiting to hear Him say well done thou good and faithful servant. God will not have a problem recognizing me for my banner will be clear. This chapter will be closed in faith "Looking Unto Christ."

When is the church truly successful? We are successful when we are making disciples who can write their testimony as a reflection on the way they live and plan to live. They must be willing to following Jesus all the way from earth to heaven. Now, we are beginning to understand what a disciple of Christ really is. We are beginning to understand what a successful church really is.

Is a church of 10,000 successful if it is only producing lukewarm, double-minded Christians? Is a church of twenty successful if it is producing whole hearted, single-minded disciples with a testimony that points that they will be obedient to the word of God? Were not Peter, James, and John like other pastors that were commanded to follow the commands of God?

Christian tradition tells us that the eleven disciples that Jesus built all were willing to fully follow Christ no matter what it cost them. That is the type of disciples Jesus built, and the type of disciple Paul and the apostles built, and it is the type of disciple that Jesus wants us to build today in our churches. If we are building this type of disciple, we will have successful churches and we will make an obvious impact on our world.

FIVE AMERICAN MYTHS OF SUCCESSFUL CHURCHES AND MINISTRIES

MYTH #1: The Size of the Church Shows Success.

There are some churches in the USA that have grown by the thousands within the first few years of their existence. That may not seem odd in certain parts of the world where the Spirit of the Lord is blowing upon a nation for true revival and evangelism (for example, Brazil, Africa, Indonesia). Unfortunately, most of the time in America, churches that number in the thousands after only a year or two of existence usually have grown so large via "transfer growth" (people who are already saved jumping from one church to another).

This happens usually in two ways: either a celebrity church (a church with an already established worldwide name brand) with a lot of money plants a church, or a celebrity leader (well-known TV personality) with a large following and mailing list opens up a church. In some cases a church without a prior name brand explodes in growth because of their talented worship team, great administrative ability, marketing schemes, or charismatic preacher, and happens to be planted in an area in the midst of many small congregations that don't offer the same level of excitement through its programs, marketing and presentation.

When churches grow like this I usually don't fault the pastors of mega churches unless they are specifically targeting a Christian audience in their marketing and even service times. For example, when they advertise on Christian media outlets or choose a time on Sunday to initially meet when most churches don't have church services, like 6 pm.

Mega church pastors can't be blamed for people leaving other churches if they have not been properly discipled or rooted and grounded in the faith. However, at the same time I do not hold up these churches as models for church growth because they are not growing organically through converting the lost, and because most likely they are gathering an uncommitted crowd rather than a true church that has members relating to one another as a family of families. (There is also a lot of turnover in these kinds of mega churches, with a different crowd every year.)

In mega churches even much of the pastoral staff eventually gets hired from outside the church because many times they do not have the capacity to develop their own leaders fast enough to keep up with their rapid growth! This can perpetuate a cycle of having a hireling and/or a professional mentality among the key staff that are not committed to long-term tenure and to the community they presently serve.

Unfortunately many saints with low self-esteem or ego need to attend one of these "successful" churches because they feel it gives them status. This is a far cry from the early church that numbered in the thousands after the Day of Pentecost because of mass conversions and the contemporary persecuted church (for example, in Muslim nations) who often meet from house-to-house, break bread, and covenant with one another as brothers and sisters, and are willing to risk their lives for the gospel by being baptized!

I am all for explosive church growth: the kind of church growth that involves mostly new converts rather than transfer growth. I am not necessarily opposed to quick mega church growth but neither am I enthralled by it or hold it up as a model for true or church expansion.

MYTH #2: The Amount of the Budget Shows Success.

Another way I have noticed people measure success in this nation is by the amount of money that comes in to support their programs. When I am in some leadership meetings, besides asking how many people attend church on Sunday, the other question that is sometimes asked is how big is the church's budget? This is not a question that should be asked by matured leaders unless out of necessity in a counseling or mentoring situation.

Another way people inflate their budget is by selling trinkets, holy handkerchiefs or holy water from the Jordan River! There are even false prophets who bring in large wads of cash because they give prophetic words on the phone for a certain fee! Having large amounts of money may not always show God's blessing because it can also come through fleshly manipulation!

MYTH #3: The Celebrity Status of the Leader Shows Success.

There are many leaders presently on television and radio. Their celebrity status has meant that these ministers are a success in the eyes of the typical American believer. However, I know many incredible preachers, teachers and ministers who are not well known outside of their communities who shun the media spotlight because they want to focus all their time and energy on the territory and the people that God has called them to!

Just because someone is well known doesn't necessarily mean God's favor and blessings are upon them. Unfortunately we have seen too many celebrity leaders living double lives. This means they started off correctly and then fell into sin or they lifted themselves up by smart marketing and were never lifted up by God to begin with!

When we lift ourselves up we eventually fall; when God lifts us up

He gives us the grace to deal with the spotlight without falling into pride because He only lifts us up into prominence when we are spiritually and emotionally mature enough to handle it. However, because of our inherent sin nature even mature leaders sometimes fall into sin because of pride or pressure. So we are all fragile and must always seek the Lord for long-lasting success!

MYTH #4: The Title of the Leader Shows Success.

In the past 37-plus years of ministry, I have seen many people who call themselves Apostle, Bishop, Chaplain, or Reverend that did not have the ministry, training, or the fruit to back it up. There are some people with small Sunday gatherings in their living rooms who print business cards and call themselves bishop or apostle in spite of having no oversight of other pastors, congregations or bona fide leaders!

The reason for this is because many believers equate success with the status that comes with a title. This quick way of achieving status seduces those who come out of a background of low self-esteem who need to be called Bishop, Apostle, or Pastor even though they have never been trained, developed and commissioned as such by a legitimate spiritual father.

In their desire to feel good about themselves they lay claim to titles they never earned or were called to, thus making a mockery of the faith and watering down these titles for many legitimate leaders who now shun these titles because so much overuse has cheapened their meaning!

MYTH #5: The Affluent Lifestyle of the Leader Shows Success.

Although I truly believe that God financially blesses and provides for believers when they seek first His kingdom (Matthew 6:33), I also believe that Christians should pursue a life of simplicity rather than extravagance, especially in this day of financial scandal and abuse! There is an unspoken assumption in certain segments of the church today in which a minister is judged by the style and expense of the suits they wear and cars they drive. They will think nothing of spending several thousand dollars for a custom-fit suit because it is necessary to keep up the appearance of God's blessing and success.

Although I have no problem with leaders wearing nice designer suits or driving an expensive car, I believe it is wrong for a leader to feel pressured to go into debt to purchase suits or cars so they can "fit in" while at the same time they cannot adequately provide for their family and/or put undue stress on their church and ministry. Besides, driving fancy cars and wearing nice suits are not always signs of prosperity because sometimes even poor people pull up for church in a Mercedes wearing fancy suits even though they may be virtually homeless or live in a small basement apartment!

I remember that in the early 1980s I was so embarrassed of driving an old car on the parking lot with Mercedes and high price cars on the lot. I would park the vehicle away from those fancy and luxurious cars. There are cases that the more you attempt to flaunt your prosperity the more it is a sign of lack! Some of the richest people I know dress very casually with jeans, tennis shoes, and wear inexpensive watches and drive old cars. They refuse to buy luxury cars and dress extravagant when those around them are asking for help. Now, again, and when I have really finished, I close the specific chapter by saying, "Looking Unto Christ."

CHAPTER FOURTEEN

THE POWER TO GET WEALTH

THERE ARE MANY schools of thought on how to get wealth. Millions of authors since the beginning of time have written scores of information on how to get wealth and keep it. This author has had the opportunity to study with some of the greatest minds on how to become a millionaire. Perhaps, you are interested in knowing how to get wealth in this 21st century.

This power that I will be writing about for the most part was not taught in schools nor was it discussed in the circle of millionaires that shared with me around the dinner table or golf course. The discussion that I may discuss is filled with revelations from God and practical and educational experiences. The real question is: are you seeking wealth from God or are you seeking wealth from the adversary? There is a big difference in how to get the wealth that God has for you and how to get the wealth that the devil promises.

Now, you are wondering how can I get the wealth that God has for me. Perhaps you have been waiting for a blessing to flow your way since you found out that it exist. This author must admit that many people have not and will not experience the biblical prosperity because of the misunderstanding of the spiritual progression which brings the manifestation of the blessing into fruition. It has been said that almost every person can quote Deuteronomy 8:18 which says: "*but thou shalt remember the Lord thy God: for it is He that giveth thee power to get wealth, that He may establish His covenant which He sware unto thy fathers, as it is this day."* There are several important points that must be understood as this scripture relates to getting wealth.

Most people start thinking about getting the wealth. However, the scripture is about you. Yes, it is about you. It is you that makes this wealth materialize as God works in you. The second point is that you are to remember God in the process of getting wealth. Also, it is imperative that you remember Him after you get the wealth. Many get the wealth and forget to remember how they got where they are. We are to remember that God gave you the brain, the strength of the body to work, and the skill set to create certain possibilities. My late father, James G. McMillan always reminded me that *"we are who we are and where we are because of who is working in us, build your hope in Christ, Jesus."* Therefore, armed with this information, we can not boast in ourselves because we live and have our being in Christ Jesus. We are who we are because He is in us. It is not by might, but by the God strength that we have our being. It is God that gives us the opportunity. Acts 10:34 says" *then Peter open his mouth, and said, of a truth I perceive that God is no respecter of person.* We are to thank God when He gives us the opportunity to get wealth. Wealth is a gift from God to you.

God wants to bless you. God sent Jesus that we might have life and have it more abundantly. What kind of gifts does our heavenly father want to give His sons and daughters in Christ? God wants to give you good gifts. James 1:17 says, *"every good gift and every perfect gift is from above, and cometh down from the father of lights, with whom is no variableness, neither shadow turning."* God has the power to give a gift that will pay off your student loans. God has the power to allow you to walk in divine healing even if the doctor has said no. God has the power to give you everlasting peace in the midst of perilous times. And He has the power to give you wealth which is an advantageous gift.

The word power has great meaning. In the Hebrew the word power is *koach.* The word means in the Hebrew strength, power, and might. Acts 1:8 says:. *ye shall receive power, after that the Holy Ghost is come upon you..then ye shall become witnesses.* With the gift of wealth, God wants us to become His witnesses. The Holy Ghost is the enabling power. Also, remember that wealth, wisdom, and understanding goes hand in hand. Wisdom energizes the owner of wealth.

Why does God have the desire that His children be rich? The simple answer is that he wants his children to fulfill the covenant He made to our forefathers. God wants us to be abundantly blessed so we can pass this wealth to the next generation. Genesis 12:2 says, *"And I will make of you a great nation, and I will bless you (with abundant increase of favors) and make your name famous and distinguished, and you will be a blessing (dispensing good to others)." (Amplified Version)*

I do not believe that God will give us anything and not expect us to use it. God has given all of us the power to get wealth. How does God expect us to use it? How does God expect us to use our finances? How do we get the power of His resurrection and put it into our daily lives and maximize His power in us to get the wealth He desires us to have?

We ought to be teaching this in our Sunday School classes. The Disciples of Christ in each church ought to be sharing this revelation to those whom God has put in their circle of influence. The church must know that God will never give you anything that he doesn't expect you to use. This is God's power and wants it used for His glory. This power is manifested through the actions of the individual. This author uses an acronym when teaching this subject at Today's Family, Inc. workshops on wealth.

P – stands for Plans
O – stands for Organization
W- stands for Work
E- stands for Enthusiasm
R- stands for Rewards

Plans

The word plan in the Greek and Aramaic language means, *thought, device, and purpose.* Proverbs 21:5 *says, "The plans of the diligent lead surely to plenty, but those of everyone who is hasty, surely to poverty."* 1 Chronicles 28:12 *says, "and the plans for all that he had by the spirit, of the courts of the house of the Lord, of all the chambers all around, of the treasuries of the house of God, and of the treasuries for the dedicated things."* 1Chronicles 28:19 *says, "All this, said David, the Lord made me understand in writing, by His hand upon me, all the works of these plans."* This author is pointing out that plans give you power.

Organization

I submit that in order to get wealth we must organize the methodical approach and present it to God in prayer for His approval. The plan should include immediate steps, twelve month steps, five year steps, and so on of how this plan will come into fruition. This plan should be written in terms of spirituality goals, financial goals, mental goals, social goals, and physical goals. Each of these levels in the plan should be well written in terms of action steps to be taken. A specific timetable should be written for the implementation for each step of the plan of action. A mental and physical goal should be created for the major areas to be completed so you will be on task. The plan should be monitored daily and prayerfully submitted to God. Praise God for each area completed before and after the plan is approved. Organization means power. Prayer is key and faith unlocks the door.

Work

Many have been told to name it and claim is the formula to wealth. Of course, this has damaged the minds of many church goers. It is called prosperity gospel. This kind of ministry is not found anywhere in God's Word. This gift of wealth between God, you, and His desire to grant it unto you is going to require work on your part. Work is not a bad word. Lasting, life-changing wealth will only come through effective, ingenious, God guided work in behalf of His children. Work means that one will have to use his or her mind, hand, and whatever is available to make it happen to the glory of God. It is very rare that supernatural capacity wealth appears without some type of work. Proverbs 13:11 says, *"wealth (not earned but) won in haste or unjustly or from the production of things for vain or detrimental use (such as riches) will dwindle away, but he who gathers little by little will increase (his riches)."* We are to examine ourselves for the purpose of wealth and make sure it is pleasing unto God and we will be doing something commendable for the Kingdom of God.

Enthusiasm

Colossians 4:12-13 says *.. labouring fervently for you in prayers, that ye may stand perfect and complete in all the will of God..he hath a great zeal for you …"* The word zeal means excitement of the mind. Zeal means to have a fervor of spirit. We are to have enthusiasm for our plan. This author wants you to understand that enthusiasm is important. It is contagious. It transfers to others how you feel about your project to make wealth, how you feel about a person, place, or thing. If you do not have enthusiasm, prayerfully ask God to equip you with it for His glory. The last four letters in the word "enthusiasm" are i-a-s-m. This author takes these letters to mean *"I Am Sold Myself."*

Rewards

Reward means that you are to be paid for your work. God will bestow rewards upon our good deeds and endeavors to build up the kingdom of God. A reward can be literally termed as dues paid for work. "If any man's work abide which he hath built… he shall receive a reward." God will allow you to receive wealth from your work by planning, organization, work ethnics, enthusiasm, and you will be rewarded by God.

God has given us the power to get wealth but not for us to flaunt it. It is for spreading His covenant on the earth. If we seek first His kingdom and His righteousness (His values for living) then He will provide for us anyway! This wealth is to be used for the glory of God. In this day of financial hardship and poverty it is more imperative than ever for ministers and leaders in His kingdom to pursue a lifestyle of simplicity. Wealth is not given for the flaunting of cars, homes, clothing, and so on. Wealth is for building up the kingdom of God and to make real His covenant with the future generations to come to fruition over and over again. There are some principles of the use of money that ought to be reflective in the actions of the leaders of the church.

Principles to consider in the operation of a church.

Principle 1 – Do not allow money to be the bottom line of all church decisions, if so then money is an idol.

Principle 2 – Balance the books based on faith and God's spiritual orders. They ought not to be run on a constant deficit.

Principle 3 – The act of borrowing money to operate ought not to be a policy of the church.

Some colleges and universities borrow regularly to get them through the summer months, but it's a bad practice. The church ought not borrow to get through certain months.

Research pointed to one Christian University trying to pay off $22,000,000 in debt that they accumulated over the many years. This is neither a sound business nor sound economic practice. Borrowing money for general operation sounds like a church wanting to close its doors.

Principle 4 - Never incur consumer debt.

The church ought not borrow money or use a credit card on anything that depreciates. For example, buses, vans, furniture, sound systems, and consumables.

If the church decides to use credit cards for travel and general purchases they should pay off the balance every month leaving a zero balance. They should not incur interest payments on credit cards. They should make it a practice of getting air miles, hotel points, and free gasoline with every credit card purchase.

Principle 5 - Borrow short-term and only on appreciating assets.

If the church must borrow for construction or existing real estate, they should pay *one- third cash* and the rest must be paid off within seven years. The property will have appreciated beyond any interest payments made.

Principle 6 - Always negotiate.

We never take the first offer as "cut in concrete" when purchasing. Negotiate with vendors and suppliers. Make sure it's a win-win situation. Remember, your vendors need Jesus too and should be interested in helping to advance the Kingdom of God.

Principle 7 – Create a staff for handling monies.

Never allow one person to be the only person handling the funds and/

or set up friendship with another in the transactions of monies. Set up security, controls and rotation systems.

Principle 8 - Develop a 13-week cash cushion.

This is to be held in a good investment account. If your average income is $1000 a week, you will need $13,000 in your "cushion account." This will be your "emergency only" fund. After the emergency, you must be committed to replenishing the account.

Principle 9 - God has a plan for a church's financial success.

This does not involve selling candy, peanut brittle, quilts, peaches, fish sandwiches and cakes or having rummage sales. Churches are to operate under God's fiscal plan. The principles of giving in love are the best plan. God calls for an offering in love and in good cheer. Malachi 3 tells us of the great promises for the giver. 2 Corinthians 9 tells of the His wonderful promises for the generous giver.

Principle 10 -Missions are important.

The monies are in the storehouse for this particular mission.

Principle 11 - Pray in faith about all financial matters in the church.

All of God's promises are yes and Amen in Christ Jesus.

> (1) Pray for,
>
> (2) Plan for,
>
> (3) Prepare for,

The Sensational McMillan Singers said, *"Pray and Pray Some More!"*

Principle 12 - OBEY GOD and keep His Commandments.

The church is not to make a decision based upon mammon. When God says build, they are to obey and begin praying, planning, and preparing, and He will show the church how to bring in the finances. The church is not to do it on their own, if they do, then they will be on their own. Now after having established these foundation principles, let's look at the practical budgetary matters.

THE GENERAL RULE

A general rule is "1/3, 1/3, 1/3." One third is to go to missions. One third goes to salaries, overhead, insurance, and others. One-third goes to building expenses, and ministries. Pray that God will send the church a Christian Business Manager that will assist the church in meeting its budget based on God's work for the church. Use the computer technology available to build up the Kingdom of God.

CHAPTER FIFTEEN

FOR A STRONGER NATION

THE UNITED STATES of America was founded on the principals of freedom and liberty rules of law. The Constitution of the United States further states that it was founded on equality for all, social compact, and desire for limited government. America wants that every citizen would have the right for the pursuit of happiness and indicated that this would be a gift from the creator. The author believes that this qualifies America to have had their forefathers real intentions to be that it wanted this nation to live under the laws and foundation of the creator.

It stands to reason that if America was to honor the forefathers wish, then it must be a civilized nation. If America is to be called a civilized nation, then this nation must adhere to what it means to be civilized and practice this process on a daily basis. When America finds that she has moved from the doctrines and meaning of being civilized, then she is practicing savagery. This author wants to remind Americans to practice civilization for she may be traveling down the road of destroying the foundation upon which she was founded.

Civilized societies consist of people who choose to be honest and caring, sharing, and pairing with one another. If America wants to be a free enterprise system then they must have a civilized system. It takes a civilized people in order for a free society to work. Civilized people will not grant favors for others expecting a special favor at the expense of others which in most cases can not afford the uncivilized gesture. Civilized people will not accept bribes to get special interest at the expense of tearing down or closing the governmental offices that provide lifesaving care to others in the society. Instead a truly civilized society will choose to be moral so that free enterprise and political freedom will and can thrive for the betterment of all people.

In a civilized culture the family will remain intact. A civilized society will accept the sovereign God as their ruler and obey His Word. This society would not attempt to change a sovereign God's laws, commandments, and doctrines. This society will not attempt to undermine and/or destroy natural law. A civilized society would consist of a man and woman as Godly married parents. Their children will be raised in loving homes, with caring parents who guide their education, training, and religious education until they reach adulthood. The civilized family consisting of man and woman and children will remain interested in the well being of each together until death do them part. This is what the creator intended and it is recorded in the Word of God. God is the creator.

Civilized people live peaceably among their neighbors. They will be an agent of helping their neighbors and will abide by the laws to protect and oversee each others success in the community. Civilized people live in peace with other civilized people. They are not racist and full of greed, selfishness, proud, and deceitful. A civilized society is able to live together in peace. In a civilized society people feel free to choose their work, their home, their family practices, their friendships and associations. They generally are self-restrained before they infringe on the rights and freedoms of others. A civilized society has the components that reflect a religious society. It has a culture base in which each person uses a uniform standard code of living, ethics, and doctrine of faith. Yes, a civilized society must accept a God-given authority as the standard of behavior. Does it sound like America is a civilized society?

Jesus Christ was asked what was the greatest commandment, He answered, and gave a second as well: "*Thou shalt love the Lord thy God with all thy heart, and with all thy soul, and with all thy mind. This is the first and great commandment. And the second is like unto it. Thou shalt love thy neighbor as thyself. On these two commandments hang all the law and the prophets.*" This points to the fact that America is to follow these commandments and use these commandments as their standard of living.

The creator gave Ten Commandments to the world so they will be able to be a civilized society. It comes from the Judeo-Christian tradition. These commandments come from these two categories. The first four commands we honor God. God is the source of human rights for a civilized society. The people in a civilized society must be free to exercise these rights without threat and/or impartial. These commandments are the ones that a civilized society must honor if they are to remain civilized.

Honor parents
Do not murder (take innocent life)
do not have sex outside of marriage
do not steal
do not lie
do not covet (want what belongs to your neighbor)

Also, civilized societies value other things and would strive to keep the following in place so that all will profit.

1. **Value Truth**
2. **Religious Freedom Is Necessary to Civilization**
3. **Extremely dislike terrorism**
4. **Value a religious civilization**

The Creator who made all things and mankind will be recognized and worshiped. The Creator revealed a moral code of behavior for happy living and peaceful living. The creator gave the created ability to distinguish right from wrong. The Creator holds the created responsible for the way they treat each other. God who is the creator has prepared a place for all humankind to live after death. Humankind can choose between heaven and hell based on his or her will. God is final judge of all humankind and He will judge. We are to live in this land as civilized people with God as our creator. This is what the founding fathers of America believed when they set up the government and wrote the constitution.

But, there are ways that people will behave that will not be considered as being civilized. These kinds of people are fixed on destroying any group of people who have the desire of being a civilized society. They exhibit these negative fruits. It is clear that the president of this nation ought to exhibit being civilized. If deportment is used then it ought to be a model for the world. When civilization characteristics are not apparent then these things will take place.

1. Religion of Savagery

Their belief system correlates the religion of savagery. They openly degrade the position of God as the Creator. They are seen as being agnostic or an atheist. This religion denies God and it is replaced with human deity. They act as if they are God. Many believe that they are God or can eventually become God.

2. Devaluing human life

Often they elevate animals above human life. They seem to worship animals and will rather see human life sacrificed to God rather than animals. They will worship animals before worshiping a sovereign God. Actually they practice beastology.

3. Destroy free will and consequences

They believe that the sun, moon and stars or things that are controlled by something out of the influence of a human being. Whatever it is controls the fate and actions of individuals. Therefore their thinking and actions are not to be held against them. They are not responsible for the actions of others nor do they seek to change their actions.

4. Degrading Position of God

They oppress the believers of God and they degrade anything the believers do. This is not a civilized practice. They oppress the believer and aim to neutralize the power of God. They also bring up a negative position and/or manufacture a point to degrade the idea that there is a creator.

There is hope for the savagery to civilization. America can get back to being civilized in this 21ˢᵗ century. What can America do to get back to Civilization?

1. Repent. Admit that their action doesn't qualify them to be called civilized.
2. Recognize. Understand that they are wrong and not denying the facts.
3. Confess. Confess openly that they are wrong and their opinions does not matter.
4. Make restitution. Ask for forgiveness from those whom they have done wrong.
5. Change their thinking pattern and began to live honorably from this point onward.

Government cannot force civilization on a people. But, the government can enforce the level of civilization agreed upon. The government can enforce equal protection under the law. The government can support the civil rights laws on the books. But, the government is not the solution for making people become civilized. The family can set a standard of living amongst family members. The church can set standards. Some schools can set standards for their students.

America can set standards, but the people must choose to obey these standards. In fact civilization can only happen when the lower level (state level) has made the changes needed. When the state, federal, and at the national overall has been civilized then, America will demonstrate the atmosphere of civilization in this 21ˢᵗ century. Changes must be made. However, it seems as though America is moving in the opposite direction. This author is suggesting that if changes are not made, then America is on the brink of becoming uncivilized. We wonder if America can answer these questions in honesty and believe that they are traveling on the road of civilization.

CIVILIZED BEHAVIORS ARE CATEGORIZED IN THIS FACTION.

Civilizations turn on the collected attitude of making it possible that all people will have the opportunity to work to support themselves and their families.

Civilized people welcome children into their family in love and commit to nurturing their children physically, emotionally, educationally, and spiritually to pass this virtue on to the next generation.

Civilized people will freely give freely from their surplus and time to assist those less fortunate than themselves during hard times.

Civilized people are honest with friends and associates, in business deals, and in personal relationships.

Civilized people are peacefully, law-abiding, and fair with other civilized people.

Civilized people don't get intoxicated or use recreational mind-altering drugs that destroy the affairs of others and the country.

Civilized people do not attack their civilized neighbors in anger, nor provoke their neighbors, and do not practice racism. If there are disputes, they work them out, with the help of the system set in place.

Civilized people obey the command of God as it relates to being married as man and woman.

Civilized people do not participate in pornography, neither in production, dissemination, nor use.

Civilized people know that prostitution is savage and will not participate in form of prostitution.

Civilized people do not commit a sexual act such as rape, incest, and child abuse.

Civilized people are quick to forgive the repentant. They will accept restitution.

Civilized people protect their country. They will not do any thing intentionally to over throw the government, shut down the government or cause it to not be ineffective.

Civilized people will support their leader and compromise and/or will agree to make their society better for the betterment of the people.

For a stronger nation we need a nation of people that are determined to go down the narrow path that leads to the components of being civilized. When a nation truly becomes uncivilized, that nation soon will collapse. America must accept God as being the creator of all things. This nation will only be civilized and strong if the people follow the commands of its creator. It is a dangerous thing to fall into the hands of an angry God for not following the commands of the creator.

CHAPTER SIXTEEN

Jesus is Coming Back For His Church

THIS COUNTRY SEEMS to be taking a vacation from facts on many facets and settings. Many churches are surfing over the waves of reality without examining the core problems that is causing it to be ineffective for today's world problems. Many churches are swimming in polluted water just to maintain regular congregations for financial gains. Many of their officers and members are lying out on the beach on Sunday morning during vacation drinking as many cocktails as their butler brings them. The church can not afford the luxury of ignoring the biblical commands that has been written in the Word of God. It is my belief that the church is under judgment. The author has been charged by the spirit to set forth these facts on page so she can be warned once again. The Word of God tells the world that Jesus is coming again for His church.

This fact is unacceptable to the world. The Word of God clearly points out that Jesus is coming back for His church. He is looking for a church without spot or wrinkle. The church is to present itself as being Holy and without blemish. Christ loved the church and gave himself for the church. God wants to sanctify and cleanse the church of all sin. The church must not be blemished. They are not to have any marks of imperfection. If the church has a spot or blemish of imperfection it means that they are not prepared to go back with Jesus. The fact is that the church must be exposed if she is not operating by the manual that God instituted. The church has a short amount of time to get their house in order. The end time is very near. Yes, I am speaking of the rapture. The church can not be perfect and imperfect at the same time. The church can not be righteous and unrighteous at the same time. The church can not be a child of God and a child of the devil at the same time. Christ is coming back for a church that is ready according to His word to return with Him.

When Jesus says come up hither, He will be speaking to the perfect or complete in God's people. (Mat.22:12) He is the judge. The bible said the Lord was not willing that any should perish, but all should come to repentance. (2 Peter 3:9) He made a way of escape. We can be holy as Jesus is Holy. (1Cor.10:13) However, we have free will to refuse to go back with Him. And if those judged by God are found to be unfit, then they will forfeit the opportunity to go back with Him.

What makes you, the church perfect? Being complete makes you, the church perfect. Complete means having all of the properties that belong to you. Jesus said, *"I will go away and I will pray the Father and he will send you another Comforter."* (John14:16, 26) Then if we don't have Him, then we are not complete. I have heard the statement that *"I have to sin a little every day."* This is not the doctrine of Jesus, the Christ. If the church commits sin, the bible says that *"they are of the devil."* (1 John3:8) The church has power over the devil. We are not to allow the devil to degrade us and bring us down to his level. The bible says that *"Satan is a liar, and father of lies."* In John 8: 44, the Word of God says, *"Ye are of your father the devil, and the lusts of your father ye will do."* Satan was a murderer from the beginning, and abode not in the truth, because there is no truth in him. *"When he speaketh a lie, he speaketh of his own: for he is a liar, and the father of it."* In 2 Corinthians 13: 11 the Word says, *"finally, brethren, be perfect, be of good comfort, be of one mind, live in peace; and the God of love and peace shall be with you.* Jesus is coming again. Church we are living in the last days. Jesus is to make His departure very soon. Soon and very soon we shall see the king. The bible tells us to be ready. The question is will you be ready?

WE SHALL ALL BE CHANGED

Well, 1 Corinthians 15: 51-52 describes the final victory. The Word says: *"Behold, I shew you a mystery; we shall not all sleep, but we shall all be changed, in a moment, in the twinkling of an eye, at the last trump: for the trumpet shall sound, and the dead shall be raised incorruptible, and we shall be changed."* Paul says this occurs at the last trump, which the Bible tells us is the seventh trumpet. 1 Corinthians 15 and Revelation 11:15 are referring to the same thing. In Revelation 11:15 the Word of God says *"and the seventh angel sounded; and there were great voices in heaven, saying, the kingdoms of this world are become the kingdoms of our Lord, and of his Christ; and he shall reign for ever and ever."* The fact is that the Word of God says *"For the trumpet shall sound, the dead shall be raised, and we shall be changed."* The fact is that we shall be changed to meet Jesus if He deems it to be so.

TRANSFORMED INSTANTLY

At the Second Coming of Jesus Christ, all born again Christians will be caught up in the clouds to meet the Lord in the air. In 1 Thessalonians 4:13-18 says, *13 "But I would not have you to be ignorant, brethren, concerning them which are asleep, that ye sorrow not, even as others which have no hope. 14 For if we believe that Jesus died and rose again, even so them also which sleep in Jesus will God bring with him. 15 For this we say unto you by the word of the Lord, that we which are alive and remain unto the coming of the Lord shall not prevent them which are asleep. 16 For the Lord himself shall descend from heaven with a shout, with the voice of the archangel, and with the trump of God: and the dead in Christ shall rise first: 17 Then we which are alive and remain shall be caught up together with them in the clouds, to meet the Lord in the air: and so shall we ever be with the Lord. 18 Wherefore comfort one another with these words."* The facts are clear. At the sound of the "last trumpet," the dead who were born again during their lifetime will be resurrected from the dead. At the same time, those who are born again and still alive on earth will be transformed instantly, from mortal beings to immortal beings. Romans 8:11 tells us that our mortal bodies will be made alive if we have God's spirit living in us. When Jesus Christ was caught up, He was seen leaving the earth. Just as they were able to see Jesus go, so will people be able to see the church go up to meet Him in the air.

No One Knows The Day Nor The Hour

In Matthew 24:36 Jesus said, *"But of that day and hour no one knows,"* Jesus said to His disciples on the Mount of Olives. The Word tells us there will be signs of the end of time. The word says that there will be perilous times. The word perilous means "dangers" in the Greek. Truly we are living in dangerous times. Jesus was speaking not only to people living in the first century, but also to the church of today. The ungodly leadership of this country is a direct signal that we are living in dangerous times. The election of a satanic leader of the free world will signal the righteous to sound the alarm even louder.

The Times And Seasons

In Acts 1:6, prior to Jesus being caught up to heaven, Jesus' disciples asked, *"Lord, will you at this time restore the kingdom to Israel?"* In Acts 1:7. Jesus replied He said, *"It is not for you to know the times or the seasons, which the Father hath put in His own power."* We will not be able know the times and the seasons? But, there will be signs given to those in Christ of His impedient return. The church is to be on watch for the signal.

The Sons Of Light Will Know

In Matthew 24:34, Jesus says, *"Verily I say unto you, this generation shall not pass, till all these things be fulfilled."* He says, *before His return there will be such things as wars, rumors of wars, earthquakes in various places, widespread famine and disease, and the Antichrist's rise to power."* Paul says, *"but of the times and the seasons, brethren, ye have no need that I write unto you. For yourselves know perfectly that the day of the Lord so cometh as a thief in the night."* *"For when they shall say, Peace and safety; then sudden destruction cometh upon them, as travail upon a woman with child; and they shall not escape. But ye, brethren, are not in darkness, that that day should overtake you as a thief. Ye are all the children of light, and the children of the day: we are not of the night, nor of darkness."* 1 Thessalonians 5:1-5 says, *"But of the times and the seasons, brethren, ye have no need that I write unto you.2 For yourselves know perfectly that the day of the Lord so cometh as a thief in the night. 3 For when they shall say, Peace and safety; then sudden destruction cometh upon them, as travail upon a woman with child; and they shall not escape. 4 But ye, brethren, are not in darkness, that that day should overtake you as a thief. 5 Ye are all the children of light, and the children of the day: we are not of the night, nor of darkness."* Paul is saying for us to pay attention to the times and the seasons, then the church will know when the time is near. If the church pays attention, then we will see the day of the Lord coming. The question is: are you a son or daughter of the Light.

THOSE LIVING IN DARKNESS WILL BE SURPRISED

1 Thessalonians 5 and Matthew 24:42-43 tells us that the day of the Lord will come as a thief in the night. The master of the house will not know what hour the thief will come. The thief represents the Lord. The master of the house was living in darkness. He was not prepared for the coming of the Lord. The unsaved are the unbelievers. They will not realize the signs of the end of times. Paul states that the coming of the Lord would only be a surprise to those living in darkness. Unbelievers are Satan's children. 1 Thessalonians 5:4-5 indicates that, unlike the situation with unbelievers, the day of the Lord will not overtake His children. They will not be surprised. This is why the church is to study and show themselves approved and rightly dividing the Word of the Lord. The church must preach and teach the unadulterated Word of God.

THE HARVEST OF THE EARTH

In chapter 14:17-20 of Revelation states *"14 And I looked, and behold a white cloud, and upon the cloud one sat like unto the Son of man, having on his head a golden crown, and in his hand a sharp sickle.15 And another angel came out of the temple, crying with a loud voice to him that sat on the cloud, Thrust in thy sickle, and reap: for the time is come for thee to reap; for the harvest of the earth is ripe.16 And he that sat on the cloud thrust in his sickle on the earth; and the earth was reaped. 17 And another angel came out of the temple which is in heaven, he also having a sharp sickle. 18 And another angel came out from the altar, which had power over fire; and cried with a loud cry to him that had the sharp sickle, saying, Thrust in thy sharp sickle, and gather the clusters of the vine of the earth; for her grapes are fully ripe. 19 And the angel thrust in his sickle into the earth, and gathered the vine of the earth, and cast it into the great wine press of the wrath of God. 20 And the winepress was trodden without the city, and blood came out of the wine press, even unto the horse bridles, by the space of a thousand and six hundred furlongs."* Here we see a vision of Christ reaping a harvest. This author repeats God's Word, And I looked, and saw a white cloud, and upon the cloud one sat like unto the Son of man, having on his head a golden crown, and in his hand a sharp sickle. And another angel came out of the temple, crying with a loud voice to him that sat on the cloud, Thrust in thy sickle, and reap: for the time is come for thee to reap; for the harvest of the earth is ripe. And he that sat on the cloud thrust in his sickle on the earth; and the earth was reaped.

In John 4:35, says: *"say not ye, There are yet four months, and then cometh harvest? behold, I say unto you, Lift up your eyes, and look on the fields; for they are white already to harvest."*

This tells of the souls in the harvest. The reaping of the good harvest is the rapture of the church. This harvest reaped is immediately before the wrath of God. Yes, the rapture of the church occurs prior to God's wrath.

The harvest signals the end of the age. Jesus, the Christ will come back for the rapture of His church. The Battle of Armageddon will take place. Jesus prophesied of the harvest. It is called the "rapture" by many, but the word is not found in the bible. Rapture means "the catching away." 1 Thessalonians mentions the *"catching away." "Then we which are alive and remain shall be caught up together with them in the clouds, to meet the Lord in the air: and so shall we ever be with the Lord."* 1 Thessalonians 4:17

AFTER THE TRIBULATION

Matthew 24 concludes that Jesus said the rapture will come after the tribulation of those days. *"Immediately after the tribulation of those days shall the sun be darkened, and the moon shall not give her light, and the stars shall fall from heaven, and the powers of the heavens shall be shaken: And then shall appear the sign of the Son of man in heaven: and then shall all the tribes of the earth mourn, and they shall see the Son of man coming in the clouds of heaven with power and great glory. And he shall send his angels with a great sound of a trumpet, and they shall gather together his elect from the four winds, from one end of heaven to the other."* Matthew 24:29-31

NOT A SALVATION ISSUE

The timing of the rapture is a controversial issue. But, whether it comes before or after, or even during the tribulation it has no bearing on the church salvation. God is able to come for any one of us at any time He wishes. Jesus said in Matthew 24, *"Watch therefore: for ye know not what hour your Lord doth come." "But know this that if the good man of the house had known in what watch the thief would come, he would have watched, and would not have suffered his house to be broken up."* Matthew 24:42-43

SIGNS OF THE END TIMES

Many people are wondering what is happening with all these disasters, wars, worldwide economic woes, animal deaths and a general degradation in society. They are the signs and it appears that the end time is very close. Christ said Himself … *"So likewise ye, when ye shall see all these things, know that it is near, even at the doors"* Matthew 24:33. *"Verily I say unto you, this generation shall not pass, till all these things be fulfilled"* Matthew 24:34.

In the last scenes of this earth's history, war will rage. There will be pestilence, plague and famine. The waters of the deep will overflow their boundaries. Property and life will be destroyed by fire and flood. This author has noticed the conflicts and wars that are raging across the globe. Disaster after disaster is unfolding on almost all nations. Economies are collapsing throughout the world. Animal life as we know it is diseased and dying. The entire world is experiencing wickedness and sin is rampant. Domestic violence is faking havoc in the eyes of children and sanctioned by many adults. Genuine Christians have the spiritual sight to see exactly what is happening in this 21ˢᵗ century. God is sending the signals and we have been warned!

SIGN - PERILOUS TIMES SHALL COME

2 Timothy 3:1-5.... *"This know also, that in the last days perilous times shall come."* These are dangerous times. Times are getting worse. There are protests most notable in Ferguson, Baltimore, and many other cities. There are riots and uprisings all over the world today. The economy worldwide seems to be ready to explode. Civilization is un-raving and those desiring to be in leadership are questionable. Many wonder if the leadership really believe in the creator. The chants of the "Black Lives Matter" movement has begun. Racism has raised its head even in the White house and gaining control in the halls of congress. America is divided on many issues.

SIGN - THOSE WHO DESTROY THE EARTH, GOD WILL DESTROY

Revelation 11:18 … *'And the nations were angry, and thy wrath is come, and the time of the dead, that they should be judged, and that thou shouldest give reward unto thy servants the prophets, and to the saints, and them that fear thy name, small and great; and shouldest destroy them which destroy the earth.'* … This applies to the end time signs and what man does to the earth. Humankind is in control of their actions, but weapons of mass destruction, the craving for war, and regulating the massive gun industry are signs of the end time. They have polluted the air with chemicals. They have polluted the waters with oil and other toxins. They have destroyed forests and so on. They have destroyed numerous animals through derelict actions. Those who destroy the earth, God will destroy.

SIGN - FALSE CHRIST AND FALSE PROPHETS

Matthew 24:4-5, 11 *"Many shall come in My Name, saying, I am Christ. … and many false prophets shall arise and deceive many."* This includes false prophets and preachers. We have had certain people claiming to be Christ, or a special "chosen one." Truly I have not forgotten people like Jim Jones and David Koresh. There are the new age spiritualist and satanic cults operating in the world. Many these are deceiving the masses in their congregation.

In this 21st century the world is full of false prophets, preachers and movements like never before. Within the churches, they preach in error and deceive millions of people. There are homosexual preachers, lesbian preachers, same sex marriage preachers, and aesthetic preachers. There are the prosperity gospel preachers. These prosperity preachers focus entirely on material wealth and prosperity. They do not even attempt to preach on sin and repentance. There is not an attempt on the behalf of prosperity or false prophets to convict people of sin. There is an emerging church movement to unite the church with the world. False prophet preachers deceive people that it is profitable to the Christian Kingdom to unite with other faiths of the world. The church and the world are not to mix according to the scriptures. The church is not to unite with other faiths that do not obey the doctrines of God, His son Jesus, the Christ, and the Holy Spirit.

The only reason people are deceived by these preachers and false doctrines is that they do not study the Word of God. Another reason is that preachers, pastors, and leaders are not teaching the real content of the bible. Many of these stand directly in the way of allowing God's Word to be taught by matured Holy Spirit filled bible teachers. There must be a concerted effort in churches to devise a universal test to ascertain if churches are preaching and teaching the unadulterated Word of God. When particular churches and pastors fail to obey God' command to teach and preach as He instructed, then they are to be labeled as false prophets and not churches of God. They are not to be categorized as Churches of God. The question is: are God's fruits being produced from these churches? Ellen White stated in her book that there are definable characteristics in true and bonafide Christian leaders to advance the Kingdom of God. The Church of God can no longer associate itself with churches designed to destroy the works of the Kingdom of God. The word of God says, "Come out from amongst them."

Sign – Famine

Matthew 24:7 ... *'And there shall be famine.'.. ...* We are living in a time of famine and hunger. In this 21ˢᵗ century, famine is all over the world. There are thousands of people dying of starvation every day. The United Nations Food and Agriculture Organization estimated that about 805 million people of the 7.3 billion people in the world, or one in nine, were suffering from chronic undernourishment in 2012-2014. Almost all the hungry people, 791 million, live in developing countries, representing 13.5 percent, or one in eight, of the population of developing counties. There are 11 million people undernourished in developed countries.

In the United States there is hunger in the land. Six years after the onset of the financial and economic crisis, hunger remains high in the United States. In 2013, 14.3 percent of households (17.5 million households, approximately one in seven), were food insecure. Children were food insecure. The report indicates that 9.9 percent of households had children. There were 3.8 million households that were not able to provide adequate, nutritious food for their children. They usually tried to shield their children from hungry; but both the children and parent went without food. In 2013, there were 45.3 million people in poverty. This is up from 37.3 million in 2007. The facts indicate that 19.9 million Americans live in extreme poverty. This means that their family's cash income is less than half of the poverty line, or about $10,000 a year for a family of four. This is a direct sign of famine in the land. The problem is not getting better.

There is famine in the land. Statistically, 1 out of 7 Americans experience the pain of famine. More than 12 million families struggle with hunger pains on a daily basis. This means that 48 million people in America are facing the reality of famine in the land. Food Banks serve 5.4 million people every week. These are figures based on statistical collections in the year of 2016. America has the ability to help the hungry children and families, but they choose not to do so. They have a desire to be politically correct. What does this mean to hungry children and families?

There are three main causes of poverty in the United States. The causes lie in the operation of the political and economic system in the United States. This system has a tendency to make sure that poor families remain poor. There are others who believe that actual physical and behavioral issues among the poor cause them to remain poor. Yet, many people are dying and going to bed hungry every day. This author believes that the intentional operation procedures of the US economic and political system has led to certain people/groups to being relatively disenfranchised.

Even in the midst of a famine, there is so much food wasted that could feed the masses of the poor. However, laws have been enacted that requires companies to through away food that could have saved the lives many people. God will be the judge of those who enact and force those kinds of laws that actively kill millions. It really stems from the sin of greed by the most fortunate. There is an overwhelming effort to put the wealthy and powerful uncaring people in the decision making authority over distributing resources to the less fortunate. In their greed they always have been known to give funds to the rich and un-needy. These people represent those with the most wealth in America. The rich keeps getting richer and the poor continues to get poorer. Based on military, political, and economic power the resources of the land ends up in the hands of the rich minority (the ten percent crowd) that live well. But those at the bottom barely survive. God will judge everyone for what they have done, and what they did not do. Nevertheless, there are signs of famine in the land.

SIGN - EARTHQUAKES IN DIVERSE PLACES

Matthew 24:7 ... *'And earthquakes in divers places.'*.. ... We can see that earthquakes are increasing in frequency, and also appearing in more "diverse places". "Current graphs clearly show a worldwide trend of increasing earthquakes in strength and frequency. The USGS statistics page shows an increase in the frequency of stronger earthquakes. (M > 5.0)." A series of massive quakes in 2012 prompted an earthquake expert to suggest that the earth is "cracking up." There are numerous earthquakes in the world such as:

1. Costa Rica sees increase in seismic activity during past 62 years

2. Over 3,000 noticeable quakes hit Japan in 2012
3. Over 5,000 earthquakes hit Mexico in 2012
4. Korea experienced twice as many quakes in 2012 than in the past
5. Pacific-Antarctic Ridge, Nepal, Papua New Guinea, FJJI, Tunga Flores Sea, ReykJanes Ridge, Argentina, and Vanuatu have reported earthquakes

The world is now experiencing 2,600 earthquakes every day! Jesus Christ said that there would be earthquakes in "diverse" places, and that prophecy is certainly fulfilled in this 21st century.

SIGN - KILLED FOR YOUR FAITH

Matthew 24:9-10 ... .'*Then shall they deliver you up to be afflicted, and shall kill you: and ye shall be hated of all nations for my name's sake. And then shall many be offended, and shall betray one another, and shall hate one another.'.. ...* Christians are being persecuted and killed all over the world for their faith in Christ Jesus. For example, they are being killed in China, Russia, Africa, Iraq, Israel, and being killed by ISIS. Soon this persecution will rise up in the western world and then the mark of the beast will be enforced. History records that The Roman Catholic Church killed tens of millions of Christians during the dark ages between 538 – 1798 AD. This evil will rise again just before Jesus returns.

SIGN - SINFUL SOCIETY

Matthew 24:12 .... *"And because iniquity shall abound, the love of many shall wax cold ... ... idolatry, adultery, violence, lust, greed, homosexuality, theft, lying."* The world is abounding in these sins, and not just the heathen world, but also within the church. It is a sad day in church when the sins of the world are not being addressed. The 21st century church is truly aching and suffering under the burden of sin. God is a God of wrath. God will not stand by and let this happen much longer. America has openly allowed since 1973 over 50 million innocent babies to be aborted. Many Christians have "waxed cold" and do not believe in the merits of the Ten Commandments. The Word of God says, *"Thou shalt not kill."* Many sins are on the increase and the church is silent. The amount of sin allowed into our homes through television is appalling. The nation seemly calls it entertaining. And what does the church call it? The church does not address the issue for the most part. It was sin that put Jesus, the Christ on the cross. But, in this 21st century, the world is allowed to call it entertainment.

I can not help from thinking how I grew up. Fifty years ago, people could leave their houses and cars unlocked without fear of a thief breaking in to steal. People dressed more modestly. Women were not dressed in a "sensual" and sexual way. People were "pious" and caring and courteous towards one another. The communities as a whole attend a church of their choice. Blue laws were enacted because the populace believed in the sovereignty of God. What appeared on television reflected the integrity of a Godly society. Society was stable and set guidelines that would enhance the growth of children to obey the dictates of God. But in this 21st century, society has degraded to an all time low. Truly we are living in a sinful society.

SIGN - PEOPLE WILL BE LOVERS OF PLEASURE

2 Timothy 3:1-5. *"This know also, that in the last days perilous times shall come. For men shall be lovers of their own selves, covetous, boasters, proud, blasphemers, disobedient to parents, unthankful-unholy, without natural affection, truce breakers, false accusers, incontinent, fierce, despisers of those that are good, traitors, heady, high-minded, lovers of pleasures more than lovers of God; Having a form of godliness, but denying the power thereof: from such turn away."*. ... In this 21st century, the world is truly following the trend cited in this scripture. The end times is being fulfilled without a doubt. The world is lovers of pleasure more than lovers of God. They love sports, entertainment, and anything else rather than God. Many are Christians only in name, but they love the pleasures of this world. This is a description of many of the 21st century church today. Yes, the majority of professing Christians of this century are more interested in the TV, sports, partying, socializing, and playing games. Worshiping and praising God as their creator is not even secondary.

SIGN - WAR AND RUMORS OF WAR

Matthew 24:6-7 … *'And ye shall hear of wars.. … For nation shall rise against nation and kingdom against kingdom.'.. …* For over the past century there have been more than 200 wars and conflicts. Not a day has past wherein a war has not been fought. President Obama announced a joint venture to go to war against ISIS, a terrorist group. ISIS are actively persecuting Christians, beheading Christians, and are threatening the entire world. Yes, we are hearing of wars. And there hasn't been one single day where a war or conflict hasn't been fought. President Donald Trump ordered a strike on Syria in response to a chemical attack on its own people.

SIGN - KNOWLEDGE SHALL BE INCREASED

Daniel 12:4 … *'Even to the time of the end: many shall run to and fro, and knowledge shall be increased.'.. …* This applies to Biblical knowledge concerning Bible prophecy. Since 1844 Bible prophecy has been opened to God's people. God has a remnant church filled with the truth. Churches must read and study this passage and teach to all their believers. Also, there is the application of worldly knowledge. Over the past 50 years, the world has been flooded with much technology. It is amazing and has been counter productive to the church as a whole. Without a doubt, there has been an incredible increase of knowledge. We can google almost anything and get an answer in seconds.

SIGN - TRUE GOSPEL PREACHED THROUGHOUT THE WORLD

Matthew 24:14 … *'And this gospel of the kingdom shall be preached in all the world for a witness unto all nations; and then shall the end come.'.. …* The end of time cannot come unless this gospel is being preached throughout the world. This means that the true gospel must be preached. After the true gospel is preached then the end times will come. The true gospel is being preached through my website, and other websites. The true gospel is being preached in this book. The true gospel is being preached from many pulpits, TVs, radios, other books and so on. In this 21st century, the gospel of Jesus, the Christ is reaching the ends of the world. The return of Jesus is near.

These signs signify that we are living in the last days, just before the second coming of Jesus, the Christ. We can see more signs in the sun, moon, and the stars. We are witnessing the threshold of the crisis of the age. The succession of the judgments of God will happen just as God said. There will be fire, flood, and earthquake, war, and bloodshed. It is time for the church to take a stand and give America and the world the kind of warning God commanded. It is my prayer that those reading this book will make every effort to seek the truth and be free. We are to follow in the footsteps of Jesus, the Christ and be saved and enter into eternity with Him. Be ready, Jesus is coming soon. Are you saved?

END TIME FACT

Daniel 2 ... *'Thou, O king, sawest, and behold a great image ... This image's head was of fine gold, his breast and his arms of silver, his belly and his thighs of brass, His legs of iron, his feet part of iron and part of clay. Thou sawest till that a stone was cut out without hands, which smote the image upon his feet.'*

In Daniel 2, verses 31-45, paints the picture of the prophecy. It tells of all the different kingdoms that were to rule the world from the time of Babylon. It continues to paint the picture until the end of the world and the second coming of Christ. This gives us the visual to see the fulfillment of the prophecy. Today, we are seated at the foot of this image. We see the divided kingdoms of the world.

Based on this divine prophecy it is obvious that we are living in the "end times." This age began in A.D.476. So, based on discernment and historical analysis it is evident in human reasoning this is the last "age" before the end. This world has been living in the last age for over 1500 years! So we are now closer than ever before. We stand awaiting the King of Kings to return. His return will signal the eternal Kingdom to assemble as commanded for the second coming of Jesus, the Christ.

THE MARK OF THE BEAST

The "Mark of the Beast" has been referred to as "666." The time will come when every one will be required to receive a mark or a number. Without this mark, I predict you will not be able to fly on a commercial aircraft, enter a federal building, drive a car, open a bank account, receive health care, or hold a job. I heard about the technology being in place today. It is happening right now.

INDIVIDUAL ECONOMIC SANCTIONS

Based on economics, politics, and religious conformity this technology can be enforced. I believe that UN pressures can be enforced into conformity. Perhaps there will be a one-world political system, a one-world economy, and a one-world religion. In Revelation 13:16-17 it states, *"And he causeth all, both small and great, rich and poor, free and bond, to receive a mark in their right hand, or in their foreheads: And that no man might buy or sell, save he that had the mark, or the name of the beast, or the number of his name."*

CASHLESS SOCIETY

The Cashless Society is around the corner. It seems that research and development is ready to completely take control over the lives of individuals. When this is in place, Satan will be able to counterfeit true worship. False Prophet under penalty of death will require everyone to worship the "Beast," the Antichrist. Mankind will be required to surrender everything which includes all financial transactions. There will be no cash circulating in the economy. This is the meaning of a cashless society. There will not be any banks to rob. IRS will have all the records needed to assess taxes and refunds at a moments notice. They will be able to withdraw taxes as if it is their money. They will be able to get your money before you have a chance to spend it.

WILL YOU TAKE THE MARK OF THE BEAST?

The book of Revelation 13:15-18 says, *"Every person will be forced to have a number, without which they will be unable to buy or sell."* In order to have a job, one must have a valid, government recognized ID. They must be in the global database. After this system is activated worldwide, the mechanism will be in place and the scriptures will be able to be fulfilled. The Mark of the Beast will be ready for implementation. This Mark of the Beast was prophesied 2,000 years ago.

ABILITY TO ENFORCE THE MARK OF THE BEAST

Revelation 13:17 … *.'And that no man might buy or sell, save he that had the mark, or the name of the beast, or the number of his name.'*… The Word of God says that during the last days the beast system would enforce the world to take the mark of the beast. Revelation 13 *says that those who don't take the mark will not be able to buy or sell.* In order for this prophecy to be fulfilled there must be a stop for people from "buying and selling. The world has to do away with the cash system. It needs to be replaced with an electronic form of payment. When this happens, then it would be easy to press a button and freeze the finances of any person who refuses to go along with the beast. America has the technology to do this. This is a sure sign of the end times that we live in.

Revelation chapter 14 tells us that whoever receives the mark of the Beast *"shall drink of the wine of the wrath of God."* The mark is a permanent designation. It is applied to your forehead or right hand signifying ownership. If you take the mark, then you will be eternally lost. This is a mark of eternal destruction. The enforcement of financial obligations will be easy. It will be disastrous because of the lost of individual control. Your financial account could be cut off instantly. It is designed to make you join the global financial system. This is an absolute certainty that this will happen. We will face this option. Apple computer chief executive has introduce an "I" phone called "ISIS" that will do all of the above. We urge you to make sure that your name is in the Lamb's Book of Life. What will you do?

WHAT WILL THE "MARK OF
THE BEAST" BE LIKE?

You will not get this Mark of the Beast accidentally. This will be your decision. You will have the opportunity to make a conscious choice to receive it. The Future Attribute Screening Technology Mobile Module enables the Department of Homeland Security to collect video images, audio recordings and psycho physiological measurements. This gets into the minds of potential terrorists which allow them to determine if a terrorist has the intention to do harm.

Let it be known that you will be pledging your allegiance to the most charismatic dictator the world has ever known. The False Prophet of the church will make worship of the beast irresistible. The false prophet will promise you protection, eternal life, peace and prosperity, if you worship the Antichrist. Those agreeing will have his special mark. Having received the mark, people will be allowed to buy food, water, medicine and clothes. Taking the mark will seem to the unbeliever to be logical, intelligent, and the patriotic thing to do.

PRECURSORS TO THE MARK

The Real ID Act requires that Americans produce compliant driver's licenses, as approved federal identification, upon demand. This act coerced states to build a national multi-billion dollar system for the purpose of identifying, tracking, and controlling law-abiding citizens. A number of states refused to comply because this is expensive. This program did not receive federal funds. Also, this program is an invasion of the privacy of its citizens. Penalties for not implementing this initiative were postponed by the government. The Department of Homeland Security announced a gradual roll out for enforcing this act. This act has the potential of being implemented in the venture of the "The Affordable Care Act." The "E-Verify" bill, a nationally mandated universal bio metric ID will require federal approval for employment. The government is also considering the implementation of enhanced drivers license, enhanced social security cards, and bio metric and DNA Identification databases. These actions are making the way for historical and religious stamp of the 666 on individuals.

A statement of John lends credence to this idea. He says 666 "is man's number" (13:18). *Man, however, is fallen, sinful and incomplete.* On the other hand, seven is the number of completeness – and would refer to God and His work. The seven days of creation in Genesis 1 is an example. If the meaning of "666" is in the number itself, then the point is simple: The beast is nothing more than human government under demonic control. In that sense, the "beast" has always been with us, and it can be seen at work throughout the ages.

The church of Christ must be on watch for the end times and teach their disciples to watch as well as pray. There is a moment coming in this 21st century that the church must be ready to contend with. By faith, the church should be able to see through the eyes of God and govern themselves accordingly. Let the church think on these things.

PROPHECIES ABOUT THE END TIMES

The bible gives proof that 2,600 years ago that America was foretold it would come out of Great Britain. The bible gives prophecies about Russia, Germany, the European Union, and Great Britain. The author speaks in detail about this proof.

NEW WORLD ORDER IS WORLD GOVERNMENT

There will be a World Court system, a World Bank, and an International law system set up prior to the Second Coming of Jesus Christ. This lesson pinpoints the actions of the government over which the Antichrist will soon rule.

ENTRANCE RAMP FOR THE ANTICHRIST

The Bible states that one out of three people on the earth will die in this war of all wars! After this global holocaust people will beg for a strong leader to get them out of this chaos and destruction. They will want peace and security. Perhaps such a person is already living. At the right moment, this person will step on the scene. He will offer leadership and direction. This war is coming and will kill one-third of the world's population.

ISRAEL'S GOD-GIVEN DESTINY

The whole world is focused on one small area of land that has less than one-tenth of one percent of the world's population. It is told that Israel will live again. The Temple Mount is the most important place on earth according to the scriptures. Why? What is the destiny for Israel?

ISRAEL – GOD'S PROPHETIC TIME CLOCK

Twenty-five hundred years ago God gave a prophecy for Israel. Their future is near. This prophecy foretells the beginning of a seven-year period that will end at the Battle of Armageddon. The beginning of this final seven years is near. What is destined for Israel?

HOLY ROMAN EMPIRE REBORN

The Holy Roman Empire was declared dead in 1806, but reborn on November 3, 2009. The prophecy also reveals where the Antichrist and his religious partner, the False Prophet, may come from.

THE ANTICHRIST AND THE FALSE PROPHET

The Bible prophesies that two individuals will rule over a system of world government just before the Battle of Armageddon and the Second Coming of Jesus Christ. One will be a political leader, the other a religious leader. The prophecy lets us know that these two personages will come out of the rebirth of the Holy Roman Empire. The power-base of the Antichrist is established and awaiting his arrival.

THE COMING ONE-WORLD RELIGION

One school of thought is that Muslims, Jews, and Christians all worship the same God. They believe that all these followers of these different religions will go to heaven. This belief that all religions are equally true and valid is called interfaithism. Totalitarian governments have always sought to enforce a uniform belief system upon their people. The Bible prophesies speaks of the Antichrist and the False Prophet. This form of religion will be enforced during the Great Tribulation.

THE SEVEN TRUMPETS

There are seven angels with seven trumpets in the Book of Revelation. The trumpets yet to sound foretell the coming of World War III and the Battle of Armageddon. This lesson gives proof that five of the seven trumpets have already happened and the sixth trumpet could happen at any time.

THE SECOND COMING

The Second Coming of Jesus to earth will be the capstone of all human history. Every person on earth should have a clear understanding of what happens at the Second Coming of Jesus Christ. Christians must prepare for Jesus' return.

KINGDOM OF GOD

Jesus told the world what they must do to enter the Kingdom of God. He also told us what the world will be like when He returns to rule over the earth. The prophecies say men will beat their swords into plowshares and their spears into pruning hooks. They also declare that men will not learn war any more. The Bible reveals that there won't be one war on earth during the entire 1,000-year reign of Jesus Christ.

This generation stands upon the recipe of the wrap-up of human history. This is all happening in the 21st century under our watch. We have all the knowledge needed to ascertain the proximity of this occurring. This knowledge and understanding has not been available to any other generation. We do not know neither the time nor the hour, however, we ought to be able to see the signs of the end time.

The prophet Daniel predicted precisely this time on God's prophetic time line. In Daniel 12:14 states, *"But thou, O Daniel, shut up the words, and seal the book, even to the time of the end: many shall run to and fro, and knowledge shall be increased"* (Dan. 12:4). The book was open and was closed by God. The angel had told Daniel the prophet that this would happen. He was told that the book of understanding would end and would remain closed until the time of the very end was reached.

But Jesus, said about His second coming, concluded, as reported in the book of Mark: *"And what I say unto you I say unto all, Watch"* (Mk. 13:37). It is therefore incumbent upon us "all Christians" to discern the signs of the times. Christians must trust, without reservation the "Word" (John 1:1-2), that God will fulfill the remaining prophecies for the future.

There are no prophecies yet to be fulfilled before the rapture of Christ's Church. Luke 17: 26-30 records this catastrophic intervention. Jesus will step out on the clouds of glory and shout "Come up here!" (Rev. 4:1-2). All Christians meaning those who accept Christ's blood atonement for salvation (born-again believers) will instantly be with Jesus above the earth. (1 Cor. 15: 51-55 and 1 Thes. 4:13-18.) Millions of people that raptured will vanish and will disappear from the planet before the astonished eyes of those left behind. They will be taken back to heaven with the Lord. He has prepared a place of eternal dwelling for them (Jn. 14:1-3). The bema judgment will take place. He will give rewards for service to the Lord while on earth. Crowns will be handed out to God's family. The marriage supper of the Lamb will occur. Christ's Bride will be made ready for the wedding, and the Wedding Feast will take place. (Revelation 19:9). Things on earth will be put in gear for the end-time storm. Second Thessalonians 2 says that God, the Holy Spirit will remove as restrainer during the times following the rapture.

The nations of earth will be in chaos. The turmoil will include civil disorder and economic calamity. The government will try to regain governmental and economic equilibrium. According to prophecy, one man will step forward to proffer a plan to quell the fears of war in the Middle East (Daniel 9:27). This prophecy correlates to Revelation 6: 2, with the rider on the white horse riding forth.

A great world leader will have the answers for a peace covenant in the Middle East. He will be able to sell a seven-year peace plan. This covenant deal is recorded in Isaiah chapter 28. This will cause God's judgmental wrath to begin to fall.

The Lord will not allow the satanic realm to go unchallenged. The Antichrist will be revealed. He is then revealed as Antichrist, the son of perdition, the man of sin. He will cause all to accept his mark or be cut out of the economic system - all buying and selling. He will order all killed, who will not worship him. The chief method of death dealing will be beheading. His partner in the satanic duo will point all worship to the beast – Antichrist.

CONCLUSION

I F GOD CONTINUES to tarry, then the organization called "the church" will move the era called the "Graying of America." Twenty percent of the population by 2030 will have 70 million older persons. Based on this projection, the church must address the needs of their membership. The culture shift will pressure churches to adopt scriptural tactics of the corporate business world into their organizational structure. God has commanded that the church continue to follow the Biblical order cited in 2 Timothy 3:5. What we need is a sweep of a mighty revival in the land that will reveal the mighty power of God and His glory. We need a lively hope. We need to place our trust entirely on God. We must preach and teach the total Word of God. We must demonstrate these truths in the marketplace as written in Hebrews 4:12.

The reality seems to point out that America will steadily decline as the major influence in the world. This decline is for the most part, because this country is shifting from core foundation beliefs to ungodly political correct marketing surveyed opinionated beliefs. I believe that the church will continue to lose respect in the community. The secular government will withhold tax exemptions and City governments will not welcome churches seeking to purchase land.

The church must remember its mission and focus on its mission to reach everyone with the Gospel of Christ. They must seek to elect only matured Christians to office. (1 Timothy 2:1, 2) The church can no longer afford to vote satanic individuals into offices to represent the needs of their congregants.

The 21st century churches are witnessing individuals who desire to undermine the office of Pastor. The bible says that wolves will creep into the local church and scheme to lead astray the faithful members of the congregation. They will seek to cause divisions over petty and insignificant issues. The God called pastor will warn the people. They will operate in wisdom and harmony according to their call coupled with wisdom, and Scripture. (Jeremiah 3:15) In addition to the wolves, the unbelieving world will direct outright hostility toward the church. Believe that open persecution will be evident in all churches. The hatred for the Gospel message will permeate the media, government, medical and research organizations, the entertainment industry, and educational institutions. What has been whispered in the dark will be shouted in the streets. The church must prepare their congregations for harassment. This is a great time for the church and they must not withdraw from working in the community. The church must double their efforts to win souls to Christ. We are living in the last days of our life (1 Corinthians 4:10-12).

It saddens my heart to say that the American family will continue to disintegrate. The core values of the home are under attack and their plan is to increase the attack. The church must teach Biblical principles of marriage, family, and child rearing (Ephesians 5: 21-33). The church must aggressively continue to preach the gospel, evangelize, feed the poor, clothe the naked, and share the love of God to all they can reach (Luke 10:1-12).

Throughout America, the distortion of the truth will intensify. Lies will saturate every institution of our nation. "Who can you trust," will be a major question. God's church will be known because His church will not be guilty of being a false witness. Jesus told us about the end of the age. He said we will be living in perilous times. He said, "When these things begin to take place, stand up and lift up your heads, because your redemption is drawing near (Luke 21:28)."

What is the great problem of the twenty-first century facing the church? There are a number of potential answers. One problem facing the church is the emergence of technology that is creating a major divide in the population as a whole. There is a rift in the quality of life in terms of those that are taking advantage of the technology and those who can not afford it or those that are functionally ignorant of it. The economic divide riddled with policies has depressed wages and increased the cost on those who can least afford it. The gap is getting wider and wider.

The simple fact is that we are living in a nation in which the wealthy are becoming wealthier. There is an increasing number of those who are poor are getting poorer and many live below the poverty line. This is a great problem. What has not been talked out in this country is the power of having access to money and those who do not have access. Those who have access are often found abusing their power. The church must recognize and defeat the ever present myth that God is the author of the form of oppression prevalent in hearts of the less fortunate. The church must continue to engage in the liberation theological movement and bring it to fruition. The church must practice an ethnic of empowerment. The church must recognize and defend its historic claim that faith is essentially empowerment. They must shout from the roof top that any church or sociopolitical or economic structure that fosters dependence, degradation, or despair is not the product of true faith. God promised His children an abundant life.

Ways To Improve The Church Of The 21st Century.

1. Focus on God in every element of the church.
2. Have clear and concise biblical support for every element in worship.
3. Pastors are to preach ex-positional sermons and not entertaining sermons to keep the congregations happy.
4. The church is to give reverence and great spiritual attention to the public reading of Scripture" (1 Timothy 4:13).
5. The church is to pray and pray some more. (Lyric by "The Sensational McMillan Singers")
6. The church must provide spiritual and practical support.
7. The church must warmly welcome guests, make them feel comfortable, and at a proper time give them a tour of the facilities and programs offered.
8. The church must develop an assimilation strategy.
9. The church must build small group structure.

APPENDIX

Semonic Outline

A Successful Church
Ephesians 5:23-27

Introduction:

1. Christ's view of the church
2. Christ views the church as his body, his bride
   Sanctified, cleansed, glorious, holy, and blameless

What Makes a Successful Church?

I. A Scriptural Church (2 Tim. 3:16-17)
   1. Bible believing, Bible teaching, Bible obeying
   2. What God says matters, discipleship making

II. A Servant Church (James 2:14-18)
   1. 1 John 3:16-18
   2. Heb. 13:16

III. A Praising Church (Ephesians. 5:18-19)
   1. Friendly, warm, alive, joyous, loving
   2. Heb. 13:15

IV. A Evangelistic church (Matt. 9:37)
1. Matt. 28:19
2. 2 Tim. 2:2

V. A Selfless Church (Phil. 2:3, 4)
1. John 13:34, 35
2. Jesus was the great example of selflessness Rom. 15:1, 2
3. 2 Cor. 8:9
4. 2 Cor. 5:14, 15

Conclusion:

MAKING DISCIPLES

MAJOR POINTS OF INTEREST

A strong prayer foundation– Churches can achieve very little without prayer. Successful churches that pray and fast will know God's will and purpose for its existence. Successful churches pray for their growth, resources, and the unsaved, engage in spiritual warfare and ask God to make them a blessing in the communities.

Bible-based preachers– A church will rise or fall on the quality of the sermons and teaching delivered from the pulpit. A growing church has ministers who can skillfully deliver Bible-based messages that people can relate to, touch on real life issues and help them become more like Jesus. All of the preachers, evangelists, and leaders will be used to God's glory. It is not to be a one man show.

Pastors that love people – Pastors will exhibit a Godly care and concern for those left in their charge. Growing churches that keep and attract people are led by leaders who care.

Lively worship services – Growing churches hold lively, enjoyable worship services that have worship teams and musicians that skillfully play their instruments. Growing churches also spice up their services by inviting guest speakers and singers so people don't get bored by hearing the same people week after week. They use all the talent that God has sent them to make the ministry grow. They do not encourage secularism in their choir, and so on.

Generous and loving members – Churches that impact the community have members that are generous and who treat each other as family.

Community initiatives – Growing churches share their resources, time and finances with others by running and supporting projects that help people in need, whether it's people in their churches, the local community or abroad.

Evangelistic teams - Growing churches seek out ways to share the gospel with those who don't know Jesus. This can and does include doing street ministry, organizing outreach services, encouraging members to bring their friends and family and by generally being a welcoming church.

Churches play a key role in their community. So it's imperative that leaders do their best to also make them effective and impact places that transform lives and communities.

Discipleship Teams- Go and make disciples is to be the centerfold of each church ministry.

ADVANCED STUDY
BIBLIOGRAPHY REFERENCES

John Adams. *A Dissertation on the Canon and Feudal Law*, 1765. John Adams Quotes on Government "Our Constitution was made only for a moral and religious people." It is wholly inadequate to the government of any other."

Lyndon B. Johnson. (n.d.). *BrainyQuote.com. Retrieved* September 20, 2016, from BrainyQuote.com Web site: http://www.brainyquote.com/quotes/quotes/l/lyndonbjo157399.html. *"The separation of church and state is a source of strength, but the conscience of our nation does not call for separation between men of state and faith in the Supreme Being."*

Martin Luther King Jr. 'Letter from Birmingham Jail' in Why We Can't Wait, 1963. *"Yes, I see the Church as the body of Christ. But, oh! How we have blemished and scarred that body through social neglect and through fear of being nonconformists."*

Martin Luther. *(n.d.). BrainyQuote.com. Retrieved September 20, 2016, from BrainyQuote.com Web site: http://www.brainyquote.com/quotes/quotes/m/martinluth384169.html. "For where God built a church, there the Devil would also build a chapel."*

Eliot, T. S. *1920. The Hippopotamus. Poems," While the True Church can never fail For it is based upon a rock."*

C.S. Lewis. Letters to Malcolm: Chiefly on Prayer *(San Diego: Harvest, 1964), 4-5.*
"The perfect church service would be one we were almost unaware of. Our attention would have been on God."

Max Lucado, By Michelle A. Vu, *Christian Post Reporter, "For years I thought my assignment or the Church's assignment was to articulate the Gospel and nothing more. Now I believe that if we don't support the verbal expression of the Gospel with physical demonstration of compassion, we are not imitating Jesus."*

"Thomas Aquinas." *AZQuotes.com. Wind and Fly LTD, 2016. 20 September 2016, http//www.azquotes..com/quote/9700, "Hold firmly that our faith is identical with that of the ancients. Deny this, and you dissolve the unity of the Church."*

Matthew Henry. *AZQuotes.com, Wind and Fly LTD, 2016,www. azquotes.com/quote/130106, accessed September 20, 2016. "The way to preserve the peace of the church is to preserve its purity."*

Ulysses S. Grant. *(n.d.). AZQuotes.com. Retrieved September 20, 2016, from AZQuotes.com Web site: http://www.azquotes.com/quote/115698, "Leave the matter of religion to the family altar, the church, and the private school, supported entirely by private contributions. Keep the church and state forever separate."*

Tertullian. (n.d.). *AZQuotes.com. Retrieved September 20, 2016, from AZQuotes.com Web site: http://www.azquotes.com/quote/579396, "The blood of the martyrs is the seed of the church."*

T. D. Jakes. *(n.d.). AZQuotes.com. Retrieved September 20, 2016, from AZQuotes.com Web site: http://www.azquotes.com/quote/144303, "And another thing is that I think as a church whenever we become politically driven, we alienate at least 50 percent of the people that God called us to reach with our political orientations."*

Gerald R. Ford. *(n.d.). AZQuotes.com. Retrieved September 20, 2016, from AZQuotes.com Web site: http://www.azquotes.com/quote/99021, "For millions of men and women, the church has been the hospital for the soul, the school for the mind and the safe depository for moral ideas."*

Database of Megachurches in the U.S., Bibliography of Scholarly Writing about Denominations, *A separate report at www.hartfordinstitute. org /megachurch/megachurches_research.html and http://www.leadnet.org/ megachurch analyzes the congregations from the survey with attendance 1800 and above.*

Scott Thumma, Ph.D.*, is professor of sociology at Hartford Seminary, the director of Hartford Institute for Religion Research, and co-author of Beyond Megachurch Myths, among other books and articles.*

Jesse Bogan. *America's Biggest Megachurches, 6/26/2009, In Pictures: America's 10 Biggest Megachurches, Forbes Magazine, Sources: Forbes; average weekly attendance figures from the Hartford Institute for Religion.*

Anderson Antunes, Contributor, Forbes Magazine, Edir Macedo & family, 2016, *Billionaires List: Dropoff, and Brazilian Billionaire Bishop Edir Macedo Is Now A Banker, Too.*

Nenanda Radio List, *Top 10 richest pastors in the world, August 16, 2014, editor@nehandaradio.com.*

B. Denise Hawkins and Adelle M. Banks, *Religion News ServiceMonday, April 6, 2015, Deseret News National, "Gardner C. Taylor, dean of black preachers, dies at 96," article on faith.*

Robert C. McMillan, *The 6G Leader, An Imprint of McMillan Group Publishing, 2012, Upstart Financial Plan, "Six Generations to release the Genius Leader Your were born to be."*

Barna Group*, "Born Again," Barna Group is a visionary research and resource company located in Ventura, California, barna@barna.org.*

Andrew Strom, *THE* "OUT-OF-CHURCH" CHRISTIANS, Why are tens of thousands of devoted Christians leaving the churches? Is it a 'movement'? What is causing this world-wide phenomenon?http://www. revivalschool.com 2003/2004.

Steve Hill, Spiritual Avalanche: The Threat of False Teachings that Could Destroy Millions, Charisma House, 2013.

Pew Research Center, U.S. Public Becoming Less Religious, *Modest Drop in Overall Rates of Belief and Practice, but Religiously Affiliated Americans Are as Observant as Before, November 3, 2015.*

American Religious Identification Survey (ARIS), *Americans Who Don't Identify with a Religion No Longer a Fringe Group, 2016.*

The KJV parallel Bible Commentary, Edward E.Hindson - Woodrow MichaelKroll - T. Nelson Publishers – 1994.

Zondervan KJV study Bible: King James Version, Kenneth L.Barker - Donald W.Burdick - Zondervan – 2002

The Message Bible: Eugene H.Peterson - The Message – 2007.

Strong, Matthew K.Manning - Fernando Cano - Joe Azpeytia - Capstone Stone Arch Books – 2014

Strong's exhaustive concordance of the Bible, James Strong - Hendrickson Publishers – 2007

Life application Bible: New Testament: the Living Bible, Tyndale House - 1987

Dr. Harold Carter, Sr. Now Faith Is, Gateway Press, Inc., 1991.

David T.Olson. Zondervan, The American church in crisis: groundbreaking research based on a national database of over 200,000 churches, Zondervan – 2008.

US News and World Report. "Populations Has Increased." Introduction, 2011.

Thom Schultz and Joani Schultz, *Why Nobody Wants to Go to Church Anymore: And How 4 Acts of Love Will Make Your Church Irresistible*: Amazon best-seller on the Adult Christian Ministry list.

Ed Stetzer, *The State of the Church In America: Hint: It's Not Dying Is the American church really dying?* The Exchange, October 1, 2013.

Harford Institute of Religion Research, Hartford Seminary,

Thom Rainer, *Thirteen Issues for Churches in 2013; Church Leaders,* September 21, 2016.

Dr. Diana Eck, *A New Religious America: How a "Christian Country" Has Become the World's Most Religiously Diverse Nation* was published in 2001, Published by Harper San Francisco.

Bodie Hodge, *How Old Is the Earth?*, February 21, 2009, Published as an AiG Daily, Feature by AiG on 21 February 2009,

Green, WIlliam Henry, *Primeval Chronology*, published in Bibliothecs Sacra, April, 1890, pp. 285-303.

Milliam, Dr. John, The Genesis Genealogies.

Francis Chan, *Crazy Love: Overwhelmed by a Relentless God,* Published May 1st 2008 by David C. Cook.

Roderick C. Meredith, *Where Is God's True Church Today?*, booklet, 2016.

The Charlotte Observer, *"Comfortable in Church*, 2016.

Larry McMillan, *Put Out Sin Revival*, Booklet, Last Supper, 2015.

Harold Lindsell, *The Battle for the Bible*, Zondervan (September 1978)

Ray C. Stedman, *Legalism*, May 14, 1972, booklet.

The Sensational McMillan Singers, *Praise Him Now*, 1981, lyrics.

Food and Agricultural Organzation of the United Nations Report, 2016.

USGS, *Statistics and information on the worldwide supply of, demand for, and flow of minerals and materials essential to the U.S. economy, the national security, and protection of the environment,* Last Modified: 10 June 2016.

THE TRUE FACE OF THE ROMAN CATHOLIC INQUISITION, NEWS1675, *"Lives of the Popes",* by Richard P. McBrien, HarperSanFrancisco, 1997.

Future Attribute Screening Technology Fact Sheet, Homeland Security, Last Published Date: March 2, 2016.

REAL ID Enforcement, Current Status of States / Territories, The REAL ID Act, passed by Congress in 2005, enacted the 9/11 Commission's recommendation that the Federal Government "set standards for the issuance of sources of identification, such as driver's licenses."

E-Verify is an Internet-based system that allows businesses to determine the eligibility of their employees to work in the United States. E-Verify is fast, free and easy to use – and it's the best way employers can ensure a legal workforce., Rep. Smith, Lamar (R-TX-21) Introduced 02/27/2015 H.R.1147 — 114th Congress (2015-2016)

REFERENCES

Hartford Institute for Religion Research. *"The Definition of a Mega church"*. "Retrieved 2013-07-17.

Hartford Institute for Religion Research, Database of Mega churches". irr.hartsem.education. Retrieved 2010-02-06.

This report is based on a marketing survey conducted by the **Barna Group**, 2009. (ww.barna.org)

David T. Olson, American Church in Crisis, Zondervan.

Russell Gregg, *"Meeting the Ancestors,"* *Creation*, March 2003, pp. 13–15.

Floyd Nolan Jones, *Chronology of the Old Testament* (Green Forest, AR: Master Books, 2005).

James Usher, *The Annals of the World,* transl. Larry and Marion Pierce (Green Forest, AR: Master Books, 2003).

Jones, *Chronology of the Old Testament,* p. 26; others would include gaps in the chronology based on the presences of an extra Cainan in Luke 3:36. But there are good reasons this should be left out. See chapters 5, "Are There Gaps in the Genesis Genealogies?" and 27, "Isn't the Bible Full of Contradictions?"

Jonathan Sarfati, "Biblical Chronogenealogies," *TJ* 17, no. 3 (2003):14–18.

Robert Young, *Young's Analytical Concordance to the Bible* (Peabody, MA: Hendrickson, 1996), referring to William Hales, *A New Analysis of Chronology and Geography, History and Prophecy*, vol. 1 (1830), p. 210.

Bill Cooper, *After the Flood* (UK: New Wine Press, 1995), p. 122–129.

Terry Mortenson, "The Origin of Old-earth Geology and its Ramifications for Life in the 21st Century," *TJ* 18, no. 1 (2004): 22–26.

James Hutton, *Theory of the Earth* (Trans. of Roy. Soc. of Edinburgh, 1785); quoted in A. Holmes, *Principles of Physical Geology* (UK: Thomas Nelson & Sons Ltd., 1965), p. 43–44.

Mark McCartney, "William Thompson: King of Victorian Physics," *Physics World*, December 2002.

Terry Mortenson, "The History of the Development of the Geological Column," in *The Geologic Column*, eds. Michael Oard and John Reed (Chino Valley, AZ: Creation Research Society, 2006).

Vardiman, Andrew Snelling, and Eugene Chaffin, eds., *Radioisotopes and the Age of the Earth*, vol. 1 and 2 (El Cajon, CA: Institute for Creation Research; Chino Valley, AZ: Creation Research Society, 2000 and 2005).

Half-Life Heresy, *New Scientist*, October, 21 2006, pp. 36–39.

Russell Humphrey, "Evidence for a Young World," *Impact*, June 2005.

Henry M. Morris, *The New Defender's Study Bible* (Nashville, TN: World Publishing, 2006), p. 2076–2079.

C.C. Patterson, "Age of Meteorites and the Age of the Earth," *Geochemica et Cosmochemica Acta*, 10 (1956): 230–237.

This does not mean that a 14C date of 50,000 or 100,000 is entirely trustworthy. This is to highlight the mistaken assumptions behind uniformitarian dating methods.

Andrew Snelling, "Conflicting 'Ages' of Tertiary Basalt and Contained Fossilized Wood, Crinum, Central Queensland Australia," *TechnicaBasalt and Contained Fossilized Wood, Crinum, Central Queensland Australia,*" *Technical Journal 14, no. 2 (2005): p. 99–122.*

John Baumgardner, "14C Evidence for a Recent Global Flood and a Young Earth," in *Radioisotopes and the Age of the Earth: Results of a Young-Earth Creationist Research Initiative*, ed. Vardiman et al. (Santee, CA: Institute for Creation Research; Chino Valley, AZ: Creation Research Society, 2005), p. 587–630.

Andrew Snelling, "Excess Argon: The 'Achilles' Heel' of Potassium-Argon and Argon-Argon Dating of Volcanic Rocks," *Impact*, January 1999.

Robert Bellah, "Civil Religion in America", *Dædalus, Journal of the American Academy of Arts and Sciences.*

Boundless. "Cultural Wars of the Nineties." *Boundless Art History*. Boundless, 03 Jul. 2014. Retrieved 06 May. 2015. History/textbooks/boundless-art-history-textbook/global-art-since-1950-cCe37/the-nineties-238/cultural-wars-of-the-nineties-845-7237/

Eck, Diana (2002). *A New Religious America: the World's Most Religiously Diverse Nation*. Harper One. p. 432. ISBN 978-0-06-062159-9.

Moltmann, Jurgen. Theology of Hope. Minneapolis: Fortress, 1993. Moltmann's groundbreaking book reoriented theological book that reflects on the expectation of the coming kingdom of God.

Taylor, Charles. A Secular Age. Cambridge, MA: Belknap Press of Harvard University Press, 2007.

Volf, Miroslav. Flourishing: Why We Need Religion in a Globalized World. New Haven: Yale University Press, 2016.

Jensen, David H., *Responsive Labor: A Theology of Work. Louisville: Westminster John Knox, 2006.

Bell, Daniel M., Jr. "Just War as Chistian Discipleship." Pamphlet 14 in the Renewing Radical Discipleship series, Ekklesia Pamphlets, edited by Daniel M. Bell, Jr., and Joel Shuman.

Cherry, Stephen. Barefoot Disciple: Walking the Way of Passionate Humility. London: Continuum, 2001.

CIA Fact Book. CIA World Fact Book. 2002. Retrieved 2007-12-30.

Barry A. Kosmin and Ariela Keysar, (2009). "AMERICAN RELIGIOUS IDENTIFICATION SURVEY (ARIS) 2008" (PDF). Hartford, Connecticut, USA: Trinity College. Retrieved 2009-04-01.

HTTP://www.gallup.com/poll/109108/Belief-God-Far-Lower-Western-US.aspx

Christian Statistics: '*Top 10 Largest National Christian Populations*". Adherents.com. Retrieved 2010-02-17.

John H. Ogwyn, *The United States and Great Britain in Prophecy*, Tomorrow's World, *Booklet, 2016.*

Black RE, Morris SS, Bryce J. "Where and why are 10 million children dying every year?" *Lancet.* 2003 Jun 28; 361(9376):2226-34.

Black, Robert E, Lindsay H Allen, Zulfiqar A Bhutta, Laura E Caulfield, Mercedes de Onis, Majid Ezzati, Colin Mathers, Juan Rivera, for the Maternal and Child Undernutrition Study Group Maternal and child under nutrition: global and regional exposures and health consequences. (Article access is free but will require registration) *The Lancet* Vol. 371, Issue 9608, 19 January 2008, 243-260.

Jennifer Bryce, Cynthia Boschi-Pinto, Kenji Shibuya, Robert E. Black, and the WHO Child Health Epidemiology Reference Group. 2005. "WHO estimates of the causes of death in children?" *Lancet*; 365: 1147–52.

Center for Research on the Epidemiology of Disasters. 2013. "People affected by conflict: Humanitarian needs in numbers."

Food and Agriculture Organization. 2012.FAO Statistical Yearbook 2012.

Food and Agriculture Organization, International Fund for Agricultural Development, World Food Program. 2014. "The State of Food Insecurity in the World 2014. Strengthening the enabling environment for food security and nutrition." Rome: FAO

Institute of Development Studies. "Hunger and Nutrition Commitment Index. Accessed March 2015.

International Food Policy Research Institute. 2014a. 2014 Global Food Policy Report.

International Food Policy Research Institute. 2014b. 2014 Global Hunger Index, Oxford University Press. 1971. *Oxford English Dictionary.* Definition for malnutrition, Population Reference Bureau. 2014. "2014 World Population Data Sheet."

Rosen, Stacey, Birgit Meade, Keith Fuglie, and Nicholas Rada. 2014. International Food Security Assessment, 2014-24. Economic Research Service, United States Department of Agriculture.

UNHCR 2014 "Mid-Year Trends" June 2014.

UNICEF, WHO, The World Bank. 2014a. "Levels and Trends in Child Malnutrition."

UNICEF-WHO-The World Bank. 2014b "Summary of key facts about the 2013 joint malnutrition estimates.

Cesar G Victora, Linda Adair, Caroline Fall, Pedro C Hallal, Reynaldo Martorell, Linda Richter, and Harshpal Singh Sachdev. 2008. "Maternal and child undernutrition: consequences for adult health and human capital." Lancet. 2008 Jan 26; 371(9609): 340–357.

World Bank. 2015. Poverty website. http://www.worldbank.org/en/topic/ poverty and the Overview page http://www.worldbank.org/en/topic/ poverty/overview Accessed March 2015.

World Bank. 2013. "The State of the World's Poor: Where are the Poor and where are they the Poorest?" http://www.worldbank.org/content/dam/ Worldbank/document/State_of_the_poor_paper_April17.pdf

World Health Organization, *Who Global Database on Child Growth and Malnutrition,* http://www.who.int/nutgrowthdb/en/ Accessed March 2015.

World Health Organization Comparative Quantification of Health Risks: Childhood and Maternal Undernutrition Accessed March 2015.

World Health Organization. "Micronutrient Deficiencies. Http.//www. who.int/nutrition/topics/vad/en/ Accessed March 2015.

Coleman-Jensen, Alisha, Christian Gregory, and Anita Singh. 2014a. "Household Food Security in the United States in 2013." ERR-173. U.S. Department of Agriculture, Economic Research Service, September 2014. Access this report by going tohttp://www.ers.usda.gov/media/1565415/ err173.pdf

Coleman-Jensen, Alisha, Christian Gregory, and Anita Singh. 2014b. "Report Summary: Household Food Security in the United States in 2013." U.S. Department of Agriculture, Economic Research Service, September 2014. Access this report by going tohttp://www.ers.usda.gov/ media/1565410/err173_summary.pdf

Center on Budget and Policy Priorities. "Welfare" Reform/TANF" http:// www.cbpp.org/research/index.cfm?fa=topic&id=42 Accessed March 3, 2015

Center on Budget and Policy Priorities (CBPP). 2012. "Policy Basics: Introduction to TANF." http://www.cbpp.org/cms/index. cfm?fa=view&id=936

Center on Budget and Policy Priorities (CBPP). 2014. "Policy Basics: Introduction to the Minimum Wage." http://www.cbpp.org/cms/index.cfm?fa=view&id=4192

Center on Budget and Policy Priorities (CBPP). 2015a. "Policy Basics: Introduction to the Earned Income Tax Credit." http://www.cbpp.org/cms/index.cfm?fa=view&id=2505

Center on Budget and Policy Priorities (CBPP). 2015b. "Policy Basics: Introduction to the Supplemental Nutrition Program (SNAP)." http://www.cbpp.org/cms/index.cfm?fa=view&id=2226

Http://www.world-earthquakes.com/index.php?option=eqs&year=2015

W.M. Easum, *"The church of the 21ˢᵗ century."*

"Future of Religion Research Page" by the **World Network of Religious Futurists.**

Phyllis Tickle, *"Re-Discovering the Sacred: Spirituality in America,"* Crossroad, (1995)

Richard Cimino and Don Lattin in *"Shopping for Faith: American Religion in the New Millennium"*

Excerpts from: Douglas Hall, *"The end of Christendom and the future of Christianity,"* Trinity (1997) at:http://www.christianism.com/

Excerpts from: Daphne Hampson, "*Theology and Feminism,"* Basil Blackwell, (1990) at:http://www.christianism.com/

Anthony B. Pinn, The Black Church in the Post–Civil Rights Era (Maryknoll, N.Y.: Orbis Books, 2002); and Dwight N. Hopkins, ed.,Black Faith and Public Talk. (Maryknoll: Orbis Books, 1999).

James Evans and Robert K. Davies Professor of Systematic Theology and past president at Colgate Rochester Crozer Divinity School. He also serves as senior pastor of St. Luke Tabernacle Community Church in Rochester, New York.

"U.S. Stands Alone in its Embrace of Religion". *Pew Global Attitudes Project*. Retrieved 1 January, 2007.

Anthony B. Pinn, http://reflections.yale.edu/article/future-prophetic-voice/prophetic-role-african-american-churches-21st-century#sthash. NDAWYhBz.dpufe Black Church in the Post–Civil Rights Era (Maryknoll, N.Y.: Orbis Books, 2002); and Dwight N. Hopkins, ed., Black Faith and Public Talk. (Maryknoll: Orbis Books, 1999).

James Evans and Robert K. Davies Professor of Systematic Theology and past president at Colgate Rochester Crozer Divinity School. He also serves as senior pastor of St. Luke Tabernacle Community Church in Rochester, New York.

Top 10 Richest Pastors in the World-2017 List Updated-The Gazette Review, http://gazettereview.com/2016/richest-pastors-in-world, 2016/02

PROFILE STATEMENT

DR. LARRY A. MCMILLAN** is the Chief Executive Officer of Today's Family, Inc. God has given him the gift to inspire families and potential couples to embark a secure journey of family life with success. He has shared the flashing lights of family, hope, joy, and happiness with families. This plan is known as "God's Plan for Life."

He is a charismatic biblical motivator, lucid speaker, marriage coach, theological scholar, author, musician, recording artist, teacher, educator, and a retired Business Manager/Educator of the Baltimore City Public School System. Also, he pastored three different churches during the tenure of his active employment. His presentations were highly effective in transforming families to higher heights in the Lord. He is entertaining, energetic, empowering, and well sought after.

Dr. Larry McMillan has established credibility in many cross denominations, community associations, and family groups. He and wife has reached the level of accountability and credibility that has earned them the title of "The Family of the Year for Baltimore City."

He is the author of many books, including "If It's Broken, Fix It." He has been praised by others in his profession for his literary work and commitment to strengthen families. Dr. McMillan is a Certified Preacher, Speaker, Licensed Pastor, and a great role model for families and children.

His specialties equips him to give Novice Presentations, Seminars, Premarital Training, online consulting and coaching services including but not limited to: Lifestyle Change, Patriot Leadership, Family Team Building, Strategic Family Account Management Skills, and Development of Community Workforce.

Born into the kind of crushing poverty that could stuff out a life or ignite a person to work, fight, and pray, Dr. Larry A. McMillan, Sr., chose to follow in the footsteps of his earthly father and mother. He chose to follow the doctrines of the laws of God. He used his God-given talents and his razor sharp intellect and boundless energy to learn how churches operate in America. He has become a remnant headlining pastor, preacher, evangelist, teacher, theologian, business manager, youth leader, and a Holy Ghost filled son of God. He has an uncompromising voice for God and is known to sound the alarm about the direction of church growth. He counts among his friends those who preach and teach the unadulterated gospel of Jesus, the Christ. He organized "The Sensational McMillan Singers." He is a recording artist of two CD's entitled, "Praise Him Now," and "Holy Step." He is an interstate and international revivalist. Pastor McMillan looks back through his extraordinary life, recalling friends and adversaries, battles waged, and church fights, while offering biblical perspectives on all issues facing the church. He is a product of the struggle in the institutionalized church, who refused to compromise the Word for personal growth, but remained steadfast always seeking to do God's will for His church.

Dr. McMillan is very much acquainted with human rights causes. He believes in the true Christian biblical concepts of Godly family living. He actively addresses the problem of sin in the house of God. The Next Gen church is experiencing problems which needs a divine cleaning solution. The lack of spiritual development and church growth as commanded by God is a spiritual problem. This book examines church history and offers solutions for a more profitable church in the sight of God. He shows the church community how to eradicate the crucial sinful problems and how to make disciples according to God's law. The next generation needs to understand the process of making sure that God's church will stand and be a powerful voice in the upcoming centuries should God tarry. This is a must read book for serious Christians.

Dr. McMillan has an earned Bachelor of Science degree in Business Education, a minor degree in accounting, a Masters degree in Theology, a Professional Master Certificate in Youth Ministry and Youth Studies, a Master's of Business Administration Degree, and many educational certificates from John Hopkins University. He has been the recipient of several Honorary Doctor of Divinity degrees. Dr. McMillan is married to Evangelist Marilyn McMillan.

As a charismatic biblical motivator, lucid speaker, marriage coach, theological scholar, author, musician, recording artist, teacher, educator, and a business manager he makes use of his talent in Kingdom Building. He makes presentations that are highly effective in transforming families to higher heights to the glory of God.

For more than 26 years, he has served as an interstate and intrastate minister. He has also served in other countries including Europe. Pastor McMillan has developed programs of evangelism, missions, education, and stewardship. He has developed family educational workshops, programs for economic stability for families, nurturing and supportive family programs, and self-actualization workshops.

He was one of the organizer of the renowned Teens for Christ. He is the organizer and the founder of the Today's Family, Inc. magazine. He is a recording artist and the founder and organizer of The Sensational McMillan Singers.

Pastor McMillan and Evangelist McMillan are the proud and blessed parents of 3 adult married sons and 6 grandchildren. Pastor McMillan has vowed to assist members of their community to meet the social and economic challenges in Christian education. His zeal is to assist in equipping families to meet the requirements of being successful in this 21st century and to foster growth in families assigned to him. It is his desire to encourage God's children to study and show themselves rightfully approved in dividing the Word of God.